ععؤ

Scenes from African Urban Life

Scenes from African Urban Life: Collected Copperbelt Papers

A. L. EPSTEIN

EDINBURGH UNIVERSITY PRESS

© A. L. Epstein 1992

Edinburgh University Press
22 George Square, Edinburgh

Typeset in Alphacomp Century
by Pioneer Associates Ltd.,
Perthshire, and
printed in Great Britain by
Redwood Press,
Melksham, Wilts

British Library Cataloguing
in Publication Data
Epstein, A. L.
Scenes from African urban life:
Collected copperbelt essays.
I. Title
307.76096894

ISBN 0 7486 0321 2

Contents

Prefatory note

In the course of producing this volume I have incurred a variety of debts to many people. Most of these I have acknowledged in the original publications, and since their names are many I hope I may be forgiven for not repeating them here. There is a smaller number to whom my debt is more immediate, and I herewith tender my thanks to Professor Angela Cheater, University of Zimbabwe; Dr Karen Hansen, Northwestern University, Illinois; and to my colleagues at Sussex, Richard Brown and Ralph Grillo. Finally, there are those to whom my debts are of very long standing and these are acknowledged in the body of the text. I dedicate this book to the memory of Max Epstein.

Allowing for minor alterations in the text on grounds of style or to avoid unnecessary repetition, all the chapters previously published are reproduced here as they originally appeared. The 'ethnographic present' relates in each case to the date of first publication. This is set out below, together with other details of publication:

1953   'The Role of African Courts in Urban Communities of the Northern Rhodesian Copperbelt'. *Rhodes-Livingstone Journal* 13: 1-16.

1958   'Tribal Elders to Trade Unions'. In Prudence Smith (ed.), *Africa in Transition*. London: Max Reinhardt.

1959   'Linguistic Innovation and Culture on the Copperbelt'. *Southwestern Journal of Anthropology* 15: 235-53.

1961   'The Network and Urban Social Organisation'. *Rhodes-Livingstone Journal* 29: 29-62.

1969   'Gossip, Norms, and Social Network'. In J. C. Mitchell (ed.), *Social Networks and Urban Situations*. Manchester: Manchester University Press.

1986 'The Millennium and the Self: Jehovah's Witnesses on the Copperbelt in the 1950s'. *Anthropos* 81: 529-554.

Chapter 8 has not previously appeared in print. However, a very abbreviated version was published in:

1979 'Unconscious Factors in the Response to Social Crisis: a Case Study from Zambia'. *The Psychoanalytic Study of Society* 8: 3-39.

Introduction

Some years ago an American anthropologist, Dr Karen Hansen, who had recently been carrying out research in Zambia, was describing some of the difficulties she had encountered in the course of her fieldwork there. Her account reminded me of some of my own earlier experiences in this regard, some of which I then described for her. At the end she remarked that the story would be of considerable interest to other anthropologists, and urged me to write it up. I did not take the matter any further at that time, partly because I was fully occupied in other tasks, partly because I could not see how such an account could stand on its own, until, more recently, it occurred to me that it would serve as an appropriate opening chapter were I to bring together in a volume my various papers on the Copperbelt. But what justification was there for such a volume? A common reason advanced for such collections is that the several items were scattered in different, sometimes inaccessible, journals and students would find it convenient to have them together between one set of covers. Perhaps this could be said in the present case, too, but I have been chiefly swayed by other considerations.

Between 1950 and 1956 I made three field trips to Northern Rhodesia (now Zambia), spending most of my time in the towns of the Copperbelt, though I also paid a number of visits to the rural areas. This research resulted in a number of monographs, each of which, as the titles indicate, dealt with a major aspect of African social life there at that time: *The Administration of Justice and the Urban African* (1953), *Politics in an Urban African Community* (1958), *Ethos and Identity: Three Studies in Ethnicity* (1978), and *Urbanization and Kinship* (1981). In addition I published a number of articles that dealt in the main with those facets of African urban society and culture that had received little or no attention in the larger works: social organisation, language, religion, and so on. They offer, as my present title plainly suggests, a set of scenes from African urban life. But while they all have their setting in an urban milieu, they are none the less rooted in the tradition of British social anthropology; stated in slightly different terms, they were originally conceived and are presented here as samples of urban ethnography, descriptive accounts intended to convey some of the detail and texture of a way of life that was taking shape as Africans of rural provenance adapted to the novel social environment of the towns.

I feel it is important to make this point because from the early 1960s there were increasingly clear signs of change in the intellectual climate as it affected the social sciences. The assumptions which underlay and had guided the urban work of Clyde Mitchell and myself as well as of Rhodes-Livingstone colleagues working in the rural areas were now being discarded in favour of modes of research and analysis being pursued by neo-Marxist scholars or the proponents of dependency theory, all insisting that developments in the Third World had to be seen in the context of the world capitalist system. Long before, Godfrey Wilson had foreshadowed approaches of this kind when in his study of Broken Hill (now Kabwe) he pointed out that

> today the inhabitants of Northern Rhodesia are members of a huge world-wide community, and their lives are bound up at every point with the events of its history. . . . [as they] find themselves transformed into the peasants and unskilled workers of a nascent nation state. (Wilson 1941: 12)

Much later, following my study at Luanshya, I myself (Epstein 1964) pointed to some of the limitations of studies of urban life approached as though one were dealing simply with local communities. I was careful to note, however, that this was not to reject studies conducted in a given urban locality as without value, and was merely reminding the anthropologist that he needed to be increasingly aware of the way events falling within the field of observation were frequently influenced by intrusive factors and so be prepared to adjust his methods where this was relevant to handling the question at issue. But by this time the tide was running strongly against the kind of study that was based upon observation of behaviour and events at a local level, and the research of Mitchell and myself was indeed singled out for criticism as the work of 'colonialist stooges' that concerned itself only with 'trivia' (Magubane 1971). Within Zambia itself the influence of this kind of perspective is to be seen most clearly in the dramatic decline of empirical research there, both in the rural and urban areas, over the past thirty years, but what I find particularly sad is that students at the University of Zambia seem to have been given no encouragement to take up the challenge of such research themselves.[1] Macro theories do indeed provide a valuable corrective to the conventional anthropological approach that even now sometimes treats local groups as though they remained self-contained entities, but in the end they are self-defeating, their underlying assumptions often as paternalistic and patronising as those of any anthropologist of an earlier day. As it happens, there are indications that the 'revolution' has run its course. Of interest in this regard is the fact that a number of papers by Continental scholars have recently appeared seeking to reassess the work of the former Rhodes–Livingstone Institute, and even suggesting its continuing relevance to contemporary Zambia (see van Donge 1985; Rossetti 1985). This, then, would seem to be an opportune moment, through this collection of essays, to draw the attention of younger scholars to an earlier tradition and even persuade some of them to follow in its path again.

I have referred to the essays in this volume as offering samples of urban ethnography. I must add at once, therefore, that this should not be taken to mean that their purpose was intended to be purely descriptive. Chapter 1 apart, which was written specifically for the volume, and presents an account of my fieldwork on the Copperbelt in the 1950s, all the papers were concerned to raise issues of method and theory. Moreover, they were written over a period of some thirty years or so. A further reason for bringing them together as a book, therefore, is that it gives me an opportunity to say something about their genesis, while offering the reader at the same time the chance to observe the unfolding of my interests as well as the continuities and changes in my approach to the anthropology of urban life.

The paper included here on the work of the urban courts was not only one of my earliest publications, it was also my first experiment with the case-method. As an undergraduate in law at Queen's University, Belfast in the early years of the Second World War, I had learnt how important case-material was in the daily life of the practising lawyer, but my introduction to the concept of the case-method itself came when a couple of American army officers, stationed in the area, who happened to

be professors at the Harvard Law School, once visited our
Department and spoke, among other things, of the use of the
case-method in the training of their students. Later I discovered
in the work of Ad Hoebel how the method could be applied to
advantage in the context of anthropological research. I found
the approach congenial because it was dynamic: my interest in
the urban courts study was not so much in recording cases in
order to draw from them the rules of customary law on which to
build an African *corpus juris*; it lay rather in the dispute
process itself, the dialogue of norm and counter-norm, and the
way in which the judges sought to resolve the matter before
them. Moreover, as Llewellyn and Hoebel (1941) had further
argued, following the way disputes were attended to led directly
into the study of the political functions of judicial bodies. Even
in my later work, when my interests had moved far beyond the
purely legal, the same basic concern with the detailed analysis
of action sequences within some delimited context is to be seen
in the way I sought to apply Gluckman's (1958) concept of the
social situation, or that of the episode employed by the social
psychologists Harré and Secord (1972).

An abiding interest in conflict also stamped my second piece
of research, conducted in Luanshya; but whereas in the urban
courts study the concern was with conflict-management now it
was with conflict as providing the dynamics of change. This
drew a response from some who complained of my tendency to
resort too readily to talk, Hegel-like, of 'contradictions'; others,
no less ideologically motivated, praised me for my dialectic
approach. One of the basic themes of the Luanshya study is
summed up and illustrated in the title of the article reproduced
here as Chapter 3: 'Tribal Elders to Trade Unions'. This refers
to the way in which, as part of an unfolding historical process,
one mode of political organisation, with its associated pattern
of leadership, gradually comes to be replaced by another. To
some of my readers, the message seemed to be the ideologically
congenial view that trade unions transcended tribes; the latter
were a relic of the past and doomed very soon to disappear. This
had always seemed to me an overly simple view of the situation,
and rather different from the one I thought I had presented.
For, to take but one aspect of the problem, while the African
Mine Workers Trade Union had indeed secured the passing of
the system of tribal representation on the mines, it was also
plain that developing cleavages within the union were apt to be

explained by Africans themselves in tribal terms. I touched on
this issue in the final paragraphs of my article as well as in the
fuller analysis in my *Politics* book (1958), but it was not until
much later that I was able to treat the complex issue of what
had in the meantime come to be referred to as ethnicity much
more systematically in *Ethos and Identity* (1978).

In the early 1950s when I was still serving my novitiate in
the discipline, structural-functionalism was still the dominant
force in British social anthropology, and *African Political
Systems* remained a basic text.[2] Among the societies represented
in the volume, a now well-known contrast was drawn between
centralised polities and stateless ones. The centralised societies,
it was noted, could be fairly readily described in the stock
categories of political science; the stateless ones presented the
greater theoretical challenge for, in the absence of the formal
machinery usually associated with the state, where were the
institutions that could be identified as political, and how,
therefore, was one to describe the political system? The situation
I encountered on the Copperbelt was far removed from anything
described in the pages of *African Political Systems*, but,
curiously enough, when I settled at Ndola for what was to be
my third and final study, I found myself facing very much the
same kind of problem as had confronted those seeking to
elucidate the political system in segmentary lineage systems.
Briefly, in a mine township the complex organisation which the
mining company had brought into being for its own purposes
provided a framework that served to regulate so much of African
life there. In what I called the 'unitary' structure of the mine,
the African Mine Workers Union itself in a sense nested within
the organisation of the mine, taking on something of that same
'unitary' structure. In Luanshya, then, the presence of a variety
of formal groups and bodies provided convenient pegs on which
to hang my analysis. Ndola presented a very different picture.
Here there was no single large-scale employer of labour. African
trade unions were represented in the town, but in most cases
they appeared to enjoy little more than a nominal existence.
For much of the time, too, even the African National Congress
was dormant. Moreover, there was much movement in and out
of the town, and even within it, and everything seemed to be in
flux. I knew of no theoretical scheme designed to handle this
kind of situation. How then to proceed?

It was in addressing this problem that I hit on the idea of

experimenting with networks. In fieldwork terms, this consisted in having a man whom I have called Chanda record his various interactions as he moved around the town and beyond it over a short period of time. It may be worth mentioning that inspiration for this did not derive from John Barnes's (1954) seminal paper introducing the concept of the network, for at this point I was not yet familiar with it; I drew rather on something that I recalled from my days in the Royal Navy. As a communications rating serving aboard an aircraft carrier, I was aware that messages received aboard ship circulated through a regular channel of communication; in theory, ordinary members of the ship's company would learn what was going on only when, finally, an item was posted on the notice-boards. In practice things did not work that way. There was what was known as the 'buzz'. By means of the 'buzz' any message received that, for example, directly affected the ship's movements was sure to sweep through the ship in a flash. Plainly, in addition to the formal or regular channel of communication, there was also available an informal or covert yet highly effective communications network. Impressed by the way, for example, strangers arriving at the bus-stop in Ndola from distant villages in the rural areas would quickly find their way to kin despite the absence of any local system of addresses, or husbands and wives with equal speed track down an errant spouse who had decamped to another town, it occurred to me that there was an aspect of social organisation at Ndola that operated in a way very similar to the 'buzz'.

At the time it seemed to me that the network concept provided a valuable corrective to the view deep-rooted in the sociological literature that urban social life was characteristically anonymous and impersonal. Furthermore, it also seemed to offer a more illuminating approach to a variety of problems touching urban social organisation, as I seek to illustrate in Chapter 5. Nowadays, of course, network analysis has achieved a theoretical salience and a methodological sophistication I could not have imagined at the time I first sought to make use of it in my Ndola research. I have myself not followed further along that path. I hope, nevertheless, that the two essays on the subject included here will be seen as continuing to have more than historical interest.

My training in the subject, as I have indicated, had been in the British tradition of social anthropology, which at the time still drew predominantly on the ideas of Malinowski and Radcliffe-Brown. My own research, of course, had been carried out in towns, which some regarded as falling outside the scope of the discipline, but the problems I had so far tackled could still be readily covered by the conventional rubrics: law, the composition and functioning of groups, social organisation, and the like. Increasingly, however, I became aware that there were aspects of urban life that escaped this kind of approach. African life on the Copperbelt, I felt, had its own distinctive flavour. Some of it is captured, I think, in Chanda's accounts around which I had built up my discussion of the role of social networks. But there was a more direct route, to some extent opened up by the greater freedom I enjoyed in Ndola for personal contact with Africans but also by the rich material being gathered by my research assistants, whose reports were studded with the vernacular expressions employed by their collocutors. I am referring, of course, to language, the new argot of the towns already so distinctive that Africans now commonly spoke of it as *CiCopperbelti*.

The response to my paper in which I presented some of this material (included here as Chapter 6) was very interesting, illustrating something of the gulf that then separated British and American anthropology. I had opened the paper by suggesting the relevance of linguistic innovation for studying the interrelations of structure and culture in situations of rapid social transformation. This prompted a letter, heavy with sarcasm, from Professor Herskovits praising me for 'discovering' what for American anthropologists had long been almost axiomatic. Other American scholars received the article more kindly, and later it was included in a reader on the sociology of language edited by Fishman (1968). By contrast, when I showed a draft of the paper to Max Gluckman he promptly dismissed it as being well below my usual standard and suggested that if I wanted to publish it I should try an American journal. The position of language within British anthropology has been utterly transformed since then and it is therefore important to remember that at the time Gluckman's reaction accurately reflected the prevailing view (see, for example, Grillo 1989: 4-7). I think it is probably fair to say that as a consequence the paper passed largely unnoticed in Britain. But Gluckman also expressed doubts of quite another kind about the paper, feeling that my material was presented in such a way as to hold the

African up to ridicule. I appreciated Gluckman's sensitivity in the matter, but it also seemed to me that, in so far as some of the matter might provoke laughter, he failed to see that there is an important difference between laughing at and laughing with people. In this way I think he also missed a more important point. In the conditions then prevailing on the Copperbelt, Africans had little choice in so many of the matters that most closely affected their daily lives: the town represented an artificial environment, created by others, to which the Africans, if they wished to continue living and working there, had willy-nilly to learn to adjust. Yet in that process of adaptation they were not wholly supine or passive. Seen from this point of view, the new language of the towns was a creative response; with its wit and inventiveness *CiCopperbelti* served Africans as a means of placing their own distinctive stamp on this otherwise alien and often oppressive milieu.

An anthropologist in the field is almost always bound to encounter phenomena that are marginal to the main thrust of his or her research but that raises such fascinating questions that they cannot easily be ignored. On the Copperbelt the remarkable evangelical success of Jehovah's Witnesses provided an example of this kind; what made the problem even more challenging was the discovery of links of continuity between the by now 'accommodationist' Jehovah's Witnesses and an earlier radical and millenarian movement known as Watchtower. As just indicated, it was what I had observed on the Copperbelt that triggered my interest in the matter, but, as I pursued it further and quickly discovered the relevance of the ethnic factor, I was also compelled to recognise the importance of developments in the rural areas, in particular the differential response to the imposition of colonial rule in different parts of the country, which had continuing implications for many aspects of the contemporary situation. Given that my interest in the problem only emerged on the spot and in the interstices, so to speak, of fieldwork directed towards other topics, I am uncomfortably aware of the many questions I ought to have inquired into, but did not, and of the many lacunae therefore in my account. On the other hand, some of the data are of a kind that has not been presented elsewhere and are thus, I believe, of historical interest; together with the analysis, the paper provides a springboard for the more comprehensive study of Jehovah's Witnesses in Zambia that we still await.

There is a footnote reference in my *Politics* book (1958: 157) to a paper, then said to be in preparation, that was to give an account of the rise of the African National Congress and an analysis of its policies. For various reasons - not least my move to Australia and thereafter my involvement for many years in research in Papua New Guinea - the paper was never completed, and in the end lost its *raison d'être* when the subject-matter came to be covered in a number of texts dealing with the history of the area in this period (for example, Rotberg 1966; Roberts 1976). By and large, however, professional historians still rely primarily on archival material and other documentary evidence, and are thus apt to pass over in silence matters which may not have found their way into the written record or to play down as marginal events which may have impressed a contemporary observer on the spot. An example of the first kind, touching the African National Congress, is my discussion of the relations between Congress and Chiefs, based on observations made on the occasion of the visits of a number of important chiefs to Ndola, which is given in *Ethos and Identity* (Epstein 1978: 28-38). An example of the second is provided in Chapter 8, which presents further information relating to the Congress. The chapter offers an account and analysis of certain very bizarre and, I believe, significant happenings that occurred in the context of the campaign against Central African Federation on which the standard historical texts have had little or nothing to say.

In writing this paper, I was also seeking to make a number of other points. Along with a number of other of Gluckman's students and junior colleagues, I was a contributor to the symposium he had organised entitled *Closed Systems and Open Minds*. One of his major concerns in this volume was with the boundaries between disciplines and what he saw as the need to adopt a stance of deliberate 'naivety' when dealing with material or ideas that lay beyond the scope of one's own discipline. Already in my contribution to the volume I had expressed some of my reservations about his position, as Gluckman himself indeed acknowledges (1964: 198-9), and my discussion of oral aggression in Central Africa that is now included here provided me with an opportunity to work out just where I stood in the matter. The paper was also important to me in other regards. I had been confronted in the field with behaviour which disclosed powerful affect at work. In a word I was presented with material of the kind I knew no way of handling using conventional sociological categories, where moreover if I resorted to what seemed relevant psychological ideas I would clearly have violated Gluckman's precepts about disciplinary 'trespass', and which at the same time I felt I simply could not avoid. Without quite knowing it at the time, I had embarked on the task of integrating affect into the business of anthropological analysis, a task which since then has become my major theoretical interest.

In dwelling so far on the genesis of each paper, I have perhaps unwittingly given too much emphasis to the particular problem or theme with which each was concerned as well as to my changing theoretical interests. In these ways I may have deflected attention from the way in which the separate analyses are also linked by certain underlying ideas and assumptions concerning method. In this connection it is important to note that for most of the time I was in Central Africa I had been associated with the Rhodes-Livingstone Institute (now the Institute of African Studies, University of Zambia) and the Department of Anthropology at the University of Manchester. Reviewing a study by one of the members of this group, Watson's *Tribal Cohesion in a Money Economy* (1958), Mary Douglas (1959: 168) remarked that it was evidently time to salute a 'school' of anthropology where 'publications are developed through close discussion, and where each individual work is enhanced by its focus on a common stock of problems'. It would be going far beyond my present task to offer here a personal account of the work of the school. But, since one of the aims of the discussion is clarification of my own position, it may be worth dwelling a little further on the matter, noting where I shared common ideas and assumptions with my colleagues as well as where we diverged.

Let me take up first the question of general orientation. I have mentioned earlier that when my *Politics* book first appeared it was criticised, on the one hand, because of its 'numbing' reiteration of such terms as 'contradiction', 'cleavage', etc. (Banton 1959: 39); while, on the other, it received praise for its use of the dialectic: in either event it seems clear that my text had been read as a Marxist analysis. Of interest in this regard is a passage from the personal journal I kept while I was in Luanshya, in which, communing with myself on one occasion about the direction and purpose of my work and my situation at the time, I remarked that the only people who appeared to have a consistent theory of society, of what it was, how it functioned, and where it was going, were the Marxists. I cannot remember whether at that time I had read Gluckman's critique of Malinowski's functional analysis of social change, but looking back it seems clear that if my own comment did not echo it certainly had much in common with the position he took there – the Marxists, he acknowledged, had a theoretical framework, but the anthropologists still had to establish a right to maintain that they were more than good recorders of contemporary events (Gluckman 1949: 21).

Gluckman's statement here is steeped in ambiguity. I think he was making evident his sympathy for Marxist modes of analysis, at the same time appearing to treat Marxists and anthropologists as though they were opposed categories. It is this kind of ambiguity, I suggest, that helps to explain why the influence of Marxism on Gluckman's own thinking has presented itself to various scholars as such a problematic issue. Thus, what Firth found striking in his reading of Gluckman was that despite the impression that 'a version of the dialectic seemed to hover at the back of much of his writing' his analyses of conflict, which was so central to Gluckman's *oeuvre*, were so curiously muted. There was, Firth observes, an apparent coyness in Gluckman's writing about Marxism (Firth 1975: 493–4). Frankenberg, who was himself a member of the Department at Manchester for many years, and has always been quite unequivocal about his own theoretical stance (see, for example, Frankenberg 1967), took a similar, if rather sharper, view. In the course of a reanalysis of some of Gluckman's Barotse material, he draws on one of Gluckman's favourite antitheses to contrast his own 'revolutionary' anti-imperialism with Gluckman's merely 'rebellious' anti-colonialism, concluding that the Marxist strain in the latter's work was stunted by the undeveloped state of Marxist theory at the time (cited in Brown 1979: 540).

Of Gluckman's left-wing sympathies and even pro-Soviet stance during his time at the Rhodes–Livingstone Institute there can be little question (Brown 1979: *passim*). On this score, for example, his favourable references to the *kolkhoz*, or collective farm, and other aspects of property in the Soviet Union (Gluckman 1943a) may not have provided the basis for the reputation he acquired in Northern Rhodesia administrative circles as a 'Bolshie', but I can vouch that they were certainly referred to by way of proving the point. There is, of course, a world of difference between being influenced in one's writing by one's political sympathies, and the regular and systematic application of a particular mode of analysis to concrete sociological problems. The point is, I think, self-evident, but an article entitled 'The Functional School of Ethnography in the Service of British Imperialism', that once appeared in *Sovietskaia Etnografia* (1948),[3] serves to drive it home. Gluckman was deeply hurt that his report offering a plan for the administrative reorganisation of the Barotse native authorities (Gluckman 1943b) had been singled out for criticism, but what he found particularly galling was to be bracketed with Malinowski as a member of the Functional School.

In his close examination of Gluckman's years at the Rhodes-Livingstone Institute, Brown (1979) has pointed to a shift in outlook from a belief in academic aloofness to a concern for active involvement with the administration, with a swing back again as he became disillusioned when his attempts to engage in practical affairs in Northern Rhodesia won him little support within the establishment. There is also some suggestion that he had mellowed in his attitudes as he established himself at Manchester (Firth 1975: 494). It was there that I first met Max in 1951 and, save for the years 1958–61, when I held a research post at the Australian National University, Canberra, I served as a member of the Department until I returned to Australia in 1966. During this time he remained politically engaged, actively campaigning against the proposals for a Federation in British Central Africa (see Chapter 8), and later participating in demonstrations at the time of the Suez Crisis. But while his political sympathies were thus clear, what was no less patent was his inability to stomach anything that smacked to him of the doctrinaire: on anthropological issues his academic judgement was always the arbiter. On the day of my very first visit to Manchester I recall that he was engaged in vigorous debate over the claim that traditional African societies were feudal. This idea, which was at that moment being canvassed by Marxist ideologues, Gluckman dismissed out of hand: he refused to accept that the feudal societies of Europe, with their sophisticated technologies that had produced castles and cathedrals, could be bracketed with the materially much simpler African societies. Much later we received a visit by a distinguished Soviet Africanist - from memory, I think, Professor Potekhin - who presented a paper on the Zulu of South Africa. Remarkably, as I recall, Potekhin said nothing of the Zulu in the contemporary South African situation but, using the classical categories of Marxist discourse, addressed himself rather to the question of where the Zulu were to be placed on the unilineal scale of evolutionary development. I do not recollect how Max responded to this - he was on occasion very courteous to guests - but I suspect that Eli Devons, one of a number of distinguished economists then on our Faculty and a very close friend of Gluckman, spoke for many of us, including Max himself, when he commented as we emerged from the seminar room that it was rather like a return to medieval theology. However, the clearest impression I received of Gluckman's theoretical stance *vis-à-vis* Marxism was on the occasion that Cliff Slaughter came to present a paper on the work he and his colleagues had been carrying out in a Yorkshire mining community, a fuller account of which was to appear subsequently under the title *Coal is Our Life* (Dennis, Henriques and Slaughter 1956). Slaughter was at that time, I believe, a prominent member of the New Left, and he offered an analysis of relations on the mine in terms of rigid oppositions along class lines. The conflict then was evident, but where, Gluckman wanted to know, was the co-operation? If Slaughter's view of the situation was accepted as valid, how was coal ever produced? Following the delivery of a seminar paper, the question Gluckman so often addressed to the speaker by way of opening up the discussion was: what's the problem? As formulated by him, it gave succinct expression to what was a central preoccupation - how the system worked. In a word, if Marx - or perhaps Engels[4] - appeared to occupy less of the foreground of Gluckman's mind, it is because Durkheim was no less a powerful intellectual influence (compare Firth 1975: 494; Leach 1963). It is worth noting in this connection that while I was in the Department Gluckman neither lectured nor gave courses on Marx or Marxism, whereas he did teach a regular course on Durkheim's *Rules of Sociological Method*.[5]

To many outsiders, then, political involvement was one of the chief marks of the school; as Leach (1973: 772) once euphemistically expressed it, the sympathies of its members were with the oppressed rather than the oppressors. In fact, Gluckman had gathered around him a very varied group of individuals who often differed widely in their political attitudes as well as on other matters. In terms of theoretical orientation, there were indeed those who were committed to Marxism, but I do not recall that they were ever a majority. There were yet others whose position on the political spectrum was never enirely clear to me, but who were almost certainly not Marxists. What, then, of my own position within the group? Earlier in the discussion I cited an extract from my journal that seems to bear on the point. But read in proper context the passage in question was written not as an expression of commitment but rather of scepticism. I had just been reading, it appears, a volume of autobiography by Arthur Koestler, and I noted that while he rejected most of the basic tenets of the Marxist doctrine, he still retained a residue of the method of approach as a valuable asset. For myself it was the notion of the dialectic as providing the motor of change that seemed to me so illuminating in seeking to understand much of what I was observing on the Copperbelt. But if I thus found this and other related concepts helpful in sociological terms, their appeal was also rooted in my understanding of processes at work within my own psyche: I had long been aware of intra-psychic conflict and contradiction as having under certain circumstances the power to cripple, but I had also come to see such tension as having a dynamic function, too. We shall see very much the same phenomenon presently in another context. What this suggests is that in my own mind there was a recognition of the interpenetration of the sociological and psychological domains, whereas for Gluckman, with his deep attachment to the Durkheimian canon, these were ever to be kept apart. In my earliest work, however, the matter hardly ever arose as an issue; that I was on a divergent path of development only gradually became apparent as I grappled with a variety of problems thrown up by my Copperbelt field data. I touch on this point further below, where I discuss my increasing difficulties with Gluckman's doctrine of 'naivety', and take it up again in detail later in Chapter 8.

My use of situations as a focus of description and analysis – what was later to become known as 'situational analysis' (van Velsen 1967; Garbett 1970; Mitchell 1983) and increasingly recognised as a distinctive hallmark of the Manchester School in South-Central Africa (Werbner 1984) – also owed much to my association with the school. As already indicated, my approach to the study of the judicial process was from the very beginning through the use of the 'case-method' (see Chapter 1). The focus on situations, so evident in my later Luanshya and Ndola studies, seemed to me at the time no more than a natural extension of the 'case-method' but applied in a wider social context. That is to say, one took some social situation, episode or action sequence – what Garbett (1970: 215) was to define as a temporally and spatially bounded series of events abstracted by the observer from the ongoing flow of social life – from the detailed scrutiny of which one sought to extract some set of regularities. The appeal of this approach lay in the way it provided a way of handling the issue of social dynamics, the fact that one was in a sense observing a form of social life taking shape before one's very eyes.

My use of the 'case-method', as I have said, grew out of my earlier background in law; in resorting to the notion of 'situations' as a way of getting to grips with the nascent structure of social and political relations in Luanshya and Ndola I drew on Gluckman's seminal paper *Analysis of a Social Situation in Modern Zululand* (1958). The situation in question was the official opening of a bridge, which brought together representatives of all the different sections of the population in Zululand at that time – Blacks and Whites, Christians and pagans, administrators and citizens, and so on. Gluckman showed how their conduct leading up to, during, and after the ceremony reflected the overall structure of South African society, not only in terms of its contemporary cleavages but also of its countervailing alliances. Thus, Gluckman was using 'situation' not simply as a descriptive device but also as a tool of analysis. More crucially, he introduced the concept of 'situational selection' in order to handle certain contradictory elements he had observed in the situation he was studying. As he himself (1958: 26) expressed it: 'individuals . . . live coherent lives by situational selection from a medley of contradictory values, ill-assorted beliefs and varied interests and techniques'. Social life on the Copperbelt too was deeply marked by discrepancy. So, for example, in the context of my own studies, I was particularly struck by the fact that in certain situations, especially those relating to the total field of Black–White relations, what we then referred to as 'tribalism' appeared to be quite irrelevant, whereas in others urban Africans continued to order their social lives according to tribal norms and values. In seeking to deal with this seeming inconsistency of response, I too invoked the principle of 'situational selection'. I have to note, however, that in doing so I drew not on Gluckman, but on Evans-Pritchard's discussion of the insufficiencies and contradictions in the Azande system of witchcraft beliefs (Epstein 1958: 227). Evans-Pritchard made it clear, of course, that he was dealing with contradiction on the abstract plane of structural relations. As it appears now, in adopting Evans-Pritchard's viewpoint for my own purposes I may indeed have diverged from it. For present purposes, however, the main point is that the image that underlay my own use of the concept was of a process of compartmentalisation, a mechanism whereby the potential for conflict set up by the holding of discrepant ideas, beliefs, and values is reduced by keeping them apart, so to speak, in separate compartments of the mind. As with the notion of contradiction discussed earlier, I found the concept of 'situational selection' congenial because it helped me to handle a sociological problem, but I believe that I was quick to appreciate its significance in this regard largely because I was already aware of the way 'situational selection' worked in my own mind.

In certain respects 'situational analysis' marked an important departure from the classic structuralist approach identified with Radcliffe-Brown. Certainly, situations were studied with a view to elucidating the structural principles that operated not simply in the particular situations being observed but also in wider social contexts. The divergence is more clearly to be seen in the position given to the individual. As van Velsen (1967: 131) was to point out, structuralist analysis rejected the particular - how Jack and Jill behaved on any particular occasion was unsuitable for 'an account of the form of the structure'. By contrast, for many of Gluckman's students, the doings and misdoings of particular persons - in some cases of particular personalities (for example, Turner 1957) - became integral not only to the task of ethnographic description but even more to the business of analysis itself. This recognition of the individual, I believe, in turn helped to pave the way for the idea of networks; certainly, it carried the approach yet further away from the classical ideal.

I have already described how I happened on the idea of networks and put it to use in my Ndola study. Here, therefore, I want to mention a rather different point. At the time I myself first invoked it, the image of the network seems indeed to have been 'in the air'; apart from stimulating a number of illuminating studies in other Central African towns (see Mitchell 1969), it was also being employed by other scholars to handle a variety of problems (for example, Mayer 1962, 1966). Around this time, too, yet other anthropologists were sharpening even further the focus on the individual in developing actor-oriented approaches. The concept of role, by now long established in anthropological discourse, seems plainly to have been rooted in a metaphor of the stage, but as employed in much structuralist analysis the major stress was on socially defined expectations, and the actor was allowed little scope for his own interpretation of his part. By contrast, the newer competing models emphasised, for example, that how an actor responded to a situation was governed by the way he perceived it and/or was able to manipulate it to his advantage. Gluckman himself was to become rather concerned about these methodological developments in which the emphasis on norms in the understanding of social behaviour was giving way to a preoccupation with individuals, whose every move was carefully calculated. I should note here, therefore, that my own handling of the network concept stressed its communicative aspect. Moreover, while it is clear that I, too, was dealing with individuals, I was always careful to locate them in their own social background and context; as with 'situational analysis', I used the 'network' as a means of getting at more general principles of urban social organisation.

There were many ways, then, in which my own ideas chimed very well with those of Gluckman and other colleagues. In other regards, however, as I have already observed, I was moving on a divergent path. I had been aware from time to time of growing points of difference, but it was the symposium *Closed Systems and Open Minds* that finally brought the matter into focus. As I discuss in detail in Chapter 8, I had encountered in my fieldwork in 1953 certain very bizarre events which puzzled me and which I strongly felt called for some attempt at explanation, but which my training to that point had left me totally unequipped to handle. Later on, in writing this material up, I made use of a variety of concepts drawn from psychoanalytic theory in a way that clearly violated Gluckman's injunctions against disciplinary 'trespass'. Gluckman, I must emphasise, was not hostile to psychoanalysis, as is very evident in the introductory note he wrote for Ritchie's (1943) study *The African as Suckling and Adult*, but he did insist that the psychological and sociological frames of reference be kept strictly separate. The aim behind *Closed Systems and Open Minds* was not to deny that different disciplines might have an interest in a particular problem, but to work out a set of procedures for dealing with situations of this kind as they arose – the solution he offered lay in his doctrine of 'naivety'. Since the matter is discussed at some length elsewhere in the volume, I am concerned here with only one point. Confronted with the issue of oral aggression, which provides the central theme of my final chapter, Gluckman would undoubtedly have advised referring the problem to a psychoanalyst. Now, as will become clear, the situation with which I was dealing had a sociological no less than a psychological dimension. It follows, therefore, that if one is to adopt Gluckman's theoretical position then his injunction against trespassing on ground that forms the area of competence of another discipline is no less binding on the psychoanalyst. In this way, what I perceived as an important problem would simply have fallen between the interstices of different disciplines: no one would have tackled it. For me this was a sticking point, signalling a basic difference of approach. I think the crux of the matter is that Gluckman had a vision of the subject the contours of which were by now well settled, whereas for myself the matter was much more problematic. For Gluckman, that is, we were well on with our task and, as he once put it to me, only the details had to be filled in; whereas, as I saw it, we had scarcely left the starting-post. More simply, I think I was always more interested in questions than in answers; there was no finality to our enquiry and every conclusion reached served only to raise further questions. The metaphor that appears most apt to fit the kind of approach I have come to develop is that of the onion-peeler: one approaches a problem by examining it first, say, in its sociological dimension, the analysis takes one some way towards an understanding of the phenomena, until one encounters other questions that do not yield to sociological analysis and then one has to pursue them from a psychological or cultural perspective, and so on. An early example of the method is to be found in my analysis of *Response to Social Crisis* which appears here as Chapter 8; I have sought to carry it much further in more recent work based on my research in Melanesia in which the role of affect in social behaviour has become the dominant theme (see Epstein 1992).

1

Retrospect: an Anthropologist on the Copperbelt in the 1950s

What were the general circumstances or conditions prevailing in the area in which the fieldworker conducted his or her research? What bearing might these have had on the way in which the anthropologist was received in the community to be studied? And what position did the researcher come to assume within it? In an earlier day, when the dominant image of the anthropologist in the field was of a supposedly objective and detached observer whose central concerns were with customs and institutions, that is with the externals of behaviour, such questions were unlikely to loom large in the resulting ethnographic report. Even so, there are ample indications in the literature that the way in which the fieldworker was received and the conditions under which fieldwork itself was carried out could vary enormously from one society to another. Thus, it would be hard to imagine contrasts more striking than those presented, for example, by Chagnon (1968: 4-9), Evans-Pritchard (1940: 11-15), or Firth (1936: 1-2) describing, respectively, their first encounters with the Yanomamo, the Nuer, or the Tikopia. Such accounts serve not merely to 'locate' the anthropologist, they also tell us at once much of interest about the groups in question and their way of life. For some time now, however, there has been a clearer recognition of the way in which the very presence of the fieldworker can influence events within the community he or she has come to study, with the consequence that the observer him/herself has to be seen as falling within the field of observation. Contextualising the research and locating the observer within the appropriate field of relationships germane to the research thus become essential to the anthropologist's descriptive and analytic tasks. Here I wish to offer a further point: that in addressing questions of the kind just mentioned touching the social context of research one is not only likely to reveal a great deal about the society to be studied but also to expose some of the methodological

1

assumptions with which one had initially approached the study; not least, the more general nature of the fieldwork experience may itself be illuminated in this way. It is with such considerations in mind that I offer this retrospective account of my own fieldwork on the Copperbelt in the 1950s.

I had arrived in Northern Rhodesia at the beginning of 1950 in order to conduct a study of the African urban courts system that the colonial administration had introduced there some years earlier.[1] I was at the time a rather naive young man with no experience, and certainly little appreciation, of the nature of a colonial settler society, and I had conceived of my study as a purely academic exercise - what I hoped would prove to be a contribution to the anthropology of law. I was very quickly disabused of this idea. I had, in fact, scarcely arrived in Lusaka when my attention was drawn to an item in a local newspaper by some anonymous contributor reporting my forthcoming visit to carry out my research project. The aim of this study, it was said, was 'to prepare a unified legal system which will apply to all [sic] African tribes and will make an end to the respective legal codes'. Making heavy play of sarcasm, the piece went on to welcome the study on the grounds: first, that it would save District officials the labour of acquiring that intimate knowledge of Native laws and customs of anything up to a score of tribes that they had so meticulously applied in the past; and, secondly, be a further step in the unification of the tribes so as to enable them the better to combine against all authority when the time comes. The item concluded:

> May we hope for an extension of this valuable service. We may see, for example, in the near future, that Mr Chin Chang Chung, an 18 year old astrologer, who has been studying revolutionary politics in Moscow for two and a half years, is coming to Northern Rhodesia to unify and develop the process of detribalization and general emancipation of the African Natives with special reference to the improvement of their methods of sabotage and resistance to all kinds of control.

> Or, Mademoiselle Sun Woo, the 17 year old Mongolian modiste, who has been studying the science of clothes with the famous firm of Paquin et Cie of Paris since she was ten, has accepted an appointment under the Colonial Office and is coming to Africa to co-ordinate and unify methods of

dress among all the Native tribes in the country so as to enable the 'African' ladies to set an example to their less fortunate white guests when dining and dancing at the Governing Houses of the territories they adorn. [*Central African Post* 8 December 1949]

I no longer recall how I reacted to this note of welcome, but I imagine that the matter receded fairly quickly from my mind as I became more fully engaged by my research. Initially, spending some months in remote villages in Bemba country and then in Kawambwa, partly for purposes of acclimatisation and partly to make a start on the learning of Bemba (the language chiefly to be heard on the Copperbelt), the world of settler politics seemed far away. But even Ndola, where on this first trip I had my most protracted stay, seemed to me at the time a rather quiet colonial backwater. At first I was totally immersed in my study of the work of the Urban court there, attending its sessions every day, hearing and recording cases and then discussing them with the African judges. At length, however, I began to feel the need to extend my inquiries beyond the court-room itself. Most of the disputes that came before the court were matrimonial disputes, and it occurred to me that I might gain a different perspective on African urban marriage and domestic life if I did some interviewing in the African housing area or location. But I was also keen to discuss the work of the Urban courts and some of the problems of the administration of customary law in a modern urban context with more educated, urban-dwelling Africans. With the help of an African Education Officer, Alex Tawe, whom I had met by chance when he was attending a course at the Institute of Education in London, I was able to bring together a number of leading Africans in the town; there followed many enjoyable meetings, which were evidently not only interesting to the Africans themselves but very helpful to me since we discussed so many matters that were of direct concern to my research.

But gradually the signs began to appear of important changes in the social climate. As the political barometer began to swing, the newspapers increasingly carried reports and comment on meetings and conferences, rallies and resolutions as the campaign for the establishment of a Central African Federation gathered momentum, as I discuss in Chapter 8. At Ndola itself a young man called Simon Zukas, whose parents had come as Jewish refugees from Lithuania and were now settled at

Luanshya, had joined the Municipality. He quickly established links with local Africans, with some of whom he formed the Anti-Federation Action Committee, and thereafter he played a prominent part in African politics until he was finally charged with intriguing against constituted authority, tried, and eventually deported to England (Rotberg 1965: 234–5, 239–40). Among Zukas's closest associates were some who had been members of the Discussion Group that I had brought together for my own purposes. Of Zukas's activities and the work of the Anti-Federation Action Committee I knew nothing at first hand for I had by then left Ndola. It is perhaps a chief mark of my political innocence at this time that when, some time later, I was called away from a hearing of the Broken Hill urban court the last thing I expected was to be questioned by a couple of members of the Special Branch about what I knew of Simon Zukas. Only much later, when I had returned home, was I to discover that inquiries about my own possible subversive tendencies had extended to a small town in Northern Ireland where my parents then lived.

I have tried to convey in Chapter 8 something of the nightmarish atmosphere I found gripping the country when I returned to Northern Rhodesia for a second period of fieldwork early in 1953, as it became clear to Africans that all their efforts to avert Federation were now doomed to failure. But here I want to focus on how the political situation impinged directly on my proposed research. In my study of the Urban courts I had concerned myself chiefly with what went on within the court-room itself, hoping in this way to grasp some of the problems that arose in the attempts to administer customary law in an urban context as well as to achieve some understanding of the nature of the judicial process in these African courts. However, given the general theoretical position I brought to the task – buttressed now, no doubt, by the item in the Central African Post mentioned earlier – I was soon led to see that there were a number of matters relating to the courts that could only be properly understood when the latter were seen as operating within a wider social context. Stated briefly, differences of opinion about the constitution of the courts, in particular the way in which the court members were appointed, and a variety of charges about the way in which they were carrying out their judicial functions, all suggested clearly that the courts had become the focus of a political struggle within the new urban African communities. This in turn suggested that the next step in the unfolding Copperbelt research programme, which Gluckman (1945) had earlier outlined in his Seven Year Research Plan for the Rhodes-Livingstone Institute, should be a study of African urban politics. This indeed came to provide the subject-matter of my second field trip.

Arriving in Luanshya in July 1953 I got off to what seemed to be a promising start. My very first call was on the District Commissioner, F. M. N. ('Tony') Heath. Heath was most unusual in that, among most of the officers within the Provincial Administration whom I had so far encountered, he at once showed himself deeply sympathetic to my research and prepared to give me every assistance he could. Not only did I enjoy the hospitality of his home, where I had an early opportunity to meet a number of leading Africans in the town, but he also took it upon himself to introduce me to various Europeans whom he felt I might find it helpful to know. I particularly valued his help in arranging a meeting for me with Mr Jack Thomson, the General Manager of the Roan Antelope mine. I think the fact that the meeting went off so cordially, and ended with the manager's promise of co-operation in my study, owed much to Heath's presence and support.

But before long it became plain that not all was to be sweetness and light. One Sunday morning I learnt from two Africans - one a research assistant, the other a man who had come to serve me as general factotum when I was in Bemba country and had then insisted on accompanying me to the Copperbelt - that the African miners at Roan intended to come out on strike on the Monday morning. Later in the day I called in at the Heath household, where I discovered that the company included the Secretary for Native Affairs as well as the Senior Provincial Commissioner. As I recorded at the time in my personal journal, I inquired casually (if, as I soon saw, foolishly) if they had heard word about the strike. I used the word 'casually' deliberately because I had assumed that as soon as word of the strike broke, the District Commissioner would have been among the first to hear of it. But this turned out not to be the case, and very soon the telephone wires were humming. By two o'clock Lusaka had come back to Luanshya to find out what the local police knew about the matter. It appeared that the police knew very little, and were now busily making inquiries. As it happened, Tony had invited me to join him and his wife that evening at the Mine Club so that I would have the opportunity to meet other Europeans socially.

While we were gathered around our table, I was approached by a man I had not met before, who asked if we could have a few words together. Once outside he told me, in words that were presumably intended to be light in tone and thus reassuring, that 'I had been passed fit for human consumption' and he then went on to suggest that 'we should get together'. His drift was perfectly clear, and I probably did myself little good by responding tersely that I was a sociologist, not a police spy. At any rate, we left one another rather coolly.

In the event the strike did not break on the Monday after all, but the atmosphere remained rather tense. Then, on the Thursday night, or rather Friday morning, at four o'clock, Heath burst into my room and woke me up. He had brought a handful of files along, together with a copy of the Witchcraft Ordinance, and we sat together for over an hour, discussing the charge that had been brought by a Mine Police Sergeant against the local branch Chairman of the African Mine Workers Trade Union, Alfred Chambeshi. Tony himself thought the whole thing had been trumped up by the mine management in order to get rid of Chambeshi, whom they regarded as something of an agitator.

Events of these kinds were disturbing in themselves, but they also have to be seen in the context of a more pervasive tension. Even before leaving England I was acutely aware of the difficulties that would face any research worker in Central Africa at this time, though I doubt if I could have anticipated the depth of feeling that had been stirred up within the African population by the failure of the campaign against Federation that I encountered on my return to the country. There was now, as I discuss at some length in Chapter 8, a profound sense of betrayal among Africans. Along with an intense suspicion of the Europeans, there had developed a marked hardening of political attitudes. Such an increasingly tense ambience was hardly conducive to social research, which depends above all on the willingness of one's subjects to co-operate. My colleagues in the Rhodes-Livingstone Institute, working in the rural areas, had already encountered much resistance and found fieldwork an uphill struggle. I expected to find the situation even worse among the much more politically conscious Africans of the Copperbelt, particularly since my interests lay in the growth of

African urban politics and thus included such bodies as the African trade unions and the African National Congress. It was an important step to have gained the approval of the mine management at Roan for my study, but it had always seemed to me that the major hurdle to be overcome lay in winning the support of those whom the research would most directly affect, above all the African population of the mine township.

My first step in this direction was to approach the branch leaders of the African Mine Workers Trade Union at Roan. Their response was quite favourable but, as was to be expected, they made it clear that I would also need to have the consent of the Supreme Council of the Union before they could agree to the kind of study I proposed. My next step, therefore, was a visit to the headquarters of the union at Nkana where, in the absence of the General President, Lawrence Katilungu, who was on a visit to Europe, I discussed the matter with the General Secretary, Matthew Nkoloma. Nkoloma was a sleek and self-assured young man - his other personal name, DeLuxe, struck me as rather apt - who evidently enjoyed the sense of power his position gave him over a suppliant White researcher such as myself. Following an unsympathetic hearing, I was not surprised when I heard a little later that the Supreme Council considered that my study was unnecessary.

It was all rather depressing since I saw little possibility of doing work in the mine compound at Roan without the union's approval and support, and I was already beginning to envisage the possibility of having to resign my post at the Institute and make a premature return to England. However, I managed to simmer down and decided to let matters rest a week or so until Katilungu's return. I had met Katilungu briefly on my previous tour when he found me at the village of Chief Munkonge, and at once we appeared to hit it off together. A tall, powerfully built man who in his physical appearance, as well as in the way he carried himself, looked so much like a Bemba Chief of the Crocodile clan - though, in fact, he held no such royal rank - I think he was vastly amused and perhaps even a little impressed at the sight of this very youthful looking European - one of my nicknames on the Copperbelt was *Bwana Kaiche, kaiche* meaning 'kid' or 'youngster' - struggling to converse in the Bemba language but otherwise plainly at home in this African rural setting. But, for whatever reasons, I felt that once I had explained my case to him his response would be more favourable

and that I could count on his support. At the same time I also
recognised the importance that attached to reciprocity in these
matters. As it happened, the Annual Conference of the Union
was to be held shortly at Roan Antelope. A number of logistic
problems were involved in the organisation of the meeting, and
I showed myself willing to help in transporting items of
furniture, union files, and personnel in my vanette to Luanshya.
I drove quite openly through the mine compound but, of course,
as I discovered later, my movements had been observed and
reported to the mine authorities. I was also able to help
Katilungu in more personal ways, as when I drove him out to
visit a daughter who was attending school some considerable
distance out of town.

Yet these links with Katilungu also presented me with yet
another dilemma. One of the central purposes of the Annual
Conference was the election of office-bearers for the coming
year. I was beginning to gather inklings of internal dissension,
intimations that Katilungu himself was coming under fire.
There was thus a distinct possibility of my getting caught up in
these internal politics and so find myself having the support of
the wrong people. Nor was there to be any easy escape from the
situation. For, to my greatest astonishment, on the very first
evening of the Conference Katilungu himself and seven other
leading members of the union descended on the house I then
occupied in the Municipal part of the town. Even today I
cannot be sure just what brought them, beyond the possibility
perhaps of finding I was able to offer them a 'proper' drink -
this, I should point out, was in itself a flouting of the law since
Africans at this time were forbidden to purchase such drinks as
whisky or brandy. And having indeed served them with drinks,
the party seated themselves around my dining table and
proceeded animatedly to continue the day's debate. As though
in recognition of a general sense of the unreality of the
proceedings, Katilungu himself remarked at one point that I
must have *bwanga*, powerful 'medicine' to make Africans talk
so freely in the presence of a European. But, much as I relished
the opportunity to be party to their discourse, I was still not
entirely happy about the situation. In fact, on the following day
it looked as though my fears were to be confirmed, for I learnt
that at one of the sessions Katilungu had stormed out in a
furious rage, threatening to resign his post, and was only
gradually persuaded to return. Happily, by next day things

had calmed down, and in the afternoon I was invited to address the Conference in order to explain the purpose of my research. I cannot at this stage recall precisely what I said, though I did record in my journal that in asking their co-operation I cited a Bemba proverb, *umunwe umo tasala nda* (one finger cannot catch a louse). This won an immediate response, and I left the meeting feeling that I had the gathering with me. There was still one man at Roan, however, whom I had been warned I had most to fear. This was Robinson Puta, holding at that time the Vice-Presidency of both the African Mine Workers Trade Union and the African National Congress, and now said to be angling for the Presidency of the union. Puta had just come out of prison after serving a sentence for assaulting a Tribal Representative. Puta and James Chapoloko, the Branch-Secretary at Roan, were both strong supporters of Harry Nkumbula, the President of the African Nation Congress, and, although the two men were both Bemba, they were politically opposed to Katilungu; Puta was also said to be bitterly anti-White. I was greatly relieved therefore when, shortly afterwards, I was able to meet him and found him prepared to be more than friendly. I quickly discovered that he had been brought up at the court of Chief Nkula in the Chinsali District, and I think he found considerable satisfaction in talking to a European who could understand the importance he attached to these things (which he was to elaborate on in an autobiographical sketch he later prepared for me).

If at this point the way ahead appeared clear for me, I was soon to learn how grievously mistaken I was. Shortly afterwards I was preparing to leave for Lusaka for a Staff Conference at the Rhodes–Livingstone Institute. The main business of these gatherings was a series of seminars at which we would present papers reporting on the progress of our research, but they also provided an opportunity to escape for a while from the tensions of fieldwork and to find relaxation in the company of colleagues and friends. On this occasion, one evening soon after we had gathered at the Institute, we had an unexpected visit from Mr D. Symington, the Chairman of the Chamber of Mines. After his departure our Director, Clyde Mitchell, reported on his discussion with Symington:[2] briefly, it amounted to advising that my proposed study at Roan had been considered by the Chamber of Mines, which had decided that it should be discontinued as soon as possible; concern apparently was

expressed that I might interfere in union affairs and influence
the thinking of African union leaders. Since the mining
companies were substantial contributors to the funds of the
Institute, the Chamber's decision was tantamount to a directive.
The incident threw a pall over our proceedings, but Mitchell at
once made it clear that he was not going to yield without a
fight, and he wrote asking the Chamber to reconsider its
decision. He added that he had complete confidence in my tact
and integrity. In its reply the Chamber of Mines observed that
at the time Mitchell wrote his letter he could not have known
that I had attended a meeting in connection with an issue that
was currently a matter of contention between the mining
company at Roan and the African Mine Workers Trade Union
(AMWTU); it was reported, indeed, that not only had I
addressed this meeting but that I had also intimated that I had
come to help the union in the dispute. This was, of course,
complete nonsense, for who in my position could have been so
crass as to address a union meeting in such terms? At the same
time, it was not difficult for me to see how the Chamber might
have arrived at its version of events. After the Annual
Conference of the union mentioned earlier, it was agreed that at
the next meeting of the Roan branch I should be given the
opportunity to explain to the local membership the nature of
the study I hoped to carry out, which would include conducting
interviews in the mine compound, and to seek their co-operation.
I planned to speak in Bemba and, since my command of the
language was far from complete, I prepared fairly carefully
what I proposed to say. At the meeting itself, a well-attended
open-air affair, I spoke quite briefly and in fairly general terms
– my experience in these matters suggested that what is
important on these occasions is not so much the content of what
one says as the image of self that one is able to project. How
much of what I had to say was intelligible to my audience I had
no means of knowing, but when I had finished there were cries
of *chaumfwika*, it is understood, though, of course, this may
merely have been their polite way of expressing relief that I had
said my piece and they could now pass on to the real business of
the meeting. The main item on the agenda was, in fact, to
discuss the possibility of a strike, the reasons or pretexts for
which I might immediately have learnt more about had I stayed
on, but I had left the meeting as soon as I had said my say.
Reports of these meetings always got back to mine manage-

ment; in this instance at least it must have been a pretty garbled message that reached the ears of the African Personnel Manager and was subsequently passed up along the line of authority.

The affair slowly dragged on. Denied access to the mine compound, I was obliged to concentrate on the Municipal location. In November I at length sought an interview with Thomson, the General Manager at Roan. I gave my version of the incidents which appeared to be responsible for my exclusion from the mine township, which he seemed prepared to accept. He intimated that he personally had no objections to my presence, but the decision of the Chamber of Mines had been made as soon as it became known that my research was to include the AMWTU. And that decision, he made clear, was final. Mitchell continued to fight the case, attempting to bring the Governor, Sir Gilbert Rennie, who was also Chairman of the Institute's governing body, into the ring. It was agreed that Symington, the Chairman of the Chamber of Mines, should be invited to meet Sir Gilbert and discuss the matter when next he was in Lusaka. So far as I am aware, no such meeting ever took place.

But Mitchell was also concerned lest Symington might seek to have me removed from the Copperbelt altogether, a not unlikely possibility in view of the fact that other Europeans who were seen to have mixed too closely with Africans – the most recent of them Simon Zukas – had been forced to leave the country. At the very least it was evident that I was under close surveillance. Thus, I received information that Special Branch had questioned Katilungu and Nkoloma about their contacts with me. Then in Luanshya itself my research assistants reported that they had been questioned about such things as my attendance at a 'tribal' dance in the location; on another occasion a young man came to the house seeking a job with me – one of my staff at once identified him as an African detective. In the general paranoia that prevailed at the time, evident not only in such dramatic manifestations as the resurgence of the belief in *banyama*, or vampires, discussed in Chapter 8, but no less in the quotidian references, picked up on every side, to the presence of informers and police spies, it was difficult to avoid becoming infected with the poison oneself and succumbing to one's own paranoid fantasies. Looking back, I am not at all clear how I survived. The final entry in my

personal journal is dated February 1954, and it is clear that at
that point I considered the whole project 'caput'. In point of
fact, I remained in Luanshya for the whole of my appointed
stay, and in the end had gathered a body of data which, for all
its many lacunae and other deficiencies, allowed me to avoid the
complete fiasco I had earlier feared. It scarcely needs to be
added that this was made possible only by the continuing
support offered by Clyde Mitchell and Tony Heath, the
enthusiasm and tireless efforts of my African research assistants
Ackson Nyirenda and Simeo Mubanga, and not least the fact
that many Africans from the mine township were prepared to
continue visiting me at my house.[3]

After completing my study at Luanshya I gave some thought
to what I might do next and, thinking to strengthen my
credentials as a 'pukka' anthropologist, I considered the
possibility of doing a 'tribal' study. But my mentors, in this
instance particularly Professors Max Gluckman and Isaac
Schapera, thought that it would be a serious mistake to abandon
the urban field, of which I now had much experience, and
persuaded me that I should seek to round off my Copperbelt
researches with a study of Ndola, the area's administrative and
commercial centre. Once having agreed upon this course, I
decided that I would focus on the domestic domain, to adopt
Meyer Fortes's term, paying attention chiefly to the relationships of family and kinship. This posed problems of approach
very different from those I had confronted at Luanshya. In
Luanshya I had been concerned with the growth of African
urban politics. Thus, the events in which I was interested were
located chiefly in the public domain. So, where the past was
concerned, I had access to the various kinds of relevant
documentary material available in government files, reports,
newspapers, and the like, much of which could be supplemented
by the recollections and reminiscences of those who had
participated in the events in question. As to the contemporary
scene, my exclusion from the mine township did pose serious
problems. Not only was I unable to carry out any systematic
attitude or other kind of survey I was also denied the
opportunity for direct observation of, and informal interaction
with, Africans living and working there. Nevertheless, there
was still a great deal of valuable information to be gained from
attending meetings of various bodies, or being present on the
occasion of some public gathering; where possible I attended

myself, using the opportunity to discuss matters with those who might be able to offer useful comment on what was going on. Where this was not possible, or was in the circumstances plainly inadvisable, my research assistants had been trained to file regular field reports on what they had observed; these were not only of inestimable value in themselves but could also provide the basis for further inquiry among selected informants. However, what I proposed to do at Ndola called for a very different approach, one that approximated more to the anthropological ideal of participant observation. I was aware, of course, that so far as I personally was concerned, this was a complete non-starter. There had been no problem about living in African villages in the rural areas, but in the towns strict residential segregation along the lines of colour - save for those African domestic servants who were allowed to occupy a small dwelling on their employer's premises - was the rule, and for me to have occupied a house in an area set aside as a location or African housing area would have been out of the question. There was another factor. Since I was to focus on family and kinship relations, it was especially important that I take full account of the female perspective. As a young White male, and still unmarried, I was not well placed in this regard. My solution to these problems was to arrange for my two research assistants and their wives to be housed in different sections of the location where I hoped they would get on friendly terms with their neighbours and over time interact with them on a wholly informal basis. I hoped that in this way I would be able to come as close in an urban setting to the conditions for research which I and my colleagues at the Institute had enjoyed in the villages.

On the whole, the arrangement worked out very successfully. No less important, I enjoyed in Ndola a freedom of movement that was utterly lacking in Luanshya, a circumstance that made life there very difficult both from the point of view of research and also in purely personal terms. By contrast, at Ndola I was able to stroll casually around the location, to visit the market-place and chat with stall-holders and customers, or call in on store-keepers or at the different offices around the place. In these ways I soon became quite well known - I have mentioned *Bwana Kaiche* as one of my nicknames, another was *musungu muBemba*, 'the White Bemba' - and people were always ready to stop and engage me in conversation. I was also able to experiment with new fieldwork methods. Thus, one of the theoretical issues I was anxious to explore was the way customary relationships – say, between husband and wife – were being redefined under urban conditions: questions were involved here about the way in which traditional norms of behaviour were being modified or even repudiated, as well as about the emergence of new sets of social expectations. It occurred to me that it would be illuminating in this regard to persuade a group of Africans to come together to form a drama club, the main aim of which would be not simply to put on performances of plays but rather to have the club members work together to write their own scripts. The underlying idea was that I would learn much about how they perceived different characters would or should behave in the various urban contexts in which the unfolding of the play placed them. I did succeed in getting the club going, though, characteristically, the early meetings were mostly taken up in drawing up a constitution for the group, but I had not reckoned on some of the difficulties we would encounter. When at last we got down to the business of writing a play, various suggestions were made about possible dramatis personae. These included well-known, if unsavoury, urban personality types, as, for example, the dealer in smuggled diamonds; unfortunately, some members took the suggestions as being directed at themselves, refused to be mollified, and the club quickly folded.[4]

But, if the circumstances for fieldwork were much more favourable for research at Ndola than at Luanshya, it does not follow that the general social context within which the research was conducted can simply be ignored. In the aftermath of Federation the African National Congress went through a period of great difficulty, marked by much mutual recrimination within the leadership. There was much despondency, too, among its erstwhile supporters, and branch life went into decline. There was a need for reorganisation and a rethinking of policy if the struggle were to be successfully revived. The treatment of African customers in the European and Indian-owned stores was thought to provide a potent rallying-call, and boycotts became the chief expression of African political activity in the towns. At Ndola, the headquarters of Congress for the Western Province, public meetings became the order of the day as local leaders sought to persuade the people to support a boycott and then to mobilise them to ensure that it remained effective. Meanwhile, in the mine townships tension was rising over the question of African advancement within the mining industry, the matter now being exacerbated by the divisions that had come to develop within the African mine community over the question of the principle of equal pay for equal work. Since I have discussed the matter at some length elsewhere (Epstein 1964: 94-9), I need only recall here that when the talks that had been going on for some time between all the interested parties finally ended in deadlock there was at once a rapid decline in the membership of the African Mine Workers Trade Union. At the same time branches of an African Salaried Staff Association began to emerge all over the Copperbelt. The upshot of these developments was a sudden intensification of strife within and between the various African organisations. This led ultimately to a protracted period of industrial unrest, marked by a series of rolling strikes and culminating in the declaration of a State of Emergency in the Western Province and the swift removal to detention camps of many of the leaders - notably within the opposition faction - of the African Mine Workers Trade Union. Ndola itself was not directly involved in these events, but could not escape the general malaise. The main road linking Ndola to the south ran close by the Municipal location, and there were reports of traffic approaching or leaving the town being stoned by Africans. Driving into the location one day I stopped by the African Hotel to drop a passenger I had picked up on the way. Suddenly I found myself surrounded by a menacing crowd of youngsters armed with stones. Fortunately, I was recognised by some older Africans, who quickly dispersed my assailants, and I was able to proceed. It seemed to me, however, that fieldwork was no longer possible in these circumstances, and, since I was in any case planning to spend no more than another month or so in the town before completing my study and returning to England, I decided to advance my departure and spend my remaining time in Lusaka. A final episode that occurred there is worth recalling. I had called in at the Secretariat to say goodbye to a young District Officer with whom I had become friendly in Kasama on one of my trips to Bemba country. As we finally stood by the door of his office we were observed by a more senior officer who had just emerged from his own room a little further along the corridor. I learnt later that my friend had been reproved. Did he not know, he was asked, that he was consorting with a known subversive who was deeply involved in the recent troubles on the

Copperbelt? This subversive record was to follow me to Australia and was responsible for the fact that my application for an entry permit to Papua New Guinea for purposes of anthropological research was initially refused by the Department of Territories. But that is another story.

In reporting my fieldwork on the Copperbelt in the 1950s I have offered a personal account, for the most part without comment or exegesis, but as an anthropologist I also feel obliged to try and distance myself a little from events in order to view the situation in more analytical terms. In this way I believe I can show that, for all the unusual circumstances and timing of the research, my own particular experience on the Copperbelt not only sheds light on the more general issue of an anthropologist in a colonial situation but also draws attention to features of the fieldwork experience itself which, so far as I am aware, have been little remarked upon in the literature. At this point, then, I need to consider - if only briefly - my position *vis-à-vis* the other major parties whose interrelations made up the social field that was under observation: the administration, the mining companies, the European settler community, and the Africans.

Consider first the administration. In his admirable contribution to the volume *Anthropology and the Colonial Encounter* (1973), Richard Brown tells the story of the founding of the Rhodes-Livingstone Institute and of Godfrey Wilson, its first Director, using it to illustrate the fundamental ambiguity at the heart of the relationship between anthropology and colonial rule. Brown (1973: 192) makes the point that friction arises here because those in authority require new social knowledge, but at the same time are also inclined to fear its implications - an observation that fits fairly closely my own encounters with officers of the administration. There were individuals like R. L. ('Rob') Moffat, a man of great personal charm, who was at the time Native Courts Officer and local supervisor for my study of the Urban courts; or the District Commissioner at Luanshya, Tony Heath, neither of whom could have been more helpful. But these were rare exceptions and most of those with whom my work brought me into contact were sceptical about its value and luke-warm in their support. I discovered how thin was the ice on which I was skating shortly after my first article on the Urban courts appeared in print. I had discussed there the relations between the African members of the courts and the

District Officers who had responsibility for reviewing their work, pointing to some of the difficulties in their relationship. It seems that this had given offence to a number of people, who responded to my analysis as an attack *ad hominem*, and the Department of Native Affairs wrote to Clyde Mitchell, the Institute Director, seeking my retraction. I myself saw no reason for doing so since, so far as I was concerned, I could find nothing in the analysis that I could not justify; nor was Mitchell prepared to bring pressure to bear on me, for his part resenting what he saw as an attempt to interfere with his freedom to edit his own journal.[5] A storm in a teacup perhaps, but nevertheless a portent of things to come as the overall political situation deteriorated and, as it directly affected me personally, was to culminate, as already noted, in my being branded as a subversive.

According to Brown, the mining companies had from the very beginning been less than enthusiastic about helping to establish the Institute, but in the end did agree to contribute funds, perhaps, he suggests, in order to retain good relations with the political authorities in London and Lusaka. The mining companies of the Copperbelt have sometimes been referred to as a state within a state, so powerful that their mine compounds could almost be said to lie beyond government writ, and to whom, as Brown (1973: 190) puts it, the Northern Rhodesia government itself rarely felt strong enough to dictate. How strange, then, that these bodies should display such nervousness confronted by the arrival of an anthropologist. In my own case the Chamber of Mines had objected to my study on the ground that the time was not right: there was a delicate situation on the mines and my presence there might serve to upset the balance. It is interesting to recall in this regard that my own experience turned out to replicate in nearly all major respects that of Godfrey Wilson at Broken Hill in 1940. Following strikes on the Copperbelt in that year, Wilson was asked to suspend his research at Broken Hill for a fortnight. Shortly afterwards there were complaints that he fraternised with Africans during fieldwork, and permission to conduct further research was then withdrawn. The Governor of the day intervened in the dispute and met the mine authorities in Wilson's presence, but they refused to alter their decision because, it was said, 'his methods . . . might cause discontent and unrest besides undermining the African respect for the

European mineworkers'. (Brown 1973: 191-2) The case of
Hortense Powdermaker is also worth mentioning in this context.
Powdermaker was a respected senior American anthropologist
who worked in Luanshya for part of the time I was there myself
and in that period shared my house (Powdermaker 1967: 241).
She had come from New York with a letter of introduction from
a prominent personality with links with the world of mining,
and she had no difficulty in winning the approval of the
authorities at Roan for her study. Assuming that this meant
she was free to move around the mine compound as she pleased,
she had gone on her own one Sunday afternoon to watch the
'tribal' dancing there. Shortly afterwards she was invited to call
upon the African Personnel Manager, who made it clear to her
that such unaccompanied visits to the compound were ill
advised; thereafter she was attended on such visits by a young
mining official acting as her chaperone. The reason given for
this step - that a European woman moving around on her own
in the compound might be raped - sounds quite implausible. It
seems to me that very much the same reasons operated as in the
case of Godfrey Wilson and myself: fraternising with the
Africans might give them 'wrong ideas'. That this is not as
ludicrous as it might seem at first sight can best be appreciated
when the position of the anthropologist is considered *vis-à-vis*
the Europeans.

Throughout much of my stay in Northern Rhodesia the issue
that continued to capture public attention was Federation, the
divergent responses that it prompted within the population at
large following very closely the pre-existing lines of racial
cleavage. There was one small group, however, who, ordinarily
quite inconspicuous, now found themselves in the public
spotlight for breaching White solidarity and identifying with
the Africans. African political leaders pointedly excepted them
from the strictures levelled against all other Europeans
(Welensky 1964: 55); by contrast, editorials in the local press
carried venomous attacks on the anthropologists working in
the country at the time. Why, one demanded, 'should the
Europeans of this country tolerate these so-called sociologists
who in the name of scientific research are injecting poison into
our Race Relations?' (*Central African Post*, 10 April 1953, cited
in Richmond 1961: 153).[6]

No doubt the fact that they gave moral support[7] to the
African cause provided a convenient stick for beating the

anthropologists, but I believe it would be a gross over-simplification to explain the attitude towards anthropologists simply in these terms. The interesting question is why a bare handful of anthropologists should appear so threatening to White dominance? In what ways precisely did the behaviour of the anthropologists give such profound offence? I think one could fairly expect that most anthropologists working in Central Africa at this time would have been driven by their personal and professional values to reject the various expressions of racial discrimination that had been almost from its inception the hallmark of Northern Rhodesian society. But I also consider that we need to push the argument much further to take account of an even more basic factor – that in their very attempts to work effectively as anthropologists they were compelled to violate norms of behaviour that were quite fundamental to the structure of this colonial settler society. If one were to work successfully with Africans one had to win their confidence and support, and this was to put oneself in a position *vis-à-vis* the African that was entirely different from that of other Europeans: it was a relationship that demanded mutuality. In such circumstances even a public handshake, elsewhere scarcely to be regarded as a momentous event, here became a subversive act because it was an acknowledgement of the African's equality.

As I have just intimated, the chief mark of Northern Rhodesian society had for long been the dominant cleavage between Black and White. There was no area of social life where this cleavage did not exert a powerful influence, and it was most unlikely, therefore, that research into the workings of the society itself would be excluded. Thus, anthropologists willy-nilly found themselves impaled on the horns of a dilemma: as I have already observed, seeking the co-operation of Africans, they found themselves forced into modes of conduct that Europeans found not only deeply offensive but also, in ways they perhaps did not fully grasp consciously, threatening. What made the dilemma particularly painful was not so much the fact, say, that one was vilified in the local press, but rather that it was apt to be experienced as part of the daily round of fieldwork. By acting on terms of equality with Africans, one also left one's self open to their constant probing, testing how far one was prepared to go. Thus, even so innocent an act as a visit to the Post Office became coloured in this way in that an

African one knew, perhaps only slightly, would ostentatiously greet one as a friend and insist on an exchange of handshakes. The problem has a further dimension. For, despite the demonstrable ubiquity and power of the dominant cleavage, account must also be taken of the cleavages that existed on both sides of the divide. So, for example, where the Africans were concerned, not even in the matter of Federation could their internal differences be wholly reconciled. Consequently, in the complex political situation then prevailing, where there was so much talk, as already mentioned, of informers and police spies, it became difficult at times for the anthropologist to know where he stood or whom he could trust: the conflicts at work within and between the groups he was studying were introjected into his own self, becoming part of his very own being. In so far as all communities are riven by conflict and division, it seems to me that fieldwork of the kind undertaken by anthropologists must always involve, although to varying degree, something akin to walking a tightrope. The Copperbelt offered an example of this situation at its most intense, but I suspect that my own experience was of a kind that anthropologists are always likely to encounter if they work in any of those conflict-ridden and politically sensitive areas with which our contemporary world abounds.

But, as I have already said, I believe that my Copperbelt experience also allows me to pinpoint another general feature of fieldwork of which I have heard few anthropologists speak personally or to which I have found little reference in my reading. I have mentioned how anthropologists working in Northern Rhodesia in the 1950s were compelled to violate many of the norms of behaviour that were so important to the Whites. Yet, observing my own behaviour in that context, it was indisputable that I was White myself and thus bound at some level of the self to acknowledge the force of those norms. So, for example, from time to time I would invite an African to join me for a meal at my house: at one level of my mind, a perfectly straightforward event that would in other circumstances call for no comment at all. But in the context of fieldwork on the Copperbelt, I was not only acutely aware that what I was doing was taboo but also conscious of an inner discomfort because of the breach. There were other incidents where I was led to experience a profound sense of shame provoked by conduct of my own which I regarded as perfectly proper, but which I also recognised would have been disapproved by other Whites. Thus, my stay on the Copperbelt produced many painful encounters with the self, but after conducting fieldwork in other kinds of community I came to realise that anthropological research in the field is always apt to be a guilt- and shame-provoking activity. There is, indeed, a sense in which it must always be to some degree exploitative. This is because the pain and distress of our subjects, who by now have often become our friends, and which as friends we share, provide at the very same time the occasions that are grist for one's notebooks. There is a paradox here which seems irresolvable. If consolation is to be found in the situation, I suspect it lies in the thought that that very fracturing of the self that fieldwork seems to involve is also crucial to the process whereby one becomes open to the forming of those attachments to others that, transcending the differences of language and culture, can make of fieldwork such a rich and rewarding human experience.

2

The Role of the Urban Courts

The growth in Northern Rhodesia of large multiracial communities has been made possible by the development of the copper mining industry over the past twenty years. Some intermittent attempts to work a concession at Bwana M'Kubwa, near Ndola, had been made from early in the century, but it was not until 1927 that large-scale mining companies at last began seriously to exploit the mineral resources of the area since known as the Copperbelt.[1] Townships sprang up immediately, and the population grew rapidly. This movement was halted for a time by the world depression,[2] the effects of which led in 1931 to the closing of all but the Roan Antelope and Nkana mines, but since about 1936 the total population, African, European, and Asiatic, has increased swiftly and steadily. Today this population may be estimated very roughly at 200,000, of whom 178,000 are Africans (NRG: 1950).

This development has been accompanied at every stage by the rise of various secondary industries, the growth of commerce, and the expansion of administrative services. In a word, we find here all the activities ordinarily associated with urban communities the world over.

There is, then, in this situation a field of social relations in which Africans, Europeans, and, to a lesser extent, Asiatics are constantly interacting and mutually influencing one another. This poses a number of problems for the sociologist. Here I touch only on one: the problem of law, the ways in which disputes arise and are handled. For ever present in this situation is the possibility of 'conflict of interest', not only because it is a multiracial one, but because such conflict is inherent in every system of social relations, and is especially marked in societies undergoing rapid change.[3]

On the Copperbelt these 'conflicts of interest' operate not merely across but also within colour lines. In this chapter I confine myself to a consideration of disputes arising between urban Africans, and in particular to those coming before African Urban courts. I 'isolate' in this way for convenience of study, but it is basic to my analysis that this 'isolation' is made possible to a large extent by the dualism which exists within the legal structure of the Territory. Everyone, irrespective of colour or creed, is subject to the laws in force in the Territory and to the jurisdiction of its courts. However, by virtue of the Charter of the British South Africa Company, 1889, it is provided that in 'the administration of justice to the [indigenous] inhabitants, careful regard shall always be had to the customs and laws of the class or tribe or nation to which the parties respectively belong'. In pursuit of this policy the High Court Ordinance (s.17) lays down that the 'High Court may enforce the observance of any Native customary law. . . . such Native customary law shall be deemed applicable. . . . particularly . . . in civil causes and matters relating to marriage under Native customary law.' This raises no great difficulties in itself. Thus, in England itself courts constantly uphold claims based on customs specific to some area or locality, or are established as the practice in a particular trade. Since 1930, however, Native Authorities, and their associated Native courts, have been recognised in all tribal areas, and all Africans within them are subject to their jurisdiction. Law and jurisdiction exist, therefore, in two distinct but interlocking systems. It follows that the European who has been wronged by an African may have a remedy before a European court, whereas the African who has been injured by a European's breach of some norm of African customary law has no claim either before a European or an African court, since the latter are proscribed from hearing cases in which non-Natives are involved.

Such a form of 'legal segregation' may give rise to cases of hardship and even to a sense of grievance on the part of the African. Its significance in the present context is that it makes plain certain assumptions which underlie the policy of the administration towards Native courts. To grasp these assumptions is fundamental to an understanding of the Urban courts system because they have hitherto been accepted by the administration as equally valid for rural and urban areas. They have determined the present organisation and constitution of the African Urban courts just as they have coloured the administration's view of the functions that these courts should serve.

African Urban courts were established by the colonial government a little more than ten years ago, and since then most disputes between urban Africans, which might otherwise have had to come before European magistrates, have been dealt with in these courts. Their place within the legal structure of the Territory is defined by the Native Courts Ordinance (Cap. 158, no. 10 of 1936), which provides for the organisation, composition, jurisdiction, and powers of Native courts throughout the country. Although Urban courts are 'established' in contradistinction to Native courts in tribal areas which are said to be 'recognised', nevertheless both types stand upon the same legal footing. The Urban court is regarded, at most, as a variant form of the indigenous model, and not as a court of a very different kind.

This is seen most clearly if we consider for a moment the way in which Urban court members are appointed. Before their establishment there was much discussion of this question within the administration. One view was that the judges should be selected and appointed from amongst those Africans already resident in the towns. Only thus could the urban African be encouraged to regard the conduct and social life of Africans in these new communities as his own responsibility. The other point of view, which came to prevail, was that the primary points of political reference for the African, whether he lived within a close-knit kinship group, linked to the soil, or in the loose-knit agglomeration of a town, were still tribe and chief. His behaviour was still to be regarded as regulated by tribal principles of law and morals, which could be invoked to settle the disputes brought before an Urban court. Perhaps the point should not be pressed too far. There was never any suggestion that customary law must never be allowed to develop. But the theme which recurs constantly in discussions affecting the development of the Urban courts system is the need to maintain a balance between customary law in the rural and urban areas. It was said that Native law must adapt itself to meet the needs of new conditions, and therefore it must change; but change must always proceed from the fountain-head. The principle adopted in appointing Urban court members was in line with this point of view. In general, court members are appointed from those tribes whose people are thought to predominate in a particular town. Their selection rests with the Native Authorities of the tribes concerned. A rule that court members must retire from their posts at the end of a six-year period, and be replaced by other nominees of the Native Authorities, emphasises further the close association of Urban courts with the tribal system.

The assumption that customary law is able to cope with the kinds of problem posed by the urban situation also affects the view taken of the function that Urban courts should serve. One illustration is sufficient for my purpose. In 1944 Administrative Officers on the Copperbelt considered a proposal to establish a Native Court of Appeal for the five urban districts that make up the area. In a minute on the subject to the Senior Provincial Commissioner, Western Province, the Acting Chief Secretary pointed out that there was a constant danger of Urban courts developing and applying a body of law that was neither English common or statutory law, nor customary law. He considered, therefore, that such a court would be more satisfactory if composed of all the members of the tribe concerned in the dispute, rather than members of mixed tribes, as in the Urban court of first instance, where disagreement as to the true custom might well produce some new decision quite at variance with the general tribal custom, and thus inevitably establish new law. In other words, it is the task of urban judges to administer established customary law, not to change it.

These assumptions can best be considered by examining the role which the courts play in the urban community. I propose to do this by use of the case-method. The chief merit of this method for the lawyer is that it enables him to discover the sets of legal principles which underlie judicial decisions on diverse, and apparently discrete, social situations. The fire which accidentally spreads and burns down my neighbour's house, the pet monkey which escapes and bites a passer-by, or the cistern which overflows and causes damage in the flat below are, on the surface, disparate phenomena, but they may yet be subsumed under some common principle of liability. For this reason, to cite Hoebel (1942: 966): 'the study of primitive law must draw its generalizations from particular cases – cases to be dissected and analyzed into their principles'. Furthermore, where the doctrine of precedent operates, as in the Anglo-American system, cases becomes guides to decision, both for judges and litigants. For the sociologist, on the other hand, the case-method has wider significance. It provides him with the framework of relationships within which disputes arise and the types of situation which produce conflict in a given community.

Further, by following the way in which these disputes are settled he gains insight into the place of judicial bodies within a power structure.

I take as my point of departure a matrimonial case, heard at Ndola, since cases of this type are among the most numerous to come before the Urban courts. The parties, both Bemba, were Mangaleti, who sought a divorce from her husband, Cewe. The complainant was accompanied by her father, Peter Mwamba. When the case was called she entered the witness box and gave her statement standing:

> While we were still at home in the village, my husband wanted to have my grandmother sent to prison because I had not come to join him quickly at Ndola where he was working. He sent a letter to Chief Munkonge to say that the Chief should have my grandmother arrested because she was the one who was preventing me going to join him in the town.

> When I came to live here my husband would give me 20*s* out of his earnings. But after I had taken only a shilling to buy relish he would come and take the rest of it off me and spend it on beer. One day my mother took the 20*s* which he had given me, and I used some of it to buy two dresses. I put the dresses away in the hut and then when I came back later, I found that he had burned them. I said nothing about it at the time.

> On another occasion he cursed my mother, yet since he married me I have never cursed his mother, nor his people. My mother had been helping us by nursing my child, and when she went away he started to complain that I should not allow her to handle the child or one day I would be left holding a corpse in my hands. 'I don't want you to let her nurse the child again', he said. That is why, you Chiefs, I want this marriage to be dissolved today. Otherwise he will finish up by killing me or even the child.

This concluded the plaintiff's statement. The court asked no questions, but called upon the defendant:

> As to what my wife says, I do not deny it. I took my parents-in-law before Adam Frog at the Location court to know why they were troubling me so because I could see that they wanted to 'snatch' my wife from me.[4]

Peter Mwamba, the girl's father then gave evidence:

> When my son-in-law arrived in Ndola I welcomed him most

warmly. I said my son-in-law has come from the village, took a hen and killed it for him, for that is how we show respect to a relative by marriage. He stayed with us for two months, and I looked after him properly. Then he sent a letter to Chief Munkonge that the girl's grandmother should be arrested because the girl was still in the village. When she arrived in Ndola she was pregnant, but her husband did not control himself. He was fornicating with every girl he saw. So you see this man is a great sinner among men - [a reference to the Bemba concept of *nchila*, which assumes that if the husband of a pregnant woman commits adultery his wife is likely to die in labour]. However, through the power of God, my daughter bore a child, and we took it to the Church to have it baptized. When the husband heard of this he wanted to go straight to the Police to complain that we had baptized the child without telling him.[5] I went and saw him at his house and told him that I knew all about his 'goings on' at home and that he was a wicked man.

Another day he brought our daughter to us saying 'Take your child. I don't want her.' But she refused and said she still wanted her husband. Then he gave her £2 and her mother took £1 of this and went to the stores to buy two dresses, but when she got back the husband became furious and said: 'No, you only had £1. There's no-one who can buy two dresses for £1.[6] He took the dresses, tore them up and burned them because of his jealousy.

This concluded the statements of the parties, each of whom was now examined by the court members. First, Peter Mwamba was questioned by the President, Malubeni:

Q. 'Now, these are your children who have brought this case here. Where were they married?'
A. 'It was at the village.'
Q. 'Is this young man well known to you?'
A. 'Yes, he is a son of Chifulo who is a real "citizen" [*mukaya*, i.e. a man well-known throughout his area].'
Q. 'Did you give him a fitting welcome when he arrived from home?'
A. 'Yes, I even killed a hen for him at the time.'

The President now addressed the girl:

Q. 'Where were you married?'
A. 'It was at home in the village.'

> *Q.* 'And how many years have you been together?'
> *A.* 'Just one.'
> *Q.* 'How many children have you?'
> *A.* 'We have only been married for a year.'

The President continued his questioning, but now turned to other matters:

> *Q.* 'So when he receives his wages he doesn't give you anything, is that it?'
> *A.* 'No, he doesn't give me a thing. He only gives me a pound, all of which is ration money [*iposo*, or money for food].'
> *Q.* 'How many times has he given you that?'
> *A.* 'Four times. But it is only ration money.'
> *Q.* 'And was the marriage registered with the Court?'
> *A.* 'Yes, it was registered at home [in Bembaland].'
> *Q.* 'You say he took all this money and spent it on drink?'
> *A.* 'No, I can't say he spent it all on drink.'
> *Q.* 'This marriage was contracted in the village, isn't that so? How then can it be dissolved here when there are those marriage certificates?'
> *A.* 'No, I want it to be dissolved, that's all. It doesn't matter about the certificates.'
> *Q.* 'Would you prefer us to advise him on how a husband should behave so that he may learn to mend his ways?'
> *A.* 'He will never change, my Chief.'

A second court member, Abraham, who was Nsenga, took up the examination:

> *Q.* 'Speaking for myself, I don't know what annoys him that he should swear at your parents. Tell me, is it during the day or at night that he curses them?'
> *A.* 'Ala [an exclamation of surprise] - only during the day.'
> *Q.* 'And were there no people about to advise him against such disrespectful behaviour?'
> *A.* 'No, nobody.'
> *Q.* 'About the dresses he burned, where are they now?'
> *A.* 'There's nothing left of them. We threw them out.'

To the husband:

> *Q.* 'Why did you burn the dresses?'
> *A.* 'Because she does not appreciate what I do for her. I gave her mother 15*s* and £1 to my wife . . .'

Q. 'Yes, but what made you burn them?'

A. 'There was good reason.'

Q. 'Was it because you gave her the money and then found the dresses in the house that made you angry?'

A. 'Yes, the money that I gave her was not enough for her to have bought the dresses, and that made me very angry.'

Q. 'Very well. Now, since this is a village marriage what do you say on this matter?'

A. 'For myself, I say she is my wife.'

Q. 'Since you have been here in Ndola, how much have you given your parents-in-law?'

A. 'I have given them £1.'

Q. 'And your mother-in-law visits your house?'

A. 'Yes, she's never out of the place.'

Q. 'Who is the one then who is creating difficulties in your marriage?'

A. 'It's my father-in-law.'

To the father-in-law:

Q. 'Well then, what are you going to do in this matter since it is a village marriage?'

A. 'No, that is not important. Let them be divorced this very day.'

Q. 'But what about the certificates? What are you going to do?'

A. 'Since I was not responsible for the marriage, I don't care.'[7]

Q. 'Would it not be better if we instructed him so that he ceased to be disrespectful?'

A. 'This is really a matter for themselves. If they want to be advised you can advise them.'

To both parties:

'Listen, we wish to advise you both so that you will cease quarrelling together.'

Complainant:

'He won't mend his ways, my Chief.'

To defendant:

Q. 'Since your father-in-law says the marriage should finish, what are you going to do?'

A. 'No, it can't finish at all. He has no power to "cut" my marriage.'

Court members in unison:

'You are a most wicked fellow. For it is just the parents of the girl who have the power to "cut" your marriage. We see now that you are completely stupid, and you must not behave like this again. We find that you, young man, have done wrong, and you will pay 30s altogether. First of all you will give your wife £1 as compensation because you destroyed her dresses, and you will pay 10s to the court. If you refuse you will go to prison for fourteen days. Finally, we are warning you that you must learn to honour your parents-in-law and treat them with great respect.'

Let us consider now the procedure adopted by the court in handling this dispute. The first point to notice is that the facts in issue are presented to the court by way of statement by the litigants themselves, and not, as in English law, by way of examination. Each party is allowed to speak at length, without interruption from the Bench. In this particular instance the issues upon which the court has been called to decide are stated quite clearly. The plaintiff, Mangaleti, makes a number of complaints of substance against her husband on the basis of which she claims a divorce. She is supported by her father, who elaborates on the unsatisfactory conduct of his son-in-law. The husband, for his part, does not dispute the facts, but charges the father-in-law with trying to 'snatch' his wife from him. He claims that Mangaleti is still his wife, and denies that her father has the power to 'cut' their marriage. In other matrimonial cases the issues are not always stated so precisely. Very often the parties are not even seeking a legal remedy in the strict sense, but have approached the court in the same way that a couple in this country might seek the advice of a Marriage Guidance Council.

Procedure in the Urban courts followed largely from the fact that litigants were never represented by advocates or other individuals learned in the law, and this in turn related to the 'uncomplicated' structure of Northern Rhodesian tribal society. I can make my point clearer if I refer briefly to practice in the English legal system. In the latter, when two persons engage in litigation, the matter is ordinarily conducted from the start by professional lawyers representing each party. During the preliminary stages counsel exchange documents - technically known as 'pleadings' - which advise the litigants of the case each must be prepared to meet. All extraneous elements are pruned away, so that when the case eventually comes up for hearing, counsel are able to present the legal issues involved in a clear and simple fashion, on which the court proceeds to hear argument. Thus, in the type of case I have quoted, the procedure would be something like this. English law allows divorce on a number of specified grounds only. Therefore the petitioner would have to establish that the charges she laid against her husband could be comprehended within one or other of these grounds of divorce, as defined by law. If the husband wished to resist the suit, either he would deny the charges against him, or he would argue that, even if the facts alleged against him were true, still they did not fall within any of the categories which would entitle his wife to a divorce. English legal procedure is dominated by a conception of the litigants as right-duty bearing units. The court reaches a decision by adjudicating between conflicting claims which are presented in terms of rights and duties.

I began my discussion of the case of *Mangaleti* v. *Cewe* by pointing out that here the legal issues are fairly clearly defined. Yet the approach of the African court differs markedly from that of its English counterpart. When the Urban court has elicited the facts it does not attempt to fit them into defined legal categories. Of course, the right-duty relation is present as a core of the case, but the court is more concerned with the wider implications of the relationships which link husband and wife, son-in-law and parents-in-law. First of all, the court satisfies itself that the marriage was properly established. In this connection the length of time the couple have been together, the number of children they have, the registration of the marriage with the Native Authority etc. are all relevant. At length the court turns to an examination of the relations between all the parties to the dispute. By careful questioning and probing, it seeks to discover where the source of tension lies. Does the husband give his wife money for herself when he draws his wages or does he waste it all on beer? Is he fulfilling his legal and moral obligations to care for her properly? Of what significance is the wife's complaint that Cewe cursed her parents? Was it during the day (implying publicity), or were the curses uttered jokingly in the intimacy of the marriage bed? Here the yardstick against which conduct is measured, and responsibility indicated, is that of 'the normative man'. To every social situation, to every social relationship, society ascribes certain norms of behaviour which define the mode of conduct that the parties to a given relationship may reasonably expect from one another. Thus, it is important for the examination of the relations between Cewe and his father-in-law to discover whether both had acted in accordance with the norms appropriate to their relationship. What presents had Cewe made to his father-in-law since coming to Ndola? Was he on proper terms with his mother-in-law? Again, did Peter Mwamba give a fitting welcome to his son-in-law on his arrival from the village? In order to impress the court with his own rectitude Mwamba himself had described in his statement how he received Cewe, adding significantly that that was the customary form of showing respect to a relative by marriage.

I have been discussing the case so far purely in terms of procedure. However, my concern is not procedure as such, but the light that a discussion of procedure throws upon the role of the Urban courts. Certain obvious features at once distinguish an Urban from a Native Authority court. For example, no chief is associated with the proceedings, though court members, as the record of the case shows, may be referred to by the title 'chief'. Again, parties do not squat on the ground during the hearing of their case, but give their evidence from a witness-box, and so on. Yet, on the surface, the court handles the case in the customary manner. When the court members ask whether it would not be preferable to give the party at fault a lecture on how to conduct himself in the future, they show that they still perceived their task in traditional terms. Gluckman's statement[8] for the Barotse is apposite here:

> The judges are not only concerned to define the legal rights and duties of the *personae* involved, which are almost invariably well known, or even their application in a particular case. (Judge) Imandi's reprimand in Mahalihali's case, 'we are moulding peace among you' sums up the judicial task. To reconcile the parties by getting wrongdoers to see the error of their ways so that in future all may live together in amity, requires that judges themselves take into account ethical ideas as well as legal rules.

Gluckman stresses that Lozi judges can and do distinguish between ethical and legal rules. I believe that this also holds true for Urban court members. The son-in-law, Cewe, is penalised by the court for destroying his wife's dresses. His behaviour towards his father-in-law is equally, if not more, blameworthy, but the court is content to warn him, to instruct him in the norms appropriate to the relationship. In this sense, the court is more than a repository of the law, it is also the guardian of public morals.

A second case of divorce heard at Mufulira will help to make my point clearer. Here it was the husband seeking divorce for reasons which in my record remain vague. Later, under examination, he admitted that he was tired of his wife because she was always bringing him before the court for his innumerable adulteries. The court delivered the following judgement:

> Go now with your wife. If you marry another woman we will refuse to register the marriage because you trouble us greatly. Why do you behave [towards women] as if you were the only man here in Mufulira? Every single day you are involved in cases of adultery, as though this were your work. If you are involved in another case, we shall fine you most heavily. That is all. We do not want you to divorce your wife. You don't seem to appreciate that your wife is a very sensible [i.e. reasonable] woman because she was trying to care for you properly. [The actual phrase used was much stronger, but is difficult to convey: its literal sense is 'to guard your life lest you die quickly'.] And yet you say she is a bad woman. No, she is good, really good, and if you leave her you will never find another woman to look after you in this way. Had she been like other women she too would have been committing adultery because of the example you set her, but see, she did not do this at all. You fellow, you are mad, you have no sense. It never occurs to you that a man of wisdom ought not to go running about loosely as though he were an animal in the bush. Go now, and stay in peace . . .

Thus, the aim of the courts is to preserve existing social relations. Gluckman has been able to show for the Lozi that the role of courts is a function of the social structure. He points out that every case must be decided by 'many people' because, in a type of society dominated by face-to-face personal relationships and not largely by an impersonal economic and political framework, the interests of many individuals and groups are directly involved. The communal need to settle disputes is great, and the people involved ought to constitute themselves into an informal court. Furthermore, because of what Gluckman

calls the 'multiplex' character of social relations in these
societies, a complex set of social and psychical pressures is
constantly operating to bring about a reconciliation should a
dispute ever arise. Sentiment, economic interest, links with
common kin, religious beliefs, proximity – all these factors may
be present in a given situation, and will be seized upon by the
informal court in an effort to bring the disputants together.
Should the matter eventually have to come before a chief's
court, the latter will strive to reconcile the parties in the same
way as do family or other 'informal' councils. 'The court', says
Gluckman, 'regards its effectiveness as depending on its ability
to work in accord with the numerous incentives and pressures
which always operate to maintain the course of social life.'

The significance of this for the Urban courts should be plain.
In the Municipal locations and mine compounds in which the
vast majority of the African urban population was housed,
social relationships are no more on a face-to-face personal basis
than they are in a Manchester suburb. The attachment to land
or the possession of cattle no longer provide a nexus binding
people together in a system of more or less enduring relations.
Neighbourhood creates social links, but these do not involve
economic co-operation. Kinship does remain an important
determinant of behaviour. For example, when Peter Mwamba,
whom I had known for some time before the case came before
the Urban court, discovered that his son-in-law was committing
adultery while his wife Mangalita was pregnant [a serious
offence known as *nchila*], he went to Luanshya to consult his
relatives about seeking 'medicine' to enable his daughter to
bear her child safely. Moreover, he hesitated a long time about
bringing the case because he feared that other relatives still at
home, who had arranged the marriage, would be annoyed with
him for having broken the union. But this, rather than
weakening the argument, in fact strengthens it. For, when the
members of a kinship group are scattered in this way all over
the country, it can no longer operate as a unit, or effectually
fulfil its traditional functions. Therefore, in seeking to preserve
existing relations, the Urban courts cannot work in accord with
those pressures and incentives which operated within the tribal
system, for these no longer obtain in the urban situation. The
pressure of neighbourliness of the two sets of in-laws to maintain
this particular marriage operates only at a distance. The
husband's kin are not present to join his in-laws in scolding him

for his wrongdoing. So the bases on which a tribal court could perhaps effect a reconciliation between the parties have disappeared. Consequently, I believe that one may now expect to find Urban courts laying increasing emphasis on the penal sanction in cases which would traditionally have been a matter for compensation (compare Firth 1951: 73). Conversely, one may also expect to find parties approaching the courts and invoking these sanctions in situations which formerly fell within the province of the family or kinship group.

Disputes do not arise only between kinsmen. The new forms of social grouping and new types of social relationship which spring up in towns create fresh sources of conflict. These pose novel problems for the Urban courts which bring out even more clearly the need to see the courts not as variants of Native Authority courts but as courts of quite a different kind, operating within a social system about which there is little specifically African.

It is useful to distinguish between those legal relations voluntarily contracted, and those which are involuntarily contracted. As an example of the latter kind, consider the simple case of a bicycle accident. The complainant states that he was coming out of the compound on his bicycle, keeping to the left-hand side of the road. Along came another cyclist on the wrong side of the road, and before the plaintiff had time to dismount he was knocked down and slightly injured. The defendant's plea was that as he was riding along he saw a child coming towards him pushing a wheelbarrow, and he was frightened of hitting him. At the same moment a European car appeared. He could go neither one way nor the other, and he rode into the complainant.

Now I am not suggesting that the members of an Urban court cannot handle this situation as competently as a trained European magistrate. Quite obviously, any court, tribal or otherwise, has to deal with cases in which one person claims he has been injured by the act of another. What I want to stress is the social framework within which the case arises, and is judicially handled. In the first place, in the circumstances being considered here, the situation is clearly dominated by the elements of material culture introduced by the Europeans - the road, the bicycles, the wheelbarrow, and the motor car. Secondly, it implies the existence of a political authority over the area, which is vested in the Europeans, and which has the

power to make by-laws concerning the use of the public road.
The Urban courts do not, in fact, apply these Municipal by-
laws, but in handling the case they must take cognisance of
them, explicitly or otherwise. Finally, the legal relationship
created by the accident involves not only Africans. Europeans,
too, are concerned, but the Urban court is precluded from
calling them as witnesses, and does not consider the matter
serious enough to warrant its reference to the magistrate.

A similar situation exists in the field of legal relations
voluntarily contracted. In the urban area the impersonal cash
nexus comes to be as important in the social relations of the
African as were his kinship ties in the tribal system. He may be
a businessman, a trader in fish or second-hand goods, or the
owner of a motor bus service. He enters into a variety of legal
relations: partnership agreements, agreements for the sale of
goods, contracts of service, of hiring and letting, and so on. The
variety and complexity of the legal problems that may be
thrown up by this situation are unlimited. Developments over
the whole field of contract and tort pose new problems that an
urban court may now be called upon to face. Let me give but a
few examples. In contract, such questions are involved as the
nature of an agreement, the reality of consent, or impossibility
of performance; in tort, the nature of vicarious liability, of
remoteness of damage, or of liability for the negligence of an
independent contractor. These are precisely the questions with
which many lawyers have to juggle every hour of their
professional lives. Urban courts do entertain these problems,
and may grope their way to some solution by the use of
commonsense or other hit-and-miss methods, but they do not
administer the law. For there is no law to administer.

Thus, the Urban courts are caught in a serious dilemma.
Fundamental to every legal system is the problem of achieving
some balance between the needs of stability and the needs of
change. As Dean Pound has said: 'Law must be stable, and yet
it cannot stand still.' While the effects of an individual decision
may often be to change the law, the primary function of a court
is to administer the law. In all developed political societies this
balance is achieved by a separation of the powers of judiciary
and legislature. Even among the Lozi, where the Kuta (Council)
exercises judicial and legislative, as well as other, functions,
these functions are regarded as quite distinct. Thus, in one case
that Gluckman cites a man was acquitted by the Kuta because

no offence was disclosed under the existing law. At the
conclusion of the case, the Kuta then in its consiliar role agreed
that the facts disclosed a need for legislation. In regard to other
tribes of the region, whatever may have been the position in the
past, today all Native Authorities are invested with legal powers
to amend or abrogate existing law, or to introduce new laws.
These powers are distinct from the exercise of judicial authority.
In the urban areas, however, there is no Native Authority, nor
is there any other African body as yet authorised to deal with
problems of this nature.

A further factor complicates the issue. The present orientation
of the Urban courts towards the Native Authorities in the
urban areas creates in Urban court members a vested interest in
upholding the application of customary law to the urban
community. Most do not see the urban situation as one in
which tribal sanctions have lost much of their compelling power,
and customary rules themselves must often cease to be
applicable. On the contrary, most court members tend to regard
the urban population as being composed for the most part of
scoundrels and ne'er-do-wells who have lost their respect for
themselves, their chiefs, and their tribal customs. The remarks
of an old Lozi, made in the course of a discussion which I
attended at Mufulira, provide an apt expression of this point of
view:

> All of you would be quite happy to forget our African
> ways, wouldn't you? If I have understood you properly,
> you want cases to be decided by well-educated young men.
> So you want your cases to be decided according to the laws
> of the Europeans, is that it? It seems you want to forget all
> the customs which have been handed down to us by our
> ancestors, and follow the customs of the Whites.

In other words, court members would argue that the problems
confronting urban-dwellers were to be met by further and
stronger injections of tribal law.

In point of fact, many departures from 'strict' customary law
have been introduced by the courts in the day to day
administration of the law. In the majority of cases the tribal
affiliation of the litigants has become irrelevant, and outside
the sphere of matrimonial disputes, cases in the 'conflict of law'
are almost unknown.[9] Nevertheless, the attitudes which court
members bring to their work precludes them from seeing the
real significance of many situations. My first case, Mangaleti's

suit for divorce against Cewe, illustrates this well. I have shown
that the court tries to handle the case in the traditional way.
This is emphasised in the court's refusal to entertain the case as
a suit for divorce. The marriage had been contracted in the
village, and registered at the chief's court, so it could only be
dissolved there, in the presence of those who were party to the
marriage contract. In fact, of course, the court was not dealing
with a 'customary' marriage, in the strict sense. Under urban
conditions the whole structure of the marriage relationship has
altered. The first question put by the President of the court to
Mangaleti: 'So when he receives his wages he doesn't give you
anything, is that it?' offers a significant clue. Although the
couple had only been married a short time, the husband was
already economically responsible for his wife's care.[10] Cewe had
already established his own household, for the rent and upkeep
of which he alone was responsible. Moreover, as a wage-earner
he was socially and economically independent of his father-in-
law. These structural changes within the kinship and marriage
system are at once reflected in demands for a change in the law
or, more accurately perhaps, in a denial that the old law is
applicable. Thus, Cewe takes the line that the marriage is his
own concern and when the parents-in-law took the child to be
baptised without his knowledge or consent, he became angry
and threatened to report the matter to the police, although in
traditional Bemba law it was the maternal uncle, not the father,
who was the legal guardian of the child. Towards the end of the
case, when the court explained to Cewe that his father-in-law
wished to see the marriage dissolved, and asked for his views,
Cewe protested. His father-in-law did not have the power to
'cut' the marriage. At once the court turned upon him and
upbraided him. He was most wicked. He had betrayed his
stupidity in denying what was patent, that his marriage was
the concern of the parents-in-law, and they were the ones who
had the real power to break the union.

I have said that the need for change, whether it takes the
form of introducing new law or of modifying the old, is present
in every legal system. Now, the development in any society of a
system of courts which have power to enforce their judgements
postulates the existence of a political organisation within which
the courts have an important place. In these societies the need
for change is met in the differentiation of functions within the
political organisation. Although, therefore, there is no urban

Native Authority on the Copperbelt with which the urban courts could be associated, it is plain that the courts do operate within such an organisation. It is the role they play within this organisation that I now wish to examine.

Urban African courts are, first and foremost, a creation of the colonial government. Although court members may be referred to by Africans as 'chiefs', and treated by them with deference, in fact their authority derives from government. Ultimately, it is the 'Boma law' that they administer. This was brought home to me quite forcibly by two cases of contempt of court which were heard at Ndola. In the first case, a woman had taken out a summons against her husband, but he refused to put in an appearance, saying that he would come when the court sent a motor car for him. In the second, a fight began in the court between two litigants. The two court messengers were called to give evidence on how the fight started. Thereafter the procedure adopted in both cases was the same. The court sent for the court clerk, who occupied an adjoining office, and asked him to read out the section of the Native Courts Ordinance relating to Contempt so that the parties would know the laws concerning the court, and would not then accuse the court members of convicting them falsely (*kufyenga*).

Furthermore, the courts are situated in the grounds of the Boma or District Office and, in theory at any rate, are constantly under the eye of the District Officer, to whom there is in every case a right of appeal from the decision of an Urban court. Although the numbers of cases which come on appeal is relatively small, there is often a considerable degree of tension in the relations between court members and the District Officer. Court members used to complain, for example, that District Officers, while helpful, and indeed indispensable, would always accept the verbal and written complaints of younger, educated Africans because, as Europeans, they were able to communicate more freely with those who spoke their own tongue. The court members, it was said, would be called into the District Officer's presence, upbraided before the litigants, and their decision reversed. Court members said the result of this kind of treatment was seriously to undermine their authority. On the other hand, dissatisfied litigants might refuse to take advantage of the right of appeal because court members and District Officer were felt to be working hand in glove. The assumption was that just as the District Commissioner was bound to support his junior, so the District Officer, in turn, was bound to side with the court members.

Such facts disclose a fundamental contradiction in the attitude of Africans towards the Urban courts. In some situations, the courts are seen as standing over in opposition to the administration; in others, they are regarded as its hand-maiden, a mere appendage of the Boma, as it were. This is not something peculiar to the urban situation. It exists wherever colonial governments continue to utilise 'indigenous authorities' as agents of the administration. Hence the difficult position of the modern African chief (see, for example, Colson and Gluckman 1951). The urban situation, however, does present an interesting variation on this theme.

I have explained that Urban court members are appointed by Native Authorities in the rural areas. In point of fact they have no 'indigenous authority'. In earlier years there seems to have been a tendency for court members to regard themselves as urban chiefs, and to call themselves by the names of their own Paramount or Senior Tribal Chief. Even if we accept the premise that it is possible to apply a tribal system of law in an urban context, it is clear that the administration of justice must break down if court members regarded themselves as tribal chiefs or their urban deputies, and they were now forbidden to speak of themselves in this way. Nevertheless, because of their continued association with the Native Authorities, many urban Africans considered that the responsibility for urban affairs, which should have been their concern, remained vested in the chiefs at home, with the consequence that the Urban courts became the focus of a struggle for political power within the urban community.

The struggle was clearly reflected in the constant complaints that were lodged against the Urban courts at meetings of urban advisory and other African representative bodies. The charges – that African court members were corrupt, that they were completely arbitrary in their administration of the law, that the did not give members of 'unrepresented' tribes a fair hearing, and so on – were in my view almost wholly without substance. This fact was sometimes taken by Administrative Officers as a complete reply to these attacks on the courts. But whether the charges were justified or not is largely irrelevant. Indeed, the fact that they were for the most part baseless only heightens their significance as an index of political cleavage. For the complaints which were lodged against the courts did not constitute an attack on the principle that justice should be administered to Africans in African courts. On the contrary, Africans had an interest in African Urban courts: they saw in their existence a recognition of the fact that the towns were not merely 'the place of the Europeans'. So the attacks on the present system were really a reaffirmation of political values that had come to vest in the Urban courts, values which in turn were a function of the multiracial community within which the courts operated.

3

Tribal Elders to Trade Unions

There is a sense in which the Copperbelt is one of the great 'social laboratories' of contemporary Africa: here one can study in relatively small compass the processes of change at work over an entire continent. I have been particularly interested, in my own researches, in an aspect of such change which has also attracted a great deal of administrative and political attention – in some quarters, even alarm. This is the development of trade unionism, particularly among African mine employees.

There is more to this development than a simple matter of Africans learning European methods of organisation and 'copying' them. It has involved a radical break with time-hallowed ideas of authority based on lineage, age, or the possession of certain esoteric knowledge. So the development and acceptance of a new form of leadership has been only gradually achieved; its emergence has to be traced in the protracted struggles for prestige and power which have been a marked feature of the African Copperbelt communities.

The Africans who first came to the Copperbelt in search of work were not only truly 'tribal', they were drawn from a host of different tribes, each with its own distinctive body of customs and values. They had, of course, no knowledge or experience of urban life: they were a people whose life was bound up in a set of social relations which centred on the land, kinsfolk, village headmen, and chiefs. At first they came as migrant labourers. Often they stayed no more than six months before returning to their villages. Even today there is a high degree of coming and going and changing of jobs; but the trend towards more stable settlement in the towns is unmistakable.

From the outset, African mine employees have been housed by the mining companies in vast compounds which are administered by a European compound manager and his staff. In the past the compound manager was assisted by a body of company police, upon whom he relied to maintain discipline among the compound-dwellers. The compound police also provided some liaison between the African work-force and the management. But this arrangement was found not to be wholly satisfactory, and at some mines a system of representation through tribal elders was also introduced. On the Roan Antelope mine at Luanshya, for example, tribal elders came into being as early as 1931.

The elders were elected at meetings of their fellow tribesmen. Tribal elders were themselves mine employees, and were drawn from all departments of the mine. Some of them were unskilled labourers, some were boss boys or charge hands, and there were a few who were employed as mine clerks; but what is significant is that in nearly every case the elder could claim close relationship with his own tribal chief. Indeed, once selected, the elder would take upon himself the name of his chief, and was normally addressed by his fellow tribesmen by that name and treated accordingly: he would receive from time to time gifts of beer, bought at the Beer Hall, and brought as tribute by his people according to ancient custom.

These elders formed a kind of advisory body to the compound manager. They were entitled to call for a meeting with him whenever they wanted to discuss matters affecting the social or working conditions of the people. At the same time, through the elders, the compound manager was able to convey to the mine employees the latest pronouncement of management policy. Individual elders were also called upon as occasion demanded to advise on points of African custom. For example, in order to claim married quarters and rations the mine employee had to show that he was legally married. Since the only form of union then legally recognised among Africans was the marriage according to Native law and custom, the elders were often called upon to assist in establishing the validity or invalidity of unions contracted by their tribesmen.

The system of elders proved most valuable to the compound manager, but there is little doubt that it was also widely popular among the people. The work of the elders extended to nearly every aspect of African life on the mine. Those who had disputes brought them before the elders and had them settled in accordance with customary modes of procedure with which they were familiar. Those who had domestic troubles of one kind or another would go to their elder so that - to translate the vernacular expression - he might 'teach them to live properly in the house'. When a stranger arrived on the mine, he was at once directed to the house of the elder of his tribe, who would feed and look after him until his relatives had been traced. Whenever news was received of the death of a chief in the rural areas, people looked to their elder to make arrangements for carrying out the traditional mourning ceremonies. But, above all this, the tribal elders were also the representatives of their people in bringing their grievances about matters relating to their life on the mine to the notice of the mine authorities.

The institution of tribal elders rested, of course, upon the assumption that the social ties which linked Africans to one another in the towns remained those of the tribal system; its corollary was that forms of authority which had their origin in that system were equally applicable in the mines. At the time there was, no doubt, some justification for that view. For example, when quarrels flared up and developed into brawls, the participants would align themselves with their fellow tribesmen. The very choice as elders of men of royal or chiefly blood was itself important in this respect. Their prestige derived from tribal political values; their appointment as elders was a reaffirmation of these values. Nevertheless, there was some indication as early as 1935 that the basic assumptions underlying the introduction of the tribal elder system were becoming out of step with the new conditions obtaining in the mine compounds.

In 1935 serious disturbances had occurred on the Copperbelt, particularly at Luanshya, where a mob of Africans stormed the compound office on the mine. A number of Africans were killed at the time and many others were injured. In the strike situation the workers rejected the authority of the elders, who had to seek refuge in the compound manager's office. In 1940 there was another strike which was accompanied by violence. At Nkana mine (Kitwe) seventeen Africans were killed and sixty-three injured. The role of the elders on this occasion is well brought out in the events which occurred at Mufulira (NRG n.d.). Here, too, it was clear that the elders had lost the confidence of the people, and they were accused of being in league with the Europeans. On the advice of the District Commissioner, the workers at Mufulira appointed their own strike committee of seventeen, and the members of this committee acted as strike leaders until the dispute was settled. The strike leaders exercised effective control throughout the strike; at Mufulira there were no incidents, and the days passed quietly until the strike came to an end. Here were the first signs that a new form of authority was emerging, a new African urban leadership.

After the strike of 1940 the tribal elders, or tribal representatives as they had by now come to be known, continued to enjoy the support of government and the mines. Government labour officers were charged with the task of 'educating the tribal representatives to become intelligently familiar with all matters relating to native labour', and to teach them 'to present cases for the adjustment of labour conditions in a reasonable manner' (see Epstein 1958: 89). But the new urban communities had begun to take root, and soon the position of the tribal representatives came to be increasingly challenged by men of a different stamp.

The gradual change in the pattern of urban leadership emerges most clearly in the urban advisory councils. These bodies were set up by the government in about 1941. They were designed to bring the administration into closer touch with the local African population. The councils met regularly under the chairmanship of the local District Commissioner, and were supposed to bring to the attention of government matters of concern to the African townspeople. They discussed such issues as conditions at the hospital, the lack of adequate water facilities in the compounds, the practice of the colour bar in European-owned shops, and so on. In the beginning the mine members of the councils were elected by the tribal representatives acting as an electoral college; and the early councils were, in fact, dominated by the tribal representatives.

At about the same time, however, bodies known as African welfare societies began to flourish in the urban centres. The welfare societies drew their membership mainly from the small numbers of more-educated Africans in the towns. The leading members were invariably teachers, clerks, and hospital orderlies. Significantly, their meetings were conducted in English, whereas those of the urban advisory councils were still conducted in the vernacular.

The welfare societies were in no sense 'official' bodies and therefore could make no claim to represent the local community. They were avowedly non-political in their stated aims, but, in fact, as they developed, they rapidly acquired political functions. They made representations to the local authorities on various matters, and were often able to get conditions improved and complaints attended to. Members of the welfare societies spoke of co-operation with the advisory councils. But the tensions between them soon became open. To administrative officers it looked as though the advisory councils were coming to take second place to the welfare societies. Eventually, the societies were granted direct representation on the advisory councils.

In the years that followed the political influence of the tribal representatives began to decline. The mining companies were persuaded to give recognition to committees representing boss boys, and clerks' associations also began to make their appearance. By 1949, when the urban advisory councils were dissolved and new elections held, the tribal representatives had been largely replaced by leading figures in the welfare societies and clerks' associations.

The challenge to the position of the tribal representatives may be viewed from a number of aspects. In one way, it may be seen as an expression of the opposition of different generations; in another, of the clash between literate and illiterate. The Africans who were led to join the welfare societies were mostly younger men, and were certainly better educated than the tribal representatives. They were also more articulate on the specific problems of town life, in particular on their position as Africans within the new multiracial communities of the Copperbelt. But these oppositions were themselves only a reflection of a wider conflict of values. The system of tribal representation was rooted in the common view among White officials that the Copperbelt was a place of only temporary sojourn for African workers: after a year or two they would return to their villages to resume the more even tenor of tribal life. Thus, for the migrant labourer the tribal elder served as a reminder that, although his home lay many hundreds of miles away, his deepest ties were still with kinsfolk in distant villages and in allegiance to his chief, and that these ties were cemented by a body of customs which divided him sharply from the people of other tribes among whom he lived and worked in the towns. By contrast, the new leaders made their bid by appealing to the African as wage-earner and urban-dweller. Like the elders, the new leaders were also of rural origin, but unlike the elders they had committed themselves to the new industrial and multiracial society that had grown up around the towns. In their professions as schoolteachers, Christian ministers, and clerks they were themselves actively engaged in pushing forward into a new form of society - a society where clan affiliation or attachment to village headman and chief were no longer of primary significance in ordering social relations. By virtue of their education, and proficiency in English, these men became the intermediaries between the mass of African urban-dwellers and the European authorities; in their conscious approximation to European standards in manner and dress they were also providing a bridge between the two cultures.

Thus it was that when trade unionism was first introduced to Africans in Northern Rhodesia, the leadership in the new unions was predominantly recruited from the class of clerks and other more-educated Africans - the very people who had been leading members of the welfare societies. Hence, too, many of the early union leaders came from Barotseland or Nyasaland, whose peoples had a much longer educational tradition, from missions and mission schools, than most of their fellow Africans in the tribal areas of Northern Rhodesia.

The African Mine Workers Trade Union was established in 1949. From the very beginning there were reports of friction between the union executive and the tribal representatives about the division of their respective spheres of jurisdiction. These squabbles continued until the union decided to press for the abolition of the tribal representatives. At length the Chamber of Mines agreed to consult the African mine employees in the matter. About 80 per cent of the 35,000 Africans employed at all mines on the Copperbelt voted against the retention of tribal representation. This was in 1953, some three and a half years after the formation of the union. Later in the year the first popular elections by secret ballot were held for the urban advisory councils. When the new councils reassembled they were almost entirely composed of the new leaders in the trade union movement and the political movement that had grown out of the earlier welfare societies - the African National Congress.

The gradual disappearance of the tribal elders as a force in urban political life may be taken as an index of the degree to which Africans have become increasingly involved in the wage-earning economy and way of life of the towns. The major problems which now confront the urban African are mostly -

though not entirely - of the kind which arise in any industrial community: for assistance in their solution he turns to the new leaders in the trade unions and the African National Congress.

It would, however, be a gross oversimplification to conclude that the passing of tribal representation on the Copperbelt also marks the demise of urban 'tribalism' itself. For example, it is interesting to note that recent cleavages which have developed within the African Mine Workers Union and the African National Congress have been interpreted by Africans themselves as expressions of tribal antagonisms. We touch here on a very complex problem. The growth of the new urban communities has been marked at every stage by increasing economic and social differentiation, so that the new leadership is not itself homogeneous in its social composition. I myself consider that these cleavages cannot be explained simply in terms of the persistence of tribal values in a modern urban context; but it remains significant that Africans themselves explain them in this way.

I mention this at the very end lest it be thought that the process I have been describing, of the movement away from tribalism in the sphere of political representation, is either finally accomplished or that it extends over the entire field of social relations in which Africans are involved. That would be a misleading interpretation. The term 'tribalism' has a number of quite distinct points of reference which are sometimes apt to be confused. Its closer definition and the degree to which it operates within the various sets of urban social relations are among the major problems facing students of African urbanisation, and certainly among the most fascinating.

4

The Network and Urban Social Organisation

I

In any social field much of the raw data of observation relates to behaviour that in itself is random or haphazard: the order imposed upon the material is achieved only after patient sifting and analysis on the part of the observer. Over the years social anthropologists have been able to develop concepts and other tools of research for isolating and examining the social regularities in pre-industrial communities. In this field they have made considerable advances, though it might be said, in very general terms, that their task has been eased by the nature of pre-industrial society itself. When we turn to anthropological studies of modern urban society a very different picture obtains. To say that custom is king may be a very misleading characterisation of 'primitive' society, but in no circumstances at all could it conceivably be applied, say, to the urban communities now rapidly emerging all over Africa. Here the dominant characteristics – high population density, ethnic heterogeneity, increasing social and economic differentiation, and a high degree of occupational and residential mobility – are more likely to foster the impression of a society inchoate and incoherent, where the haphazard is more conspicuous than the regular, and all is in a state of flux. It is not surprising, then, that in this field of study there is as yet little consensus amongst anthropologists on aims and methods, and that we should still be at the beginning of our quest.

The general problem I am addressing emerges most strikingly in a town like Ndola. Ndola began as a small administrative post, railway junction, and trading settlement. It has not yet come to develop any major industry, and still possesses no single large-scale employers of labour such as are found in the neighbouring mine townships of the Copperbelt proper. Ndola's recent expansion has rested, therefore, on its ability to develop

49

its original specialised functions and provide administrative, commercial, and transport and communications services for the Copperbelt as a whole. As an administrative centre Ndola serves as the headquarters of the Western Province, which embraces the whole of the Copperbelt as well as considerable areas of the rural hinterland. By virtue of its situation, Ndola also provides the vital road and railway link between the towns of the Copperbelt, as well as the Belgian Congo (now Zaire), and the south. As a communications centre of increasing importance, it has become the main depot of various bus companies and haulage contractors; garages, motor-repair shops, and body-builders abound. Again, the goodsyard established to handle the heavy traffic in freight provided the facilities which have encouraged the emergence of Ndola as an important wholesale and distributing centre. Firms of importers have their warehouses, and other business concerns of many kinds have offices or agencies in the town. Ndola has become a rendezvous for commercial travellers, who use the town, which now possesses a fair number of hotels[1] and guest-houses, as a base from which they can cover the Copperbelt. Thus, Ndola reveals a greater diversification than other Copperbelt towns, and this process has been intensified in the rapid growth of the town in the post-war years, when the European population increased about sevenfold in the course of a decade.

But the general condition of flux associated with rapid growth and diversification is exhibited perhaps most markedly among the African inhabitants of the town. All told there are probably about 50,000 Africans living in Ndola today. Some – still a very small proportion – were born and brought up there; others have been continuously resident for the past fifteen or more years; but the great majority are newcomers who have come to live in the town within the past five years. They have come from other towns, and from the many tribal areas of Northern Rhodesia as well as from the neighbouring countries of Nyasaland (now Malawi) and the Belgian Congo (Zaire). Ethnically mixed, the African population also shows a concomitant diversity of culture which is expressed in the wide range of languages spoken, in the distinctive and sometimes exotic modes of dress of different ethnic groups, and in differences of manner and behaviour. Ndola's African population is not only mixed it is also highly mobile. There is a constant coming and going of people. Individuals move from one part of the town to another. This continuous circulation of people within the town is partly accounted for by various legal provisions which place the responsibility for housing Africans in the town on the employer and tie housing to the job: when an African gives up or loses his job he loses his house, too, and has to move elsewhere. But the growth of the town itself also exacerbates the tendency towards circulation, for as new housing areas are established new residents move in from the older parts of the location, and their vacated houses are taken over by those coming from parts of the location marked down for demolition. Then, again, people decide to move to other towns or even to return to their villages, while all the while yet others are moving in at such a rate that the number of Africans in the town has doubled in the space of only a few years. In these respects, of course, Ndola does not differ greatly from the other towns of the Copperbelt. What distinguishes Ndola is the absence of any large-scale organisation that would provide a common framework of behaviour for a substantial proportion of its inhabitants in the way that a mine administration tends to structure the social life of Africans in a mine compound. In my study of Luanshya I used the term 'atomistic' to contrast the fluidity of social relations in the Municipal location there compared with the 'unitary' structure that touched almost every conceivable aspect of social life in the compound of the Roan Antelope mine (see Epstein 1958: 153-4, 191-2). There is perhaps even stronger justification for applying the same term in the Ndola context.

Yet, despite the apparent confusion of the urban scene, it is equally patent that the Africans who live in Ndola do not compose a mere aggregation of individuals nor a disorganised rabble. As a town Ndola exists to serve certain specialised functions, and complex economic and administrative institutions have been built up which ensure that the tasks necessary to these functions are, in the main, effectively carried out. Thus, economic and administrative organisation introduce at least a minimum of social order. It also becomes apparent that within this framework the Africans have elaborated a complex system of organising social relationships among themselves. One of the most striking ways in which this organisation manifests itself is, despite the continuous coming and going of people, the apparent ease with which strangers to the town are able to discover their friends and kinsfolk, or husbands and wives to track down their deserting spouses. The fact is that each individual African is involved in a network of social ties (compare Barnes 1954; Bott 1957) which ramify throughout the urban community and extend to other towns and to the tribal areas. The immediate aim of this chapter is to demonstrate the importance of this network in urban social organisation, and to indicate some of its characteristics and functions.

The procedure I propose to adopt is to set out *in extenso* and without comment an account based on a number of texts prepared for me by an African, whom I shall call Chanda, which records his movements around Ndola and elsewhere and the contacts he made with various people in the course of a number of days. This method may be considered to impose a heavy burden on the reader, and some may object to it on other grounds, too. My justification for following this course is that it illustrates vividly the random or haphazard character of urban social life. However, I am not primarily concerned with the texts as illustrative material only; rather, I take the behaviour they describe as the subject-matter for analysis whereby I seek to establish some of the regularities present in urban life. In this respect my analysis looks towards the development of a methodology or systematic approach to the anthropological study of urban communities. The detailed evidence of the narrative which follows puts the reader in a position to check my own analysis and, where this is inadequate, to suggest alternative and more satisfactory interpretations of the material.

II

It was shortly after noon when Chanda left off work. He decided to do a little shopping in town before returning to his house in Kabushi Suburb, the new African Housing Area that lay beyond the old Municipal location (see Figure 4.1). On the way to town, and just by the African Hospital, he met a woman who had just arrived in Ndola on the bus from Fort Rosebery (now Mansa). She was of his own tribe, a Lunda of Kazembe, and he greeted her. At first she did not recognise him for it was a long time since they had last met when Chanda was on a short visit to his rural home. He introduced himself as ShiChomba, father of Chomba, and said that he was the former husband of Agnes K of Mulundu. At length the woman realised who he was and apologised for having forgotten him. 'Now I remember you well', she said, 'because your daughter resembles you so much.'

After some further conversation, in which they exchanged

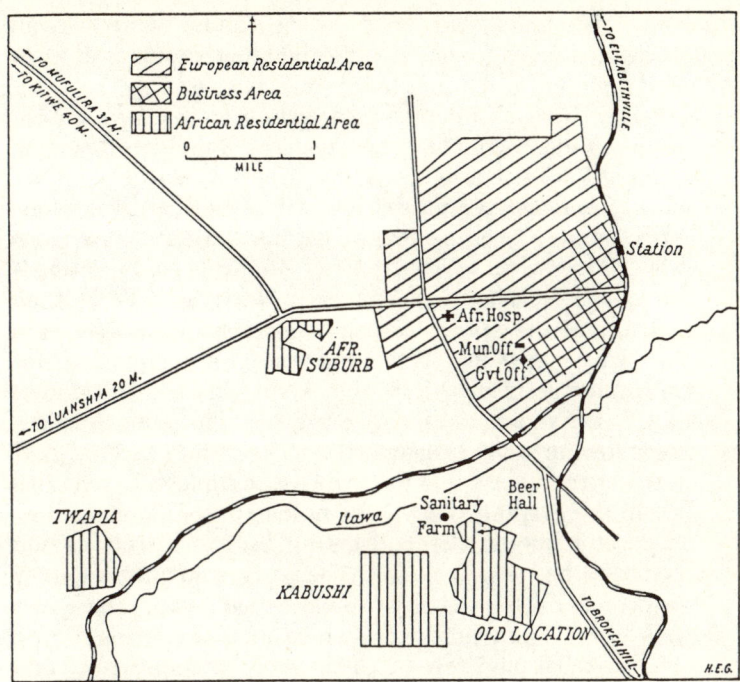

Figure 4.1. Map of Ndola

news of friends and acquaintances, Chanda bade the woman farewell and set off again on his bicycle. Near the Government Offices (the 'Boma') he ran into his friend Thompson. Thompson was employed by the Municipality as an African Health Assistant. He was one of a small number of African assistants whose duty it was to maintain regular inspection of the location and ensure that people there adhered to the standards of hygiene laid down by the European authorities. Thompson at this time was having an extra-marital affair with a girl called Paula who was Chanda's classificatory sister. As they greeted one another a co-worker of Thompson called out from behind to ask if he were going home, but Thompson replied that he had met his 'brother-in-law', who would persuade his girl-friend to be nice to him. 'You have to keep in with your brother-in-law if you are to have a good "friend"', he added. Thompson accompanied Chanda to a store, where the latter bought a broom, and then they rode off together in the direction of the location.

At one of the main road junctions they found many African cyclists headed for the location. They had just knocked off work and were rushing for lunch. Thompson remarked:

Mulamo [brother-in-law], better get off the road with these people riding crazily like this. You know, *mulamo*, they are running for lunch and then come back very soon. Some are allowed only thirty minutes and will be back at two o'clock -- but people like ourselves, we get home without having to sweat. Then we have a wash and rest awhile before eating – but not they. They will just eat quickly as soon as they arrive, and I'm afraid that some of them won't even find their wives at home. This time women like going out for charcoal and firewood in the bush. These poor fellows sweat very much . . . There are some who don't even get home for lunch. They leave their houses very early at 5.30 in the morning and don't see their wives and children until late in the evening. They have no bicycles – I wonder why they can't one day stop drinking beer and start saving money to buy a bicycle . . . Their wives commit adultery very much during the day. You know, *mulamo*, their wives cook *bwali* [the traditional Bemba dish of porridge] with chicken relish and take it to their boy-friends while their husbands die of hunger. Ah well, let them suffer: it is their turn now for when we were going to school they thought we were wasting our time, and laughed at us . . .

At length they reached the location. Then, nearing the market-place at Kabushi, someone called out to Thompson, using the appropriate greeting in Bemba for someone seen returning from work. They stopped and Thompson spoke to the man, whom Chanda did not know. The stranger told Thompson that his father had had to leave his job on the mine at Luanshya because he was no longer considered fit to work. As they parted and went on their way Thompson remarked: 'You know, it is as though those who have stayed in the villages would bewitch us because we no longer visit them. Let's go, Chanda, that man's a real *lichona* [one considered to have severed his ties with his village completely].' They approached the Bottle Store where Thompson noticed a Southern Rhodesian girl passing by. 'She's an Ndebele', he said. 'If you want I'll call her so that you can "play" her.' 'But she does not know me, and anyway I don't speak Ndebele so how shall I coax her?', Chanda enquired. 'You know I've been to Buluwayo, and I know how to approach them; they're easy-going people.' Thompson replied. 'Moreover, you look very smart, *mulamo*, she wouldn't deny you.' But Chanda seemed unconvinced. He reminded Thompson that only recently the latter had jokingly threatened to expose one of Chanda's own peccadilloes. 'And is that Ndebele not also a woman?', he asked. 'No', said Thompson, 'because she is not related to me, nor is she your tribeswoman. Such women are our "ration" here in town.' The two men parted and agreed to meet later in the day.

When he reached his house Chanda found that his wife was not at home. His next-door neighbour said that she had gone to Bwana M'Kubwa, which is about six miles outside Ndola. This news upset him for his wife had said nothing about going out. He was suddenly afraid that the Mobile Police Unit which was based at Bwana M'Kubwa might have arrested her and taken her away. He spoke to another neighbour, who assured him that there was no cause for alarm. She told him that the first neighbour was of the Nsenga tribe who had probably misunderstood what Mrs Chanda had said since she knew little Bemba. Eventually, his wife returned and prepared food. Later he went off to deliver a message to a teacher at the school in the Old location. He returned shortly and he and his wife spent the rest of the day quietly at home.

The following day was a Saturday and Chanda went into town early in order to do some shopping. Outside the butcher's shop he met a young man called Godfrey. Godfrey was a Lozi. He and Chanda had once worked together for a short time when Chanda was employed as a clerk in the Public Works Department in Ndola. At the moment Godfrey was unemployed and looking for work. Chanda asked him to accompany him to a shop where Chanda bought some meat pies which they proceeded to eat on the spot. They were joined by another young man, a Lala by the name of John. John expressed surprise at seeing Chanda in Ndola, for the last time they met they had both been working in Luanshya, the nearest town about twenty miles away. John, indeed, had been carpenter's assistant to Chanda's elder classificatory brother, who still lived there. John had come over to Ndola and found work with a European as a house-boy, but at present he, too, was unemployed. Chanda introduced him to Godfrey and while they were chatting together another man came up and greeted Godfrey in Lozi, which neither of the others understood. The

Lozi was an African detective stationed at Ndola and when he departed Godfrey commented: 'That man is very cruel – he arrests people very much. He will stay near the butchery because he knows that the butchery boys steal much meat and then sell it privately. See him standing there by the back-door . . .' John looked around. 'Does he also arrest "loafers", that old man?'

Together the three young men walked along the main street of the town. As they reached one of the oldest established and best known of the European stores Chanda was hailed by an orderly in the Public Works Department on his way to the Post Office to collect mail. 'Hallo, hallo, Mr Chanda. Are you well, father?' He also greeted Godfrey. 'And have you still not found work?' he asked. Then he explained to Chanda: 'This man, father, suffers greatly through unemployment, and it's all the fault of Leonard T., that fellow you used to work with in the PWD. He led Godfrey astray . . .' The orderly was about to launch into the story when a Land Rover pulled up outside the store and two Government Messengers got out. They immediately recognised the PWD orderly and greeted him warmly. Chanda noted that all three were Aushi from the Fort Rosebery District. Chanda was introduced to the newcomers and soon they were giving him news of a number of his friends temporarily engaged on a job there. At length the Messengers went into the store to buy shot, but there was none in stock and they drove off. Chanda bade his friends farewell and set off home.

When he reached his house he found he had visitors. His wife's grandmother, Ella, had just arrived from Fort Rosebery. With her on this occasion was her younger sister, Rose, and Alice, his wife's elder sister, who was also living in Kabushi. Although she was a grandmother, Ella still looked very young and, indeed, prided herself on her youthful appearance; she regarded herself as a 'modern' woman and was still working as a nurse at the Fort Rosebery Hospital. She began to tell Chanda how when Laura, his wife, was a girl it was she herself who had paid for her schooling. She had hoped that Laura would not marry early, but would continue her education at a school in Southern Rhodesia. But then when Laura was in Lusaka her mother had forced her into marriage with some Lala fellow whom she did not love. When next she went to Lusaka, Ella continued, and saw Laura's mother she was going to tell her something . . . and not even to write a letter all the time! While they were talking, there was a knock at the door and Chanda's sister, Anne, who was on a visit from Elizabethville in the Belgian Congo, came in. Chanda made the introductions, and began to explain something of his family tree. Ella soon interrupted him: 'Do you know, ShiChomba, that this is your own grandchild you have married?' She went into a lengthy account of how they were all related, and finally concluded: 'You *machona*, you never bother to write letters to those who remain in the village. One day when you go there you will find yourselves lost for those you left behind will already have gone.' They all laughed and agreed it was so. 'But time is short, grandmother.' Laura went and prepared food for the guests. Chanda sat apart and read the newspaper.

Early next morning Chanda set off to visit his friend James who lived in another part of the town known simply as the African Suburb, and whose wife had just given birth to a baby. Jmes had worked with Chanda's elder classificatory brother, Michael, on a carpentry course given at a mission station in their home district. Michael had introduced James to Chanda when he came on a visit to Ndola a few years previously. James was employed as a carpenter in the Public Works Department where Chanda himself was a clerk at that time, and the two became very close friends. On his way to the African Suburb, Chanda passed through the Old location and called on another friend, a 'home fellow' from the Luapula Valley, whom Chanda had known from boyhood. His friend was not at home; a younger sister's husband who was staying in the house said he had gone off to Chingola and would not be back for a fortnight. Chanda did not stay, but rode off for the Suburb.

James's wife was standing in the doorway when Chanda arrived at the house. He spoke to her in Bemba, using the special greeting customarily addressed to a woman who has just given birth to a child. They spoke a little about the baby, and then she told him that her husband had gone off to another house where there was said to be beer. Chanda left and eventually found James with another fellow whom he did not know but who also lived at Kabushi. They entered a house where beer was for sale. But it was not to their liking so they moved to another place. But here they did not even enter because the owner of the house would not allow them to park their bicycles nearby for fear the police would suspect the presence of illicitly brewed beer and come to arrest them. James said: 'Let's go and look for beer at Maria's – though I know she will have taken it to *mikotokoto*', referring to those small clearings in the bush where beer is taken for sale in order to avoid the attentions of the police.

James had guessed aright. Maria greeted Chanda with an excited outburst: 'Good heavens! ShiChomba. I'd almost forgotten you, it's so long ago . . . So you're back in Ndola again?' Maria was a friend of James's wife and remembered Chanda from the time he himself had lived in the African Suburb. They bought beer and then another 'home fellow' called George came in. They sat drinking and chatting until an Ngoni man interrupted and begged Chanda for a cigarette. George told Chanda not to be foolish, the fellow was a born scrounger: when he knew he was coming to drink beer he should have bought a packet of cigarettes for threepence at a tea-room. 'If you give him cigarettes next thing he'll be begging for beer.' George continued to abuse the Ngoni, but none of the company intervened. Altogether there were six Ngoni and nine Bemba women present, as well as a number of Ngoni, Lala, and Bemba men. But they were mostly older people. George joked: 'The beer is no good for here we are in the bush with only a lot of "old girls" – there's not a young 'un among the lot you could have some fun with.' He made some further ribald remarks and rose to go. James was keen to go on to the African Township of Twapia, a mile or so further along the road, where there was certain to be more beer, but Chanda said he had no more money and, after escorting his friends part of the way, he returned to Kabushi.

It was still quite early so, before going home he decided to call in and see his sister Anne. Anne was staying with a classificatory sister married to a businessman called Martin. At Martin's house there were a number of visitors, including Martin's own elder sister and a classificatory brother, and another man whom Chanda did not know. Martin introduced him as a friend, adding that he had been in Northern Rhodesia so long that people no longer recognised him as a Kasai. 'He speaks Bemba very well, and his face and manner do not reveal him as a Kasai.' Martin himself had just returned from a business trip to Elizabethville, and after a while Chanda asked him whether he had seen Anne's husband Jackson there. Martin said that he had and had delivered Chanda's letter to him, but that Jackson had said he was unable to answer it for the moment. 'But why can't he write us a few lines?' Chanda asked. Martin explained that Jackson was busy: he had just bought a new vanette, and he spent his time moving between the various government offices to have his documents endorsed before he could put the vehicle on the road. 'Oh, that is very good – that he is a rich man.' Chanda appears to have been suitably impressed, and he quickly changed the subject. 'What about the "fever coat" I asked you to buy me?' he demanded. 'You know the last time I went I found the coats all right', Martin replied, 'but you hadn't given me the correct size so I didn't buy you one. This time they were all finished. I tried hard to find you one, but I failed. Most of the ones I saw were of inferior quality which you, *mulamo*, as a gentleman could not wear.' 'Oh, then I am unlucky', Chanda said. Shortly afterwards he left and went home.

A short while after these events Mrs Chanda had to go to Bancroft, the new mine township near Chingola, for a few days. Chanda saw her off at the bus station and then rode off to town to collect some photographs of himself he had had taken recently. Returning home later, and passing by the Beer Hall, he ran into a number of close kinsmen who had just arrived in Ndola from home. They were talking to Crawford, an official of the African National Congress who was based at Ndola, the Congress headquarters for the Western Province. Chanda, who had himself been a branch official in the movement when he was living elsewhere on the Copperbelt, knew Crawford very well, but now he learnt that they were also kinsmen, for it soon emerged in the course of the introductions that Crawford was Chanda's classificatory father – although they belonged to different tribes, they came from neighbouring districts. Neither had known of the relationship before, and now they both expressed pleasure in its discovery. 'So you are related to Francis, my brother-in-law here', Crawford exclaimed. 'You know', he went on, 'Francis's sister is married to my own brother. Now it is good that our relationship is revealed today. That is why we get on so well. It is the blood of kinship. Very fine, indeed.'

Francis, who worked for his maternal uncle as a bookkeeper, clerk, and bus conductor, had come down to Ndola with one of his uncle's buses which required servicing. Now he insisted that Chanda give him a lift back to the garage on his bicycle. Passing through the town, Francis pointed to one of the offices and explained: 'This morning I went to those people to place an order for a new bus from Johannesburg at £3,000. You know, father, the ladies and the African clerks were looking at me very much and nodding their heads when they saw me signing the indenture papers with the manager. They saw me as a very high chap. . . . One of the European ladies gave me a cigarette. You know, father, I had two bottles of beer in the morning before I came into town so when I was talking I was very careful that my language was moderate.' 'Yes, indeed, you made an impression', Chanda commented. 'It was a landmark!' At the garage Chanda produced the photographs of himself. Francis looked at them and exclaimed with a gasp of astonishment: 'Yaa – you look just like a European, father, truly. I know you are not coming home [to the village] any more because you are very particular about things.'

On Sunday afternoon Chanda dressed up properly and set off for the Welfare Centre to watch the football match between teams from Ndola and Mufulira. But at the entrance to the ground he met his sister-in-law and her husband Robert on their way to the Beer Hall together with another elder sister of his wife. They enquired after Mrs Chanda and the baby, and when he told them that she had gone off to Bancroft they upbraided him for not having informed them before. 'Who is there to sweep up the house and fetch water for your bath? You did wrong by not telling us', they said. Robert then invited Chanda to accompany them to the Beer Hall.

At the Beer Hall they found seats in one of the chalets and immediately Chanda found himself being introduced to a large number of people whom Robert addressed as brother, maternal uncle, and so on. Together they all set to drinking the large supply of bottled beer that Robert had provided. Robert himself was a Lamba of the Ndola District. He had married Alice nine years ago. Once he had visited his wife's kin in the Kawambwa District and appeared to have been greatly impressed by what he saw there. He began to tell his relatives how well he had been treated in Kawambwa, and sought to persuade them to go there in search of wives who would be respectful and docile. All present seemed to be growing increasingly drunk. Alice asked Chanda, who tended to become intoxicated rather quickly, why he was drinking so little and sat there so quietly. Chanda replied that he was perfectly all right; he was afraid to say much lest in an unguarded moment he let something slip which might give offence to his freshly introduced affines. A Bemba woman sitting nearby agreed, and said it was always wise to watch one's step when drinking with one's in-laws. But Robert, carried away by his theme, began singing lustily: 'I am a man grown old in the town who has married a beautiful lady of Kawambwa, and that's where I'm going to settle', until his wife grabbed him by the shoulder and quietened him down. At six o'clock the Beer Hall closed and, as it was raining, Chanda made his way back to Kabushi and went to sleep.

III

Chanda, from whose accounts I have built up these 'scenes from urban life', is a young man in his early thirties. He comes from the Luapula Valley, where his father is a village headman in the Lunda kingdom of Kazembe. Chanda spent his boyhood in the valley, and received an elementary education at a mission school in the Kawambwa District. On leaving school, he accompanied an elder relative to Elizabethville, where eventually he got a job as a clerk in a European firm of importers and exporters. After some years he decided to return to Northern Rhodesia. At Luanshya he was employed as a filing clerk with a medical research unit on the mine there. More recently he had worked as an assistant in an African store and tearoom at Bancroft before he decided to come to Ndola again, where he had previously held a number of posts as a typist-clerk.

Chanda is not a typical urban African; for, as Ellen Hellmann (1949: 271) has remarked, there is no such person. Nevertheless, running through the accounts I have presented of his activities in Ndola, we may discern a number of motifs, recurrent themes in the overall pattern of the social life of the town. I should note at once that the events recalled in these accounts mostly took place at week-ends, when Chanda was off duty and free to enjoy his leisure. Yet we are also reminded on a number of occasions of the paramount need for a job in this community. The African of the towns no longer lives on the produce of the soil he has cultivated himself. Although a great many African women in Ndola do prepare gardens in the areas of bush which fringe the town, the produce of these gardens remains at most a valuable supplement to a diet of which the basic items are bought with cash. The urban African is essentially a wage-earner, dependent for his livelihood on the opportunities and services chiefly provided by others, particularly Europeans. He has come into

an urban world in which, as Louis Wirth (1956: 123) has aptly
put it, the clock and the traffic signal are symbolic of the basis
of the social order. Employment of some kind, then, is a
necessity in the town. The reflections of the Health Assistant
on the African workers scurrying back to the location at lunch-
time demonstrate how the kind of work one does not only
shapes the daily round but also affects the regard in which a
man is held by his fellows. The effective functioning of a town
demands a complex division of labour within a single economic
order. Thompson's remarks also suggest important social
divisions within the community which are based on occupational
differences and expressed in significant differences in patterns
of behaviour and ideology. When he wondered why African
labourers did not save instead of squandering their money on
beer, his observations were not necessarily valid; nevertheless,
he was giving clear expression to the same kind of 'middle-class'
attitude which elsewhere views improvidence and thriftlessness
as among the chief characteristics of the English working class.

Where so much depends upon having a job, unemployment
must count as a major hazard in African urban life, though it is
not yet the chronic sore it has become in other more
industrialised societies. Although no reliable quantitative
evidence is available, there are ample references in the
contemporary records to the incidence of unemployment among
Africans during the economic depression of the 1930s. Undoubtedly, the ability of many to return to their villages in the
tribal areas and live once more off the land mitigated the
general hardship, but the widespread distress of those days is
recalled in the word *cipoyoyo*, a vernacular term coined at the
time and still commonly used to refer to the slump.[2] After the
Second World War Northern Rhodesia entered upon a new
expansionary phase, and for some years now Government
Labour Officers have consistently reported general demand for
labour in excess of demand. Full employment, of course, does
not mean there are no unemployed. There appears to be a
considerable amount of transitional unemployment, particularly
in the building industry as one contract comes to an end and
others have yet to begin. There is also a very high labour
turnover due to personal and other causes, and young men like
Godfrey and John, referred to in Chanda's account, who give up
or are dismissed from one job may have to wait for some time
before finding another and may, as the Public Works

Department orderly remarked, 'suffer much through unemployment'. As I have indicated, there has been no serious
unemployment throughout the period of my various field
studies. At the same time, the possibility of unemployment is
always present as a potential threat to the personal security of
the African in the town - a threat, moreover, to which he is
especially vulnerable in certain respects. Since a strong body of
official and unofficial European opinion still insists on regarding
the African worker primarily as a temporarily displaced
tribesman with only minimal rights and responsibilities in the
town, no provision yet exists for social insurance schemes and
the payment of unemployment benefits. Secondly, wages are
generally paid on a 'ticket' basis, the ticket normally being
completed in just over a month. But few families ever manage
to make their wages stretch over the whole period so that they
rarely have any savings behind them to withstand a spell of
temporary unemployment or other emergency. On top of all
this, houses are tied to jobs in such a way that loss of
employment is likely to involve immediate eviction,[3] with its
attendant problems of moving furniture and possessions and
finding temporary accommodation for wife and children.

The risk of unemployment does not, of course, affect equally
or in the same way all categories within the African urban
population. Obviously, the pressures of the urban system do
not weigh so heavily on the younger men who are still bachelors
or have only recently married and are relatively recent arrivals
from the rural areas; and it is within this category that the
highest rate of labour turnover is found.[4] Nevertheless, the
various factors just outlined do underline the economically
dependent status of the African in a Northern Rhodesian town.
Socially and politically, it is also an uncertain status. While
there are a number of ordinances whose provisions aim to
protect the interests of the Africans, there are various
administrative measures designed to control the movement of
the African population, the general effect of which is to make
even more manifest his insecure position in the towns. Thus,
while local authorities are required by law to set aside special
housing areas or locations for their African residents, no African,
for example, may lawfully remain in such an area for more than
twenty-four hours without the special permission of the Location
Superintendent. In recent years there has been increasing
concern in many quarters about the growing incidence of

violence among Africans in the urban areas, which is commonly
attributed to the presence of large numbers of 'loafers' believed
to be residing illegally in the locations.[5] In Ndola, accordingly,
raids for 'unauthorised persons' are carried out regularly by the
location police. During my fieldwork there in 1955–6 one such
large-scale comb-out was undertaken by the Mobile Police Unit
based at Bwana M'kubwa at the request of the Location
Superintendent. Such was the manner in which they carried out
their task that for days afterwards I continued to hear of
women who were said to be sleeping in the bush for fear of being
arrested. At the next meeting of the Urban Advisory Council
the African leaders vigorously protested against the provocative
and offensive behaviour of the police. They drew attention to
the fact that women who were in possession of the correct
residence permits had been arrested and subsequently fined in
the Urban court because they were not in possession of marriage
certificates. Such arrests were, of course, illegal since there was
no law in force in the Territory which required the compulsory
registration of marriage among Africans. The District Commissioner, in reply, explained why the Mobile Police Unit had
been called in. The police as a whole were under strength, he
said, but occasionally it was possible to borrow a platoon from
Bwana M'kubwa for a couple of weeks. The Location Superintendent had gone away on a short leave, and he himself did
not know what instructions had been given. However, the
District Commissioner continued, as soon as he heard about the
question of marriage certificates he got in touch with the officer-
in-charge and told him to withdraw the instruction. The District
Commissioner said that he was very sorry for what had
happened: there had been a misunderstanding of the instructions
to the police. When he sought to reassure the Advisory Council
that the same mistake would not be made again, one member
was quick to point out that a raid of precisely the same kind
had been carried out at the same time in the previous year.[6] It
was the possibility of such a raid that sprang to Chanda's mind
when he returned home one day and was told by his neighbour
that his wife had gone to Bwana M'kubwa.[7] In a Northern
Rhodesian town the African is never a full and free citizen as
that term would be understood elsewhere.

Environment is a relative concept: its bounds are never set,
but what it shall include varies according to the social units
isolated for the purposes of analysis. Viewed from the standpoint

of the Africans dwelling in the location, the themes I have been discussing so far may be described as environmental constants: they refer to institutions and policies operative within the urban system over which the African has little direct control but which impinge upon him at every turn. Economic organisation and the local system of administration will vary, of course, according to the kinds of economic functions that the town has come to serve, to the aims and practice of central and colonial governments, to the presence and role of minority groups, and so on. But whatever form these take, the economic and administrative institutions of the town form the major part of the new social environment to which the urban African has to adjust. They provide a basic institutional framework, moulding and at the same time circumscribing the pattern of social relations amongst Africans in the town.

Within the limits set by this environment there are also areas of greater or lesser autonomy in which other sets of social uniformities are to be found. The first of these relates to the pattern of social relationships among Africans in the town. Here, again, Chanda's accounts provide a useful point of departure. These accounts show Chanda in personal interaction with a wide variety of individuals. The nature of his association with these people differs greatly in degree and kind. Some are purely casual and fleeting encounters, as when he accompanied his friend James to the beer-drink at *mikotokoto*, though it is noticeable here how he at once categorised the company in terms of its mixed tribal or ethnic composition. In other cases, although the people were previously unknown to him, they fell into an acknowledged social category which required some modification of his conduct. Such was his introduction at the Beer Hall to the kin of his wife's sister's husband, whom he at once treated as his own affines in accordance with tribal custom, although they were in fact of a different tribe from his own and one, moreover, that enjoyed low prestige in the ethnic ranking system that had developed in the towns (Mitchell 1956b). In yet other cases the encounter was again casual, but friendly interaction took place on the basis of a former relationship, as with the orderly or the young man Godfrey, who had once been fellow employees of Chanda in the Public Works Department. Or the effect of the meeting was to reaffirm ties that were still in existence, but temporarily dormant or inactive as in the case of his kinsmen who had just arrived in Ndola from home. Finally, there was a range of people he interacted with regularly, and with whom his relationship was relatively intense.

Each person within the total range of contact thus had a different role in relation to Chanda. For the most part, though not entirely, these roles reflect and emerge out of the different forms of grouping that operate within the urban field. It is obviously beyond the scope of the present chapter to embark on a detailed analysis of these groupings; all I shall attempt here, therefore, is to indicate them and sketch them in a preliminary fashion. To begin with, there are the social relationships associated with neighbourhood and locality. Social ties are brought into being by the mere fact of social contiguity and proximity. There are parts of Africa where the housing of the African population proceeds relatively free of government or Municipal and other controls, and the African citizen has some degree of choice over how and where he should live. But in a town like Ndola choice of this kind is more restricted, for the responsibility for providing African housing is shouldered mainly by the local authority, while the actual allocation of housing is controlled by the Location Superintendent. The usual procedure in applying for a house is to approach the Location Office through one's employer. Since the housing shortage is so acute, the newcomer will probably have his name added to a list and may then have to wait for some months or even longer before he is housed.[8] Through this system of allocation the new occupant of a house has no idea what sort of neighbours he is going to have. Although the system does allow of a certain amount of selection of householders by the authorities, the Municipal Council does not follow a policy of attempting to concentrate members of certain tribes in particular sections of the location. Any one section or ward, therefore, will show considerable diversity among its residents in terms of ethnic origins, and to a lesser extent in terms of occupational and other criteria. In short, one is rarely in a position to choose one's neighbours or one's neighbourhood.

Nor is it always easy to isolate oneself from uncongenial neighbours. Houses in the location are small and their physical proximity imposes a certain minimum of co-operation. In order to reach one's house, it is often necessary to cross a neighbour's yard. There is a communal water tap for each section and there are slabs for washing clothes. Here the women gather and have to take it in turn to fetch water or do their chores. The water taps are a frequent source of quarrels, but they also provide an opportunity to learn about one another, to make new friendships, and they become a focal point of interaction and gossip. The neighbourhood is socially a more important unit for women than it is for men. Men go off to work during the day and do not have the opportunities to form the same attachments within the immediate neighbourhood as do the women, who spend more of their time around the house. Many African women still spend most of their time outside the house itself: they prepare the vegetables, cook their meals, and do their washing-up in the open. In this way, they see their neighbours doing exactly the same sort of thing and they carry on conversations together. Often they will pop over the fence, so to speak, and do their chores together. Neighbours help one another in a variety of ways: they borrow money from one another, or household items if they should suddenly run out, or they may put up your mother-in-law if she should come on a visit and you consider it would be a breach of the in-law taboo to have her sleep in your own house. Beyond this, sets of adjoining houses become small gossip clusters in which the affairs of the neighbours are made known, discussed, and criticised. Neighbours tend to know a good deal of one's private life and movements. Whenever a man returns from work and finds his wife absent, as did Chanda on one occasion, his first recourse is to one or other of his immediate neighbours.

The boundaries of the neighbourhood are, of course, necessarily vague and, at its further reaches, shades into locality. Each part of the town, and each division or ward of the location, is distinguished by the name or number conferred upon it by the local authority. But, as I discuss further in Chapter 6, the Africans themselves also invent and employ other names to express the special character or value which a given locality has come to enjoy in their own eyes. Furthermore, in casual social intercourse, as when Chanda found his friend James in the company of a man from Kabushi whom he did not know, individuals are categorised according to the locality in which they live.

At the time Chanda prepared his accounts for me he had only recently moved into a new house and his neighbours do not figure prominently in them. In terms of numbers at least, the most important single category of persons with whom he interacted was composed of a varied body of kinsfolk. The *extent* of kinship, using that expression to cover the number of actual personal contacts with kin, is most striking. Nor, of course, do those individuals mentioned in the text exhaust the full extent of his kinship connections. There were a number of other kinsmen living in Ndola whom he saw more or less frequently, and there were many others visiting the town who would call upon him, or whom he would encounter unexpectedly on the way. In Luanshya, too, he had an extensive kinship connection, and whenever the opportunity afforded he would make the journey there by bus or bicycle to visit them. But what is equally, if not more, striking is the *range* of kinship, that is, the nature and degree of spread of kinship ties, which may be seen plainly in the skeletal genealogy I have prepared to link those persons who find a place in his narrative. None of Chanda's immediate kin was in Ndola. Two sisters were living in Elizabethville, and two others elsewhere on the Copperbelt. His father and his three brothers lived at home in Lunda country. Nevertheless, even in Ndola he remains surrounded by kinsmen, for he recognises and maintains close links with those to whom he claims relationship however remote, in both the male and female lines as well as by ties of affinity. In this way he speaks, for example, of Paula, the daughter of his father's father's brother's son, as his sister, and is addressed as father by the slightly younger Francis, whose maternal grandmother was a classificatory sister of Chanda's own father.

It seems clear that a classificatory system of kinship of this kind performs the same general function in an urban milieu as it does in tribal society. More accurately, perhaps, it serves a dual function. On the one hand, it reduces all possible relationships of kinship to a limited and readily manageable number of categories of kin, to whom behaviour is adjusted according to the appropriate kin relationship. On the other hand, it allows and even provides for the extension of these patterns of behaviour to an indefinite number of persons with whom actual genealogical connection may be extremely remote. In this respect, therefore, and in this sense, kinship provides one of the most important principles for ordering social relationships among Africans in the towns. At the same time, kinship involves more than a mere indication of the appropriate forms of behaviour to be adopted in social intercourse. The recognition of ties of kinship involves also recognition of reciprocal responsibilities, obligations, and privileges. At this time, for

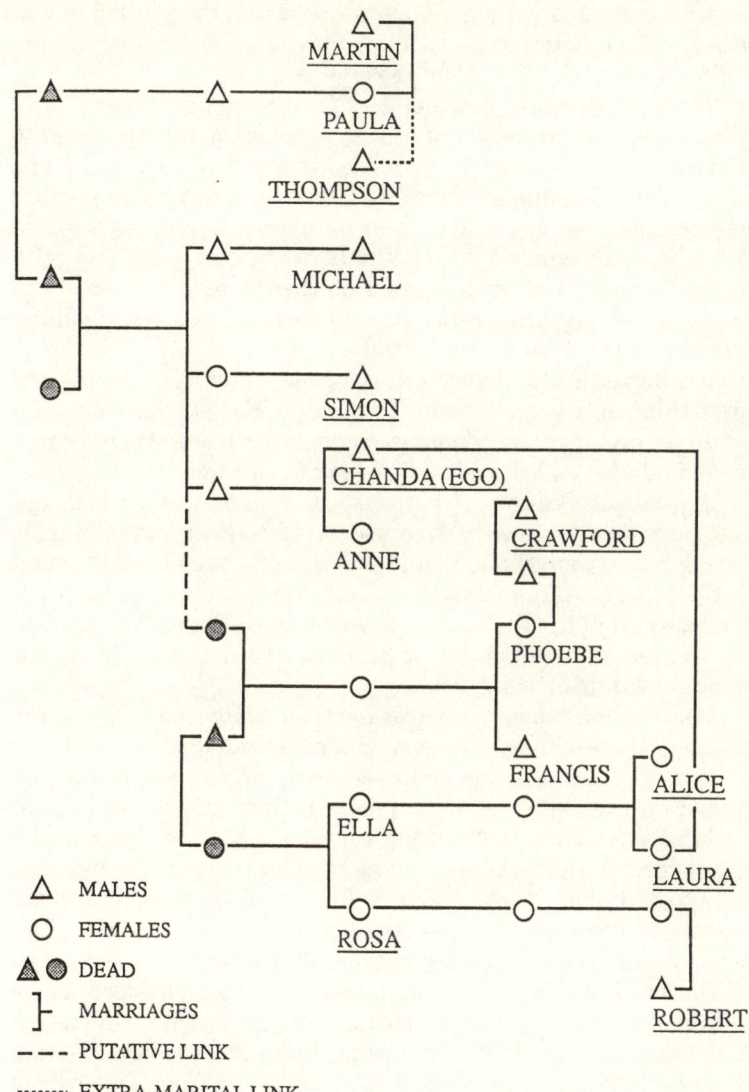

Figure 4.2. Chanda: skeleton genealogy

instance, Chanda's burdens were particularly heavy. He was keeping at his home and feeding his patrilateral cross-cousin Simon and his wife until Simon got a job and a house of his own. A conversation with Thompson, whom he met one day at the Location Office in Kabushi as they were coming home from work, illustrates the difficulties he was facing.

'*Mulamo*, I know you are in a fix', Thompson began after Chanda had shown some reluctance to accompany his friend to the Beer Hall. 'You are very worried about your financial state. Your sister [meaning Anne] has come for a very important matter, asking for 10,000 francs to buy a plot of land in Elizabethville where all your sisters in the Congo can live with their families. Your wife's grandmother is here too. And you need money for your rations and pleasure, and I understand you also have a high account at the stores. So if you go home this time you will feel very sad. To make you forget all this, the best thing is to come with me to the Beer Hall so that you feel a little happy.' Chanda elaborated on his distress. 'Where can I ever find the 10,000 francs my sister is looking for?' he asked. 'If it were just clothes she wanted, it wouldn't be so bad, but she only wants money. When she wrote a letter from Chingola she didn't say anything about all this, just that she was coming here. 10,000 francs is nearly £150. I don't know what to do.' 'I understand fully the troubles you have,' Thompson replied. 'Moreover, you keep a lot of people at your home. But let us just go and drink some beer.'

The ties of kinship impose onerous obligations which are frequently resented and even on occasion ignored; but the responsibilities are also matched with privileges. If Chanda found his duties to kinsfolk irksome at times, he also knew that in other situations and at other times he would be able to claim from them hospitality and support. Thus, when his wife was away on a short visit to Bancroft he was entitled to ask her sisters to come and help in cooking for and looking after him and, indeed, they upbraided him mildly because he had not told them that Laura had gone and he was staying on his own. From others, too, he was able to demand favours, even if sometimes, as when Martin failed to bring him back a jacket from Elizabethville, he was sadly disappointed. In the towns, where social relationships are so often casual and transitory, and where the status of Africans is so uncertain and insecure, the maintenance of widespread ties of kinship helps to ensure that there will always be someone around on whom one can rely for support and assistance now and for the future. Ties of kinship, of course, alter in their degree of intensity as the result of

absence and the movement of people, but the ties themselves
are permanent and enduring for they are fixed by the system of
descent. The wide extent and range of kinship recognised in the
towns thus introduce an important element of stability into
what is an extremely fluid situation.

Where kinship appears to serve such important social
functions in the towns, it is not perhaps surprising that its
values should spill over into, and colour, other social relationships. Thus, the modes of address and forms of behaviour
appropriate between particular categories of kin are readily
extended to unrelated persons, and close relations with
neighbours and friends are frequently translated in this way
into the idiom of kinship. What is even more illuminating as
illustrating the high value that attaches to kinship are those
cases where the parties to an already existing relationship are
later found to be kinsmen as well. Such discoveries are usually
made in the course of social introductions, which are frequently
accompanied by a detailed recital of ancestry and family
connections, and they will be received with expressions of deep
pleasure. For example, when it emerged that Chanda was
married to a girl whom he could properly call his grandchild,
everyone present immediately chorused approval: they saw the
link as lending additional strength to the bonds which already
united them. The tracing out of Chanda's tie of kinship with the
Congress leader Crawford was greeted with a similar display of
approbation. In neither of these instances was the discovery
likely to affect the behaviour of the parties to one another in
any noticeable way. Nevertheless, the establishment of the kin
tie was seen as something valuable in itself, lending to the
relationship a tone it had previously lacked.

The nature of this 'additive' element emerges most clearly in
Crawford's case, and offers a clue to understanding the value
which kinship comes to assume in the urban areas. As mentioned
earlier, Chanda had known Crawford already for some considerable time. Indeed, they were quite close friends and often drank
together at the Beer Hall. But when he met his kinsman Francis
together with Crawford one day, Francis at once explained that
Craford's own full brother, a schoolteacher in the Kawambwa
District, was married to Phoebe, Francis's sister and Chanda's
classificatory mother.[9] Chanda therefore immediately recognised
Crawford as his own classificatory father. But what is important
to note is that recognition did not involve any change in their

conduct towards one another. Chanda did not now treat
Crawford with the respect or deference due to a member of the
senior adjacent generation, even allowing for the fact that in
the matrilineal systems in which they had both been reared the
relationship of father and son is much easier than it is among
the patrilineal peoples of the region, for whom it is the father
and not the mother's brother who exercises authority over his
children. On the contrary, their behaviour remained that of
friends and equals. Indeed, this was emphasised by Crawford
himself when he remarked: 'We play together, share our gifts,
and so on just as friends and yet we are related by blood. . . .
Ah, this is fine, indeed!'

Of course, even in the routine of ordinary life under tribal
conditions the intercourse of kinsfolk often lacks formal
precision. On the other hand, among the tribes, kinship
frequently provides a basis for the formation of corporate
groups, for common residence, claims to land, and so on: as
such it is articulated with the whole political and social system
of the tribe. In the towns this condition does not obtain at all:
here, moreover, it has to be remembered that the urban African
population is made up predominantly of men and women of
working age, that is up to about 40, and that members of the
senior generation are conspicuously absent. Thus, kinship
relationships under urban conditions are in a sense largely
'destructured', and kinship consists essentially in broad
categories of persons who stand in different degrees of
relationship of blood and affinity to one another, but who tend
to treat one another as equals and recognise a general obligation
to help one another. This does not mean that the appropriate
forms of behaviour as between, say, adjacent generations or
affines are overlooked or minimised; what it means is that the
further one proceeds beyond the range of immediate kin, the
greater is the tendency to regard all kin, whatever their actual
genealogical connection, as falling within the same broad
category. It seems significant in this regard that in modern
Copperbelt parlance such persons are spoken of as being related
mu cibululu, an expression now used by Africans of every tribe
to express the notion of kinship which derives via Fanagolo
from the Afrikaans word *broer*, meaning brother. The deep
value which attaches to kinship in the urban context lies in the
fact that at its furthest extension it becomes synonymous with,
and gives expression to, the fundamental values of brotherhood.

Closely related to the ties of kinship, though really of a different order, are those which stem from membership of a tribe. Every African in Ndola is a member of a tribe, and the veriest tot will answer without hesitation if asked to what tribe he or she belongs. All told, there are probably some fifty and more tribes represented in the population of the town. They are drawn mainly from the Northern and Eastern Provinces of Northern Rhodesia, but important sections also come from the Western and Central Provinces, and from the neighbouring countries of Nyasaland and the Belgian Congo. The members of these different groups are scattered indiscriminately over the whole location, though here and there about the town small tribal pockets may be found. Thus, the small settlement known as the Sanitary Farm, which is slightly apart from the location, is composed almost entirely of Lovale, and is commonly regarded among those of other groups as the haunt of sorcerers and ghouls. To all Lovale, irrespective of the jobs they actually do, the collective term *Nyamazai*, scavengers, is contemptuously applied because Lovale alone have shown themselves prepared to undertake the work of night-soil removal. Lovale and Lunda from the Mwinilunga District in the far west of the country are also said to be concentrated in various contractors' compounds around the town, and in the African Township of Twapia, which caters for petty traders and other self-employed Africans, but I did not check these statements carefully in the field.

Although in the main they are, thus, interspersed and intermingled, the tribes are also set apart from one another by language, custom, and other marks of distinctiveness. A wide variety of languages is spoken in the town and these are often mutually unintelligible. In the Urban court, or in other contexts where Africans of different ethnic groups have to come together, recourse may have to be made to interpreters. In these circumstances, misunderstandings of the kind attributed to Chanda's Nsenga neighbour are common. On the other hand, most Africans I have known well showed a remarkable ease in acquiring the languages of other groups. Customs, too, particularly those relating to dress or adornment, serve as important diacritical indices which readily disclose one's tribal identity. Even physical appearance may be a relevant factor, as is suggested in Martin's introduction of his Kasai friend to Chanda, though it is also apparent from Martin's remarks that what are physical characteristics and what cultural may not always be easy to determine. On the basis of these and other criteria, tribes become important categories of social interaction among Africans in the towns, as Mitchell (1956b) has shown. Support for this view of urban 'tribalism' is to be found throughout Chanda's account. Whenever he comes into the presence of strangers, as at a beer-drink or on encountering the Government Messengers from Fort Rosebery, he reacts at once by placing them in a category in terms of the distinguishing characteristics that have come to be associated with their tribe, and he adjusts his behaviour accordingly. But Mitchell was able to carry his analysis of this categorising process much further: he was able to demonstrate how, despite the large number of tribes represented on the Copperbelt, the whole of the African urban population was, in fact, broken down and contained within a very limited number of broad ethnic categories. Knowledge of an alien tribe, its language, culture, and system of internal relations is related to geographical and social distance. Tribes that territorially adjoin one another will be acutely aware of the hostilities and the cultural and historical differences which divide and separate them from each other; but such matters lie beyond the ken of the remote outsider living in another part of the country. His knowledge of the distant tribes is likely to be fragmentary, so that he tends to overlook or to be unaware of their internal differences and so to bracket them altogether, treating them as a single tribal entity. In this way, for example, the Bemba of the Northern Province ignore the considerable differences that exist between the tribes of the Eastern Province, and in the towns lump them altogether as Ngoni, the dominant group of the region. Similarly, all Africans from the Belgian Congo who come to stay on the Copperbelt are known simply as Kasai. For a long time I myself lingered under the impression that the term Kasai referred to a specific tribal group; it was only late in my fieldwork that I came to realise that the usage was only a further illustration of the categorising process.

'Tribalism' in the sense just defined operates in a wide range of situations, but its influence is most noticeable perhaps in the field of personal interaction. Kinsfolk apart, a man like Chanda finds his most intimate associates among those he calls 'home-fellows' - his fellow tribesmen. These are the ones he will put himself out to go and visit, and with whom he prefers to sit and chat and drink beer. In the urban context Lunda of Kazembe are associated with the numerically preponderant Bemba, with whom they share a common language and many common customs and traditions. Chanda has a number of friends, like Thompson, for example, who are Bemba, but he appears to have no close friends outside the range of Bemba-speaking peoples. But, as in the case of kinship, 'tribalism' involves more than a mere delimiting of the range of interaction. Membership of a tribe also imposes an obligation, vaguely defined though it may be, to give mutual aid and support. Among fellow tribesmen one is always at home, for all share certain common interests which set them apart from, or in opposition to, the other tribes among and with whom they live and work in the towns. At the same time it should be stressed here that 'tribalism' is always situational; it does not operate equally or with the same degree of intensity over the whole field of social relations in which urban Africans now participate. The young man Godfrey was linked with the African detective as a fellow Lozi; but he associated himself with alien tribesmen in their common opposition to the other in his role of policeman.

One concept that finds repeated expression throughout Chanda's account is that of prestige. In broad terms, prestige refers to the esteem and regard which are accorded to a person (or group) in virtue of his personal qualities, his special abilities, or his general mode of behaviour and way of life. In the Ndola context some of the marks by which a man of prestige is known are indicated in Chanda's account of his visit to his brother-in-law and in his conversations with Francis. He had called on the former in order to see his sister, he said, but it is likely he was more interested in learning whether Martin had brought him back a 'fever coat' from Elizabethville. A number of observers of the Northern Rhodesian urban scene have already remarked the importance which Africans attach to matters of dress. At this time it seems that the 'fever coat' - a long, loose-fitting jacket - was particularly prized and would have enabled Chanda to cut a considerable dash. Here, then, prestige accrues to the African who dresses smartly in the 'European' fashion. Again, Chanda himself acquires prestige because of his light complexion - 'you look just like a European' - and because in his mode of dress and in other ways he comports himself like a 'gentleman', as will be seen again later one of the many terms now in common use on the Copperbelt to convey the notion of superior social status. On the other hand, in other contexts and in other company his incapacity for consuming large quantities of beer might count against him and stamp him as something less than a full man. Evaluation in terms of prestige extends even to the tribes themselves: this is clearly reflected, for example, in the boasts of the Lamba who had married 'a beautiful lady of Kawambwa', for the Lunda in general have a reputation for sophistication, while the Lamba are collectively designated by others as *Bapwapwa*, a term of contempt originating in the alleged propensity of the Lamba for eating the lungs (*pwapwa*) which is commonly regarded as 'dirty' meat.

In this context, then, prestige emerges as a pervasive concept in the sense that it enters into almost every social activity and into every social relationship; or, rephrasing it more forcefully, there are very few facets of human behaviour which may not be seized upon in evaluating prestige. This is perhaps what one would expect, given the general fluidity of the urban situation, the heterogeneous and differentiated character of the African urban population with its concomitant diversity of norms and standards of behaviour, and the marked emphasis on achieved as against ascribed status, all of which serve to create a set of conditions in which the struggle for prestige becomes a major preoccupation of the new urban-dwellers. Accordingly, the criteria of prestige are extremely varied, often ill defined and frequently inconsistent. There is, therefore, no one single principle which embraces all the various criteria of prestige, and no single prestige system which comprehends the whole community. In this sense, prestige may be said to be 'particular' in that its conferment always involves reference to a particular situation and to a particular set of people. In another sense, however, prestige is 'general', and it is important that the two usages of the term be kept distinct. By 'general' I mean here that despite the variability in the components that enter into the whole notion of prestige, certain of these will tend to run together in clusters, and have widespread recognition throughout the community. Thus, white-collar occupation, secondary school education, smartness in dress and appearance, a well-furnished house, etc. are in themselves important and independent criteria of prestige. When they run together - as frequently they do - they mark out readily the man of acknowledged superior status. It is this 'clustering' which has enabled Mitchell and myself to speak of 'the European way of life' as providing a scale in terms of which the African urban population is stratified (Mitchell 1956b; Mitchell and Epstein 1959). In other words, such clusters or configurations provide the basis for the emergence of social classes as a further important category of social interaction. Social classes arise out of consciousness of kind: among the members of a class there is a ready and mutual acceptance of one another as social equals; they interact more frequently, exchange visits, develop common interests and activities and even distinctive modes of behaviour which mark them off clearly, at least in their own eyes, from other classes. It was precisely in these terms, for example, that Thompson and Chanda saw themselves as set apart from the scurrying African labourers who had once laughed at them for wasting their time at school.

Thus, prestige in its 'general' aspect provides a working model of the class structure which Africans themselves employ in a wide variety of situations. But it does not follow from this that in practice the lines of demarcation between classes can always be rigidly drawn. The fact that 'general' prestige is built up around a cluster of criteria allows of different combinations and permutations which may make 'class placement' in practice extraordinarily difficult. This lack of rigidity in turn serves to promote and intensify the struggle for prestige within and between the strata, so that increasingly refined 'particular' criteria of prestige come to be invoked to advance one's status. Thus, while 'general' prestige provides an overall framework for categorising the urban population in terms of class, in terms of actual social interaction 'particular' prestige becomes increasingly important in marking inclusion or exclusion from class membership. The variety and diversity and the generally pervasive character of the 'particular' criteria of prestige thus open the way to a complex pattern of changing allegiances and cross-cutting ties both within and between classes.

We have already had occasion to remark on the high degree of diversification as a characteristic of urban communities. With this process there goes, too, an increasing segmentation and specialisation of social interests. A further mark, therefore, of urban communities is the development of various kinds of formal association for the protection and furtherance of those interests. Indeed, it is a common assumption in the literature of urban sociology that, with the progressive displacement in urban society of 'primary' by 'secondary' groups, the association comes to have overriding importance in the social organisation of the town. In recent years this view has come to be increasingly challenged (see, for example, Dotson 1951; LaPiere 1954); certainly, there is little support for it to be found in the Ndola material. Thus, throughout Chanda's account there is mention of only one association, the African National Congress – and even then the reference was incidental. Here Chanda's lack of emphasis on the associations accurately reflects the relatively limited extent to which social relationships among Africans in Ndola are organised through membership of these bodies.

Apart from the churches, to one or other of which the vast majority of Africans in Ndola give at least nominal allegiance,[10] those associations which affect potentially the largest number of people are the African National Congress and the various African trade unions. The African National Congress is a political body organised on a territorial basis, with central headquarters in Lusaka and local branches throughout the country organised on a provincial basis. Ndola is the head-quarters for the Western Province. Congress claims to represent the voice of African opinion in the Territory, and since its inception in 1949 has organised a number of campaigns to rectify African grievances or to protest about 'matters considered detrimental to African interests' (Epstein 1958: 162). Despite the widespread popular support Congress has enjoyed, it is a loose-knit organisation, in some respects extraordinarily haphazard, with a very small registered membership and little funds. Indeed, the concept of a regular membership has very little meaning when applied to a body like Congress in present circumstances. Anthony Sampson's (1958: 41) description of the African National Congress in South Africa is equally apposite to the situation in Northern Rhodesia: 'there are times of sudden indignation in the locations when nearly everyone claims to be a Congressman, others when Congress appears to consist only of a hard core of enthusiasts.' The activities of Congress are intermittent, and as a political association Congress acts to organise the community only in spasmodic eruptions and for specific purposes. So far as trade unions are concerned, the analysis which I offered (Epstein 1958) of the 'location' unions in Luanshya seems equally relevant to Ndola. There are a number of African unions in the town, but with the possible exception of the Municipal Workers' and the Railway Workers' Unions, they are small, poorly organised, and ineffectual. Indeed, in a few cases, the organisation has so broken down that it is only in a nominal sense that one can speak of the union as continuing to exist. Finally, there are a number of recreational bodies such as the Football Club or the Ballroom Dance Society, and the tribal dancing teams of the kind described by Mitchell in his paper on the Kalela dance (1956b). Conspicuously absent in Ndola is the profusion of tribal associations, mutual aid, or burial societies, and the variegated assortment of social clubs reported so frequently of other urban communities elsewhere in Africa.

The apparent paucity of associational life, and the general role of the associations in the community raise questions which go far beyond the scope of my present task. What is important in the present context is that they involve a very different mode of ordering social relations from those considered hitherto. Typically, the association has a clearly defined formal structure, and to this extent the relationships in which the members participate are themselves 'structured' or formalised. However, the associations, too, have a categorical aspect. Voluntary associations tend to arise out of the interaction of persons who see the formally constituted body as the proper or more effective way of furthering the avowed aims and interests they hold in common. Once established, the association may extend further its membership and so come to include many strangers, but all members now interact consistently within a new structural framework. On the other hand, interaction within the association also gives rise to new sets of ties which continue to operate outside this framework. Thus, Chanda knew Crawford primarily as a leader in the African National Congress, but when they met casually at the Beer Hall and drank together their behaviour reflected a categorical rather than a 'structured' or formalised relationship. In precisely the same way relationships developed within an institutional setting, such as at school or at work, provide a basis for friendly social intercourse of a different kind outside that particular setting. Apart, therefore, from the more specific role that they play in the political, economic, and other sectors of urban life, formal institutions and associations have a further importance in providing a major principle of recruitment to the network of social relations in which every urban African is involved.

IV

In the preceding section I have used the account of his activities presented by Chanda to illustrate the random character of much of urban social life. I have also tried to show that within this extremely fluid field there are also elements of regularity, and here, too, I have made use of Chanda's material in illustrating some of their properties. Briefly, I have drawn attention to the importance of various categorical and formalised relationships in urban social structure. But Chanda's material also has a further and more direct bearing on our problem, for it draws immediate attention to another principle around which social relations are ordered. As I have already noted, Chanda's accounts show him interacting with a fairly wide range of people to whom he is linked in varying ways: he acknowledges certain general obligations towards most of them, and he treats them in the main as his social equals. Together these persons represent a section - in all likelihood a fairly limited one - of the total range of his social contacts in the town. However, they do not in any sense constitute a group, for they lack any co-ordinating organisation. They do not even form a collectivity, for they have no corporate existence whatsoever: all they may be said to possess in common is the social tie which links each of them individually to a central figure, Chanda. Chanda, that is to say, is in touch with a number of people, some of whom may be in touch with each other, and some of whom may not. Barnes (1954) speaks of a social field of this kind as a network, and I find it convenient to follow his usage.

A network in the sense employed here is always egocentric: it exists and can be defined only with reference to a particular individual. As Barnes remarks, each person sees himself at the centre of a collection of friends. It follows, therefore, that the network is always 'personal', for the set of links that make it up are always unique for each individual. Chanda has his network, but the individuals who compose it are each also at the centre of his or her own. Many members of their networks will be unknown to Chanda, as is indeed evident throughout his account. In parenthesis, it may be remarked that even his wife has her own, separate, network. While there are many kin and friends who form part of their common network, she has her own range of contacts which she maintains independently of her husband. This is consistent with their highly segregated conjugal roles, suggested by Chanda's material in which his wife is never once mentioned as accompanying him on his visits.

A network is made up of pairs of persons who interact with one another in terms of social categories, and who regard each other, therefore, as approximate social equals, ignoring in this context the slight differences in social status there may be between them. Since it is essentially 'personal', the network allows of many different configurations, and these in turn may provide the basis for a typology of networks. Thus, in handling problems of urban family structure in London, Elizabeth Bott (1957) attempted to relate variations in conjugal roles to different types of network. Briefly, she distinguished between close-knit and loose-knit networks. A close-knit network is defined as one in which there are many relationships between its component units: in a family which has a close-knit network many of its friends, neighbours, and kinsfolk will know one another. In Bott's terms, such a network has a high degree of connectedness. By contrast, a loose-knit network exists where friends, neighbours, and kin are not known to each other, and the degree of connectedness is therefore slight.

Applying Bott's distinction, Chanda's network would appear to be of the loose-knit variety. However, closer examination of the data suggests that this may not be an adequate formulation. To begin with, not every link in the network has the same density; as we noted at the outset, Chanda does not interact with everyone in the network with the same degree of intensity. There are those around him with whom he has close ties and who are also more closely knit together than others. There are others, again, with whom his ties are more or less close, but whom he sees less frequently and who are strangers or have only tenuous links among themselves. Thus, there may be a relatively high degree of connectedness among those with whom Chanda interacts in terms of social class, or among those whom he counts as kin, but as between the two categories themselves the degree of connectedness may be slight. In short, the network may not be connected in its totality, but highly connected in its parts. Those people with whom Chanda interacts most intensely and most regularly, and who are, therefore, likely to come to know one another (that is to say that part of the total network which shows a high degree of connectedness) I propose to speak of as forming the *effective* network; the remainder constitute the *extended* network.

Barnes (1954: 46) has observed that it is only pairs of persons who are directly in contact with one another in the network who regard themselves as approximately of equal status; but he also points out that each person in the network does not necessarily regard everyone else in it as his equal. In the *effective* network the tendency, of course, is for status differentiation to be minimised; but in the *extended* network, although interaction takes place between approximate social equals, the likelihood of some status differentiation being recognised is much greater because of the different social categories from which the network is recruited. For example, when Chanda meets Thompson, or the orderly in the Public Works Department, or his wife's sister's husband, Robert, he reacts to each of them as his social equals. Thompson himself, however, who counts as part of Chanda's *effective* network, knows neither the orderly nor Robert, and he would regard them both as his social inferiors: in the one case, because of the orderly's lowly occupation; in the other, because Robert belonged to a tribe that ranks low in popular esteem on the Copperbelt, and because he was a lorry-driver to boot. The *effective* network, then, consists of clusters of persons fairly closely knitted together. The limits of such clusters – to use Barnes's term – are vague, but in some situations they show an exclusiveness so marked as to suggest the existence of groups in the strict sense, and point to recognisable divisions within the community. The *extended* network, on the other hand, which makes greater allowance for the gradations of social status, tends to cut across such divisions. The network as a whole, therefore, provides a covert or informal structure composed of interpersonal links which spread out and ramify in all directions, not only criss-crossing the whole of the local community but knitting together people in different towns and in town and country.

In exploring the social system of Bremnes, Barnes was concerned with the concept of network as one among a number of possible tools for use in the analysis of the phenomenon of social class. Elizabeth Bott has also used it for somewhat similar purposes. For Bott the network of friends, neighbours, and relatives mediates between the family and the total society: perception of the society as a whole, and in particular of the class structure, is thus related to experience within this primary social world. More immediately, however, Bott was concerned with the concept of network in explaining variations of conjugal role within the family. It seems clear that all of these uses would be equally valuable in probing the social system of a town like Ndola. However, in concluding this present discussion of the concept, I want to suggest that it may also have considerable relevance to the investigation of other problems arising within the urban field, such as the question of social control. For example, Mitchell (1957) has expressed the view that African marriage on the Copperbelt is gradually assuming a character of its own. He then raises the question of what mechanism, in lieu of the kinship system, operates to enforce the norms of marital behaviour, and suggests for an answer that it lies in the African Urban courts. The role of the courts is clearly important here, but I suggest that a fuller understanding of the growth of new norms of married behaviour, and the pressures towards acceptance of them may be found in the operation of the network.

The evidence to support this view would take me far beyond my present purpose, and here, therefore, I am able merely to sketch in the general argument. In the discussion hitherto I have treated the network simply as a series of links in a chain of personal interaction: nothing has been said of the content of that interaction. When we follow a young man like Chanda through these various links, what we observe is a number of individuals conversing together, recounting experiences, exchanging news of acquaintances and friends, discussing personal matters or ideas, and so on. Implicit in much of this conversation are the norms, values, and attitudes, of general or special application, recognised in the society at large or within some segments of it. An important part of such exchanges is made up of gossip, that is discussion of the affairs and behaviour of other persons in their absence. Viewed, then, in terms of the content of interaction, the network may also be seen as a mechanism of communication, providing what often amounts to a series of links in a chain of gossip.

In common parlance gossip is frequently associated with idle chatter: in sociological analysis, however, it represents an activity of considerable importance (see, for example, Colson 1953). Much of gossip is condemnatory; but this implies the existence of some norm in terms of which one's character or

conduct is evaluated and condemned. In this sense the function
of gossip is the reaffirmation of norms of behaviour held in
common by those who participate in it. A further property of
gossip is that its victims are rarely seized upon at random. To
adopt Oscar Wilde's epigram, there is only one thing worse
than being talked about and that is not being talked about. To
be talked about in one's absence, in however derogatory terms,
is to be conceded a measure of social importance in the gossip
set; not to be talked about is the mark of social insignificance,
of exclusion from the set. In other words, gossip denotes a
certain community of interest, even if the limits of community
can only be vaguely defined. It is within the *effective* network
that gossip is most intense, and the marriages, *affaires*, and
conjugal relations of those within the *effective* network are
among its major themes. In this way continuous gossip leads
not merely to the reaffirmation of established norms but also to
the clarification and formulation of new ones. When we recall,
too, the importance that attaches to prestige in Copperbelt
society, so that breach of the norm is also likely to involve loss
of esteem in the eyes of neighbours and friends, the importance
that the network may assume as an instrument of social control
readily becomes apparent. Given, also, this emphasis on
prestige, the ensuing struggle to which it gives rise must be
expressed in the continuous adoption of new norms and patterns
of behaviour, for only in this way can those who already enjoy
high prestige ward off the challenge of their competitors. I
suggest that new norms and standards of behaviour will tend to
arise more frequently within the *effective* network of those who
rank high on the prestige continuum, and that through the
extended network they gradually percolate throughout the
society. From this point of view, the network would also appear
to have importance as an instrument in examining the processes
of social and cultural change.

V

So far in this chapter I have been discussing social regularities
in terms of social relationships, and the ways in which these are
ordered within a particular kind of institutional framework. It
remains now to consider a quite different set of uniformities
also amply illustrated in Chanda's account. These may be
regarded as behavioural constants, regularities to be perceived

in the actual modes of behaviour of Africans in the towns: they relate not to the form but to the content of social relationships. These behavioural constants consist in customs and usages, and the values and attitudes which they express. Many of these derive from indigenous African culture. Such are the custom of teknonymy, as when Chanda is addressed as ShiChomba, father of Chomba; and the continued expression of traditional standards of courtesy in modes of greeting and address, as when he was addressed by the Public Works Department orderly as 'father', or when Chanda himself greeted James's wife in the customary way on seeing her for the first time after the birth of her child. Or, again, tribal custom is exemplified in the occasion when Chanda's wife provided food for her female visitors, while he himself sat apart reading a newspaper. Among most, if not all, of the Northern Rhodesian tribes, men and women normally eat separately, and the custom is still widely followed in the towns. But, while traditional practice and belief are often present at the core of a given behavioural complex, particular customs may be considerably modified under urban conditions, or perhaps survive only in fragmentary form. Finally, Chanda's accounts provide many instances of customs and modes of behaviour which are specific to the town. They are the expression of African urban, as distinct from or even opposed to tribal, culture. A good illustration is to be found in the incident involving the Ndebele girl, which argues a certain free-and-easy approach to extra-marital relations, an attitude which is also evident, incidentally, in Chanda's acquiescence in his friend's liaison with his classificatory sister. In certain circumstances urban Africans will express considerable concern about the extent of 'adultery'[11] in the towns, and can on occasion castigate profligacy as roundly as would any traditional guardian of tribal mores. However, in everyday life sexual laxity is taken lightly and, indeed, is accepted by many as one of the more amiable aspects of the urban way of life, provided, of course, that one's *affaires* remain undetected or one is not one's self the injured party. On the other hand, the acceptance of 'laxity' is not the same thing as condonation of promiscuity. The urban areas do have their own code of sexual behaviour, which includes norms for the regulation of extra-marital relations. Thus, the Ndebele girl was fair game for Chanda because she was of an alien tribe; but more important is

Thompson's comment that she could not refuse Chanda because
of his smart appearance. In general, Southern Rhodesian girls
have a reputation for sophistication. Many of those who come
north are relatively well educated, speak some English, and
have a sense of dress which ranks them as more desirable than
the local womenfolk. The implication of Thompson's remark
was that such a girl could not demean herself by consorting
with any Tom, Dick, or Harry around the location, but a man of
prestige, of high social status, she would not refuse. Similarly,
for Chanda himself, the liaison would have been quite 'legitimate',
and would have caused no stir so long as it was not discovered
by the girl's husband or by his own wife.

Reference to the concepts of prestige and social status have
been made at a number of points, and we have also had occasion
to note some of the marks by which a person of prestige is
known. Here, therefore, it only remains to observe how the
notions of prestige and status as they have developed in the
towns also provide norms of behaviour which different
individuals can appeal to, and manipulate, in handling their
own relations. For example, Chanda was obviously disappointed
when he learnt that his brother-in-law had not brought him a
'fever coat' from Elizabethville. I suspect that Martin had not
done so because he knew so well Chanda's propensity for
purchasing goods well beyond the range of his pocket, and his
chronic inability to pay his debts. But Martin was too diplomatic
to say so openly. Instead, he explained that most of the ones he
had seen were of inferior quality and unworthy of a 'gentleman'.
Since it was precisely in these terms that Chanda liked to see
himself he could say little in reply, and he was compelled to hide
his chagrin.

The persistence in the towns of tribal customs and values,
the abandonment or modification and adaptation of others, and
the emergence of specifically urban customs, usages, and
attitudes raise complex problems of a somewhat different order
from those considered in the earlier sections of the chapter.
They raise questions about social and cultural change, and the
relationship between them. It was, in fact, the emergence of
these problems rather than the nature of urban society itself
which first drew the attention of anthropologists who had come
to do research in the towns of Africa. Thus, there developed in
these studies a tendency to view the urban situation against a
model of the tribal system, with a consequent failure to grasp

that the new patterns of behaviour were also frequently specifically urban responses. Today there is an increasing readiness to accept, as a point of departure, the assumption that urban life everywhere shares certain common characteristics, and that these provide the basis for a minimal definition of urbanism. It follows then that the social life of urban Africans will more closely resemble the way of life developed among urban dwellers in other parts of the world than it will the traditional folk-ways of the tribe. This must not be taken to mean that the African who comes to the towns at once abandons his tribal culture. It is, of course, clear that the African who leaves his tribal area to seek work in town will take with him a whole set of customs, values and attitudes, beliefs, and so on. Not only will he continue to utilise these in the towns, but their persistence in the urban milieu may in turn influence the ordering of social relationships there. However, the point is that for the urban African the town is something given, with which he has to come to terms and to which he has to adjust. In other words, the problem of cultural continuity has to be set firmly, in the first instance, in the context of the urban social system, the major elements of which I have sought to outline here; and, secondly, in the context of the wider system which consists in the interrelations of town and country. Urbanisation is one of the most notable features of our age, and all over the world new towns are rapidly growing up or ancient cities being transformed. For the most part, they draw their populations from among peoples of widely differing cultures who hitherto had followed a peasant or a tribal way of life. These towns likewise differ widely among themselves, and yet, as towns, they may be expected to share certain structural resemblances. In terms of the argument presented here, I suggest, therefore, that these emerging urban communities provide for the anthropologist a potentially fertile field for exploring the interrelations of social structure and culture.

5

Gossip, Norms, and Social Network

In the previous chapter I sought to draw attention to the value
of the concept of the social network, as enunciated by Barnes
(1954) and later used by Bott (1957), in the analysis of problems
of urban social organisation in modern Africa. I pointed out
there how each African urban-dweller may be regarded as the
focal point of a number of social relationships, defined in terms
of different roles: some deriving from the tribal system; others
a product of the wider social system that has developed in
recent years. Pursuing this perspective, it followed that the
social structure of the town could be viewed, at least in part, as
made up of a complex series of links in a chain of innumerable
dyadic interactions. The further argument, which I was not at
that time able to develop in detail, was that when the content of
such interaction was itself taken into account, the concept of
the social network also helped to shed light on some of the
problems of social control in African urban society: how norms
of behaviour come to be set; how they are maintained or
sanctioned; and how they come to be diffused. In this chapter
my aim is simply to document this argument, and at the same
time to clarify a number of points made in the earlier analysis.

The incident

In my earlier discussion of the network the procedure I adopted
was to follow one man, Chanda, in his movements around the
town, and to trace out the nature of the various social contacts
he made over a limited period of time. The emphasis there was
on the network seen simply as a series of linkages. Here my
concern is more with the content of social interaction: in this
context the workings of the network principle seem best brought
out in charting the involvement of a number of persons in an
incident, that had no great significance in itself, which I recorded
in the course of fieldwork in Ndola. The background to this
incident was as follows. After I had been in Ndola for some

time, I decided to select two areas for intensive study – one a section in the Old location; the other a section in Kabushi Suburb – and I was able to arrange for one of my African research assistants to live in each. I hoped in this way to be able to carry out formal interviews intensively over a period of time, as well as to achieve some approximation to the conventional anthropological ideal of participant observation, if only vicariously. One day my assistant called in the ordinary way at one of the houses in his section. He was met by a young lad who explained that he was the younger brother of the occupier, whom I shall call Charles, and that Charles was at present out of Ndola. When my assistant asked whether Charles would be back soon, the lad appeared reluctant to answer, and my assistant departed.

The reasons for Charles's absence emerged shortly afterwards. It appeared that he had been found committing adultery with a girl called Monica, who was the wife of Kaswende. Kaswende was at this time employed as a lorry-driver by a firm of brewers which supplied bottled beer throughout most of the country. His duties, therefore, often took him on long journeys, and he was frequently absent from Ndola for days at a time. During these absences Charles and Monica used to meet at Kaswende's house. Somehow Kaswende's suspicions became aroused and before his departure on one trip he asked his younger brother to keep an eye on Monica. One evening when Kaswende was absent the younger brother called at Kaswende's house. He received no reply to his call, so set about forcing his way in. Charles thought that the best way out of this awkward situation was through a window; but the window-space in Kabushi houses is somewhat tiny and as he was scrambling through, he lost a shoe, which was taken by Kaswende's younger brother. When Kaswende eventually returned to Ndola he was, of course, duly informed, and he immediately sought out the adulterer. Confronted with the evidence of the shoe Charles was forced to admit his guilt, and Kaswende gave him a severe thrashing. He warned Charles, moreover, that the matter had not ended there, and that he would beat him again whenever he saw him. Kaswende turned out to be a man of his word, and he assaulted Charles on two further occasions. Charles then decided to leave Ndola, and I heard later that he had found a job in one of the other towns of the Copperbelt.

There is nothing peculiarly urban nor indeed African about

an act of adultery, and there is certainly nothing very unusual in the circumstances of the present case. Cases of adultery in the towns of the Copperbelt are indeed legion (compare Powdermaker 1962: 164–9). Thus, at Ndola one young African woman had agreed to keep a daily journal for me in which she would record her daily activities – whom she met and what they discussed, for example. Each day brought its regular tale of somebody's adultery until, out of a mixture of tedium and embarrassment, I felt compelled to ask her to stop. In any case, at this stage of my research I had already spent a considerable amount of time attending the sittings of the African Urban courts and recording the cases heard there, a substantial proportion of which were grounded in complaints of marital infidelity. Why, then, should I linger on the present case? What aroused my interest was not the incident itself, but rather that within a short space of time I heard the story from a number of different sources. This suggested that the *affaire* was known to, and had possibly been discussed by, quite a wide range of people. It occurred to me that this was something worth looking into in order to try and trace out at least some of the ways in which the story had ramified.

The 'gossip' network

I myself received the story in the first instance from my assistant in Kabushi, Ponde. Ponde first came to Ndola in 1947 to attend a course on social welfare, and it was at this time that he first met Charles, who was then working in one of the location tea-rooms. Subsequently, they came to know each other better, for both were keen footballers and belonged to the local club. However, they were acquaintances rather than friends, and although before Charles's departure from the town they had both lived in the same section of Kabushi, Ponde had not visited Charles save for the occasion mentioned earlier. Ponde, in fact, did not hear the story 'in the course of his work', but from his side-neighbour in the section, Besa. Besa was a young man in his early twenties. His parents had brought him from Bemba country when he was a child, and he had gone to primary school in Ndola: in fact, he had not gone back to his rural home since then. At this time, he was employed as a market supervisor. Besa and Kaswende, the husband in the present case, had been class-mates at school: they had grown up together and were still close friends. One day Ponde was being visited at his house by a close friend Simon, an African Welfare Assistant. They were discussing the case of adultery of a mutual friend when Besa came in. After Simon's departure, Besa told Ponde the story of Charles and Monica.

I also received the story independently from Margaret, whom I had come to know through her husband, a senior African clerk and a member of a number of African bodies in the town. He was quite well known throughout the Copperbelt. Both Margaret and her husband were Bemba from the Luwingu District. Margaret had attended school at Mindolo, then the only boarding school for African girls on the Copperbelt. Margaret knew the story at first hand from Monica herself, with whom she had been at Mindolo. Margaret had also heard the story from Mrs Mutwale while they were combing out each other's hair one day. Mrs Mutwale and her husband came from the Luapula area. He was an accounts clerk in town, and said to be earning unusually high wages for an African at that time. Mrs Mutwale was another product of Mindolo, and as Margaret was telling me this she commented: 'We Mindolo girls like to go about together, and don't like to go about with others.' Margaret in turn had related the story to a number of other women as well as to a young man called Nicholas, who held a supervisory position under the Municipal Council. Nicholas also came from the Luwingu District, that is from the same area as Margaret and her husband. There was some element of a joking relationship between Nicholas and Margaret whom Nicholas addressed as sister-in-law, although there was no traceable connection between himself and Margaret's husband.

Finally, I heard the story again from my second assistant, Phiri. Phiri was a townsman, born and brought up on the mine compound at Mufulira, where his parents were still living. He himself had first met Charles in 1947 when they boxed each other at a scouts' jamboree. They met again when Phiri came to join me in Ndola. The introduction on this occasion was made by Monica, who was herself a Mufulira girl. Monica and Phiri had, in fact, grown up together as children and, although they were of different ethnic backgrounds, Phiri told me that he had always regarded Monica's family as being in some way vaguely related to his own. He himself had actually heard the story of Kaswende's case while visiting Monica's mother, who was then living in one of the settlements a short distance out of Ndola. It appears that a preliminary meeting of the parties had been arranged to discuss the whole affair. Monica's brother, however, refused to attend the gathering because Monica herself was not in Ndola at the time – she had run away. Phiri was present when the brother arrived to inform his mother of the latest developments. Later Phiri was to hear the story again from Nicholas. They were good friends and with a few others formed a regular drinking group at the Beer Hall. Nicholas confided to Phiri that he was rather worried about the whole business because he himself was indirectly involved. Monica, he explained, had a friend and confidante called Alice. Charles and Monica used sometimes to meet at Alice's house, for Alice's husband was a businessman who was out of town from time to time. But at length Alice grew fearful that her husband might come to learn of her part in the intrigue and, what was worse, might come to doubt her own moral rectitude. Alice therefore arranged to find another rendezvous for her friends. But in the end her secret could not be contained. Returning from one of his trips her husband found some clothes belonging to Monica in the house. Somehow he divined what was going on, and he chased Alice from the house, saying she could go and live on the money she had earned in adultery. It was these circumstances which led Nicholas to disclose his fears to Phiri, for at this time Alice was his own mistress, and he was afraid that his *affaire*, too, would be publicly exposed. He spoke bitterly against Margaret, whom he accused of being a great gossip-monger and always spreading false stories about him. As a result he was having a troublesome time with his wife, who was threatening to divorce him. Finally, he told Phiri that he was no longer on speaking terms with his 'sister-in-law' Margaret.

What these events reveal is how the discovery of an apparently trivial act of adultery triggered off a chain of gossip, and even came to affect the relations of a number of people. I should add that my own attempts to trace out the path of all this gossip were less than systematic and far from complete. In order to avoid overburdening the text with detail, I have not included in my account all the names which appear in my field notes; on the other hand, I did not discuss the matter with all those whose names I have mentioned. Each of these presumably was involved in yet another 'gossip set', so that the story was probably known to a much wider range of people than I have been able to indicate. Margaret remarked to me, indeed, that it was known all over the location (*umulandu waishibikwa ku mushi onse*). This is almost certainly an exaggeration, but it does not affect the main point that in a town like Ndola, whose African population is so young in terms of urban experience and so heterogeneous in terms of ethnic origins, occupation, and church affiliation, a considerable number of persons can be shown to be interconnected through their common interest, expressed in gossip, in a case of adultery. Of course not every such case that occurs in the town will be the subject of so much talk. My research assistant Phiri was quick to point out that had the *affaire* involved some of the people living in the Old location little would have been heard about it. Why, then, the widespread interest in the present case? For answer we need to look at the way in which social relationships are organised in the town, and at the norms of behaviour which inform those relationships.

In tracking down the sources from which my informants heard the story, and the others to whom they in turn passed it on, I have merely traced out the links making up a number of individual's personal networks. I have treated the town, in Barnes's terms, as a social field, within which each person is in touch with a number of people, some of whom may be in touch with each other, and some of whom may not. Each person's network, as I showed in the earlier discussion, is built up in different ways: it may include neighbours, fellow members of some formal organisation or association, or others drawn from the categories of kin and tribe and so on, each of which represents a distinct principle of social organisation in the town. But, while it is possible to isolate these various principles for purposes of analysis, what is striking is the way in which in the actuality of social life such principles are often found operating simultaneously. In other words, any given dyadic relationship tends to have built into it a number of different and, for this reason, sometimes conflicting, roles. For example, although Charles and Ponde were neighbours in the sense that they belonged to the same section and lived fairly close to one another, the neighbourhood principle had never been activated, and their relationship had its source elsewhere. In the case of Ponde and Besa, however, the neighbourhood principle was stronger, though here, too, other roles affected the character of their interaction and defined their relationship. When Ponde moved into his house, Besa was already in the section. They soon struck up a friendship, and since Besa was still a bachelor

he used to drop into Ponde's from time to time to share a meal.
Both were observant Roman Catholics and they took to
attending services together. In this way Besa came to be
introduced to Ponde's friend, Simon, and then to Simon's sister,
to whom he eventually became engaged. From this time he
began to address Simon as brother-in-law, a mode of address he
then extended to Ponde, whose relations with Simon were so
close that to Besa it appeared as though they were brothers – in
fact, they were unrelated, being of different tribes and from
different parts of the country (though they belonged to the
same linguistic group). This translation of social ties which
have grown up between unrelated persons into the idiom of
kinship and affinity is seen also in the case of Nicholas and
Margaret, and Phiri and Monica.

In these instances the use of kinship terms serves to buttress
or give 'tone' to a relationship that is already quite close. On the
other hand, the greater the number of roles present within a
single dyadic relationship, the greater the opportunities for
division within that relationship. Thus, attendance at the same
school and membership in the same religious body were each
important bases of association within the networks being
considered here, but they sometimes ran counter to each other.
Ponde and Phiri, for example, had been close friends at
secondary school, where they had also known Margaret's
husband. In Ndola they shared many interests in common,
including an enthusiasm for football. But they had been brought
up in different religious denominations, and their views in
matters religious differed radically: sometimes they had heated
arguments which threatened to disrupt their friendship. In
matters of politics there were associated differences of attitude
and conviction, too.

Norms and the gossip network

In defining the character of a network, then, one has to take
account of a number of variables: the role-components that
enter into the network; the degree of 'mesh' or consistency
between these roles; and the relative weight or intensity of each
particular link. For, even when relationships are built up out of
the same role-components, it does not follow that they are of
equal 'quality'. The intensity of a relationship may be gauged in
some measure by the frequency of interaction, but even more so
by its content. Every social relationship involves the idea of

exchange, and what helps to define it are the kinds of information, views, and talk which are interchanged. Hence, as Gluckman (1963) suggests, the closer the bonds of relationship, the more intimate or even esoteric the gossip, and the more trite or meaningless it will appear to outsiders. For one of the functions of gossip for those who are party to it is to define or reaffirm the norms regulating behaviour among themselves, and marking themselves off from others. Here, I think, we have the key to the amount of gossip that gathered round the *affaire* of Charles and Monica. The gossip did not consist in a bare recital of the 'facts' of the case - implicit in the telling was an evaluation of those 'facts'. Unfortunately, I did not gather any version of the story from Kaswende or his friends and kin. From the accounts which I did receive, however, the 'slanting' was quite plain: there was little expression of sympathy for Kaswende or even recognition of his position as an injured husband. Thus, Ponde's comment was that the marriage of Monica and Kaswende was a strange one and that many people had wondered at it. Many asked how a girl like Monica should have come to marry a man like Kaswende. The point was, Ponde then explained, that Monica was widely regarded as very beautiful whereas Kaswende was quite an unprepossessing fellow. Moreover, he added, Monica was more highly educated than her husband, and could have found any number of men who would have been pleased to marry her. Phiri, who had known Monica from childhood, was able to fill in some of the background. Monica had at one time been engaged to a man with whom Kaswende went about. Then she contracted venereal disease and had been very ill. Kaswende had been struck by her beauty: he sought medicines for her, and in the end she was cured. In gratitude Monica's parents were quite happy that Kaswende should marry their daughter. But Monica herself was less pleased with the arrangement. She found, moreover - or so rumour had it - that Kaswende was impotent, and it was said that the child she bore was not his. She had then started going around with other men so that Kaswende would be forced to divorce her.

The clear implication of all this was that Monica had married a man of inferior social status, and I took up this and other points with my assistants on a later occasion. I pointed out that as a senior driver Kaswende must have been earning relatively good wages, and thus would have been in a position to provide his wife with those things to which I knew African urban women attached importance. My assistants were quick to reply that although Kaswende was indeed quite well off, his manner of dress was really quite poor. In a word, Kaswende lacked those qualities such as education and 'civilised' taste which, as discussed, are necessary to confer prestige in modern Copperbelt society. Here, too, presumably lies the explanation for Kaswende's unwillingness to divorce his wife. When I asked why he had not done this earlier in view of his wife's previous infidelities, Ponde replied that it might have been because of her beauty. What he had in mind, I suspect, was not so much Monica's physical attractiveness for Kaswende as the prestige which could accrue to a man of Kaswende's stamp who could boast such a beautiful wife.

The exchange of gossip, I have said, denotes a certain community of interest: it marks off the 'set' from others of whose intimate affairs they are ignorant, or which they would consider too unimportant for their concern. Through such gossip is expressed the norms of behaviour specific to the 'set'. Both of these points emerge in the present discussion. Although much gossip tends to be condemnatory, it is worth noting that in all the talk I recorded about the *affaire* of Charles and Monica I heard no word spoken in condemnation of the act of adultery itself. None spoke maliciously of Charles or charged him with breaking up a home; on the contrary, as I have indicated, the sympathy appeared to lie with Charles rather than with the injured Kaswende. This must not be taken to mean that all my informants condoned adultery. The standards of sexual morality on the Copperbelt may be highly permissive, but they are still far from outright promiscuity. In any case, the point here is that marital fidelity is a norm of general application, accepted by all in theory if not in practice, and is not specific to any particular group or category within the population. Moreover, while an element of 'spice' is probably a necessary ingredient of a good deal of gossip, it is not the 'spice' alone which is of interest to the 'set'. What is important is their own social position and that of the person who is the subject of their gossip.

If we examine the social characteristics of those involved in the present account, it will be seen that we are dealing mainly with those who fall within the upper ranges of the prestige continuum (Mitchell and Epstein 1959). All the men whose

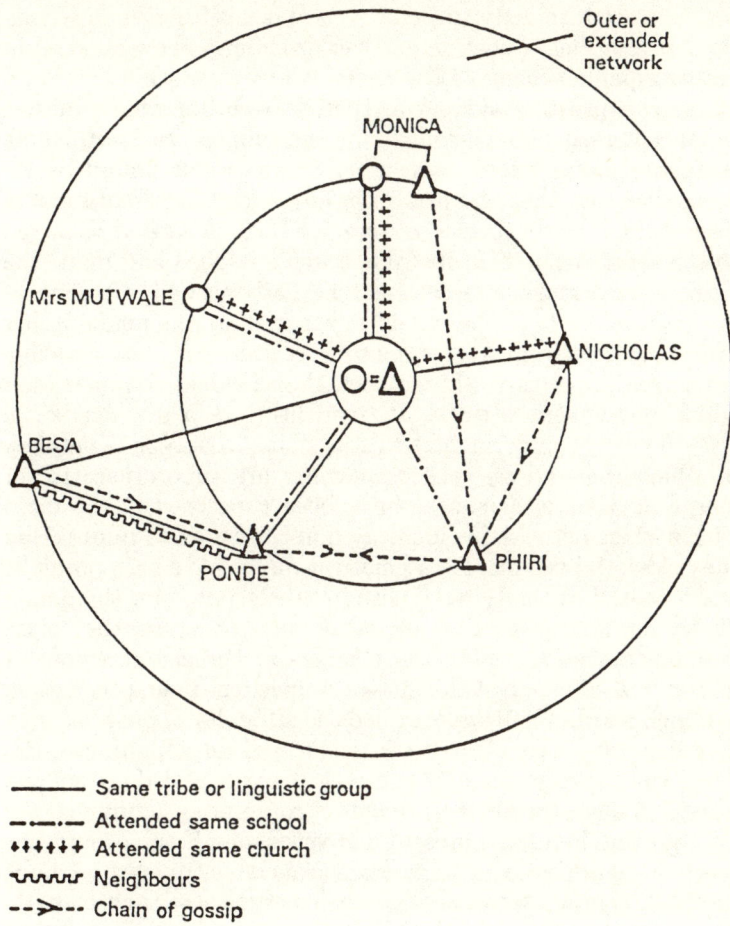

Same tribe or linguistic group
Attended same school
Attended same church
Neighbours
Chain of gossip

Figure 5.1. Section of 'class network' (centred on Margaret) showing the interlocking chain of gossip

names appear in the account, save for the husband, Kaswende, and Besa, the market-supervisor, were white-collar workers holding relatively responsible and highly paid jobs. Besa himself aspired to a similar position, and his constant problem was how to achieve a style of life on the miserable pittance he received from his job at that time. As for the object of all the gossip, the central figure was undoubtedly Monica herself. In terms of the modern standards of the Copperbelt, she was one of the most

sophisticated, smartly turned out, and beautiful girls in Ndola.
By virtue of her education and her grooming, she embodied in
her own person many of the norms and values which serve to
define the prestige system of these new urban communities.
Monica herself thus belonged to the 'upper crust' of Ndola
African society, but as a member she was also bound by its
rules. The fact that she had an *affaire* with Charles did not in
itself call forth any special censure, for Charles himself belonged
to the same social stratum. What was criticised and made the
subject of discussion was that she had married someone of
lesser social status. The gossip of her friends who made up her
own social network (or at least a section of it) provided a
reaffirmation of the values which they held in common, and
which gave them their sense of identity as a distinct social
class. Thus the material here relates mainly to a type of network
in which the various role-components are subordinate to, or
merge in, that of class; we have been concerned in the main
with a 'class network' as illustrated in the attached figure. Had
the fieldwork been more systematic it might have been possible,
and it would certainly have been instructive, to plot the points
at which gossip tended to peter out, or cross the 'class
boundaries', and to note the changes in the character of the
gossip as it did so. But this does not upset the main contention.
Mitchell and I (1959) have argued the difficulty of postulating a
contemporary class structure in urban African communities for,
while the prestige scale is relatively clear cut, it does not yet
provide a basis for the recruitment of corporately acting groups.
On the other hand, the present analysis shows how, through the
mechanism of the social network, social classes or status groups
in the Weberian sense are able to emerge, how they come to
articulate the norms of behaviour which define their distinctiveness, and develop means for reasserting their validity when
they appear to have been challenged.

6

Linguistic Innovation and Culture on the Copperbelt

This chapter sets out to discuss some of the linguistic usages which have developed among Africans in the emerging urban communities of the Copperbelt. Comparable data on those aspects of linguistic change to be considered here appear to be scanty in the literature: I hope, therefore, that the material I present may prove to have intrinsic linguistic interest. At the same time, I seek to show how the use of such data may also be valuable in shedding light on the present way of life and social organisation of urban Africans. Here I want to suggest that the study of linguistic innovation may have wider theoretical significance in providing an avenue for exploring the inter-relations of structure and culture in situations of rapid social change.

Before turning to the theme of linguistic innovation itself, it is first necessary to sketch the general situation in regard to language on the Copperbelt. The Copperbelt's population is, of course, entirely immigrant and is drawn from a welter of different ethnic and national groups. Mine managers and bureaucrats, engineers and geologists, skilled artisans and supervisors - are all 'Europeans', but they include those who have come from South Africa (of whom a high proportion are Afrikaans-speaking), the United Kingdom, and, in earlier days, Canada and the United States. The further diversification of the ethnic structure has gone hand in hand with the country's economic growth and the increased rate of White immigration after the Second World War. In addition to the Europeans, there is a relatively small Asian element which occupies an important role in the trading and commercial life of the towns. Finally, there are the indigenous peoples themselves, the Africans, of whom there are now probably well over a quarter of a million living on the Copperbelt, and claiming membership of a hundred different tribes. Africans participate in the economic life of the Copperbelt as casual, unskilled, and semi-skilled workers, though an increasing number are beginning to occupy posts that call for a greater measure of skill and responsibility. Socially, however, the practice of residential segregation, whereby most Africans are bound to live in areas known as compounds or locations, reduces to a minimum the extent of contact between Africans and Europeans outside the actual work situation.

This heterogeneity of population, with its accompanying diversity of custom and culture as well as wide differences in economic, political, and educational status, provides precisely the kind of polyglot setting in which one expects to find the emergence of pidgin and 'creolised' languages. Thus, on the mines it was imperative that there be some means of communication between White overseers and Black labourers if instructions were to be understood and properly carried out. A high proportion of the early European miners came from South Africa, while many of the Africans who now came to the Copperbelt had previously worked on the Rand or at Wankie in Southern Rhodesia (now Zimbabwe). Thus, many were already well acquainted with Fanagolo or 'Mine-Kafir', long well established in the south, and they introduced it to the Copperbelt. The term Fanagolo itself is rarely heard in Northern Rhodesia, where Europeans generally speak of 'Kitchen-Kafir' and Africans of *Cilapalapa*, presumably because of the continuous iteration of the term '*lapa*' which seems to recur with the same unwavering frequency as the words 'long' and 'bilong' in Melanesian pidgin. Fanagolo is a hybrid of Zulu, English, and Afrikaans. Its vocabulary is roughly 70 per cent Nguni (mainly Zulu), 24 per cent English, and 6 per cent Afrikaans in origin, but it retains hardly any of the phonetical, morphological, or syntactical characteristics of the Nguni or other Bantu languages (Cole 1953).

Fanagolo is thus a 'true' pidgin in that it is native to none, or virtually none, of those who speak it. Moreover, it is sharply reduced in complexity of structure and vocabulary as contrasted with the languages from which it is derived (Hall 1955). In these respects it is similar to Melanesian pidgin, and shares many of the defects, for example, limited range of expression and lack of subtlety, frequently alleged against the latter. Unlike Melanesian pidgin, however, Fanagolo has never developed – and in Northern Rhodesia shows no sign of ever developing – into a native lingua franca. Undoubtedly, the reasons for this lie in the very different linguistic situations obtaining in Africa and Melanesia. Africa, too, has its bewildering variety of languages and dialects, but language groups, at least in Central Africa, are frequently measured in tens and sometimes hundreds of thousands and are rarely, if ever, confined to a small cluster of neighbouring villages as is often the case in New Guinea. In my experience, it is only on very rare occasions when they can find no other common tongue that Copperbelt Africans resort to Fanagolo among themselves. Fanagolo tends, therefore, to be restricted to certain kinds of situations in which Africans interact with Europeans. Despite its many inherent limitations, Fanagolo is not a completely impoverished jargon. Among skilled speakers it lends itself readily to fluent and intelligent conversation on a variety of subjects. Nevertheless, in the eyes of Africans, it remains essentially the language of command and direction, and by more educated Africans at least is invariably associated with European racialist attitudes and the refusal to acknowledge Africans as their equals.

If, in the sphere of Black-White relations, Fanagolo is the mark of social distance, English is the mark of social acceptance and even equality. For an African to address certain Europeans in English would be regarded as the height of 'Kafir insolence'.[1] Conversely, the use of English in the context of casual interaction between Europeans and Africans indicates a more 'personal' relationship, and even a degree of friendliness. On more formal occasions, such as at meetings of bodies in which Africans and Europeans participate jointly, it is now rare to hear an African speaking in the vernacular, and English has become the standard medium. The use of English in these circumstances has obvious advantages, but it is also a reflection of the prestige which is accorded the ability to speak English in the African section of the community. Nowadays at least some command of English is indispensable to the African who aspires to urban leadership on the Copperbelt, although it should also be noted that too ready a fluency in it may sometimes be bitterly denounced by other Africans who accuse their English-speaking fellows of 'leaning too much to the side of the Europeans'.

The use of English as a criterion of prestige among Africans makes sense, of course, only because adequate knowledge of the language is still confined to a small minority. What proportion of urban Africans speaks English it is impossible to say. Any measure we might devise would be completely arbitrary and largely meaningless for we have to deal with a continuum, at one end of which is a very small number whose command of the language is well-nigh perfect, while at the other are those whose efforts are fluent enough but frequently result in gibberish and almost complete incomprehensibility. In most cases the quality of English spoken merely reflects the poor standard of teaching in African primary schools, but even the best speakers employ usages deriving from the construction and idiom of their mother tongues. Nevertheless, there are circumstances when imperfection may become a source of virtue, for Copperbelt English often achieves a striking freshness and vividness of imagery which often elude more orthodox modes of expression. One example must suffice here. The African Urban Housing Board at Ndola had been discussing the question of shop rents in the Municipal location. One of the speakers, whose command of English was extremely good, was arguing against a proposed increase in the rents. He complained of the difficulties that beset the African storekeeper, and the heavy expenses he had to incur. Finally, he exclaimed: 'The result is that the shopkeeper remains with nothing. If these shops were our own we would be fighting for something. As it is we are fighting a goalless football.'

The value that attaches to the speaking of English is best seen in the different kinds of social situation in which it is used. Among educated Africans the principal criterion appears to be whether their social status is involved. At meetings of associations and societies in which all the members enjoy equivalent educational status use of English is the general rule. Among close friends gathered in the privacy of the home the vernacular will probably be preferred; but if a less intimate acquaintance should join the company the talk will be continued in English. Similarly, the parents of a girl who hope to marry her off to an educated young man will urge her to write her love-letters in English in order to make a good impression. Here I have been referring to those Africans who have achieved at least a moderate competence in the language. But the vast majority of urban Africans remain largely illiterate, having received the most rudimentary schooling. Nevertheless, there are few who have not acquired some smattering of English. Those who have the closest acquaintance with Europeans outside a purely working context, such as house-boys or hotel waiters – and it is worth noting that at this time domestic servants constituted the third largest labour category in paid employment – often acquire quite an extensive English vocabulary, and their conversation is interlarded with English words and phrases even where the vernacular would be perfectly adequate. The following is perhaps an extreme example, but it does reproduce fairly the distinctive flavour of much of everyday Copperbelt speech. Visiting one day a section of the Ndola location where we were working at the time, my research assistant found a man whom he had not met before. Other people present – they were drinking beer at the time – introduced the stranger as Juwi Dick, and then explained to Juwi that my assistant was a newcomer from Lusaka engaged in social research. Juwi Dick at once greeted him:

'Welcome, Charlie, to Ndola. Ndola Commercial Centre for DDNM [Daily Drinker Never Miss]. The day I miss I will be in the grave.'

He began to address the others:

'Uyu muntu umweni sana muno Ndola but ni well known pantu wa social kabili ni DDNM. E member tufwaya muno Ndola.' [This man is very much a stranger here in Ndola but he has become well known as a social worker and a daily drinker. These are the sort of people we want in Ndola.]

And then to display his largesse, and to indicate that he was a man of some status, he added:

'Please, Bamayo, peni member uyu five cups pali two na six . . . [To my assistant] OK my boy, I'll sign cheque for you.' [Please, mother, give this chap five cups of beer for half-a-crown . . . I'll pay for you.]

Thus, in a purely African context prestige is sought and conferred through the use of English. But according prestige is not its only, or even perhaps its major, function. The vernacular languages of Central Africa are often extremely rich in idiom, metaphor, and expression; they are complex, and subtle, and particularly well adapted to the handling of personal relationships. However, they are not always fully adequate to cope with the varieties of experience of a modern urban and industrial society. English, on the other hand, at once offers a whole range of new concepts and ideas; it makes available to the African newspapers, journals, and the world of books. Secondly, it provides a means of communication which cuts across tribal-cum-linguistic boundaries. Therefore, when young men began to come together in meetings of the welfare societies (which were among the earliest forms of indigenous association to develop in the urban areas) and discuss the problems of the colour-bar and unemployment or complain of the designation 'boy' applied indiscriminately by Europeans to any African irrespective of his age or status, their insistence on the use of English was an expression of a growing awareness of themselves as Africans in a new multiracial society. The new regimen was a source of much confusion and resentment, but their numerous grievances did not amount to a rejection of the system as such: rather, they were beginning to claim a proper place for themselves as Africans within this society. Their use of English was the expression of their desire to enter fully the modern world. And because they were aware of the many new problems of urban life, as well as the role of intermediary between the African urban populace and the European authorities that their jobs often led them to fill, these young men gradually established themselves as leaders in the community. Yet competence in English in this kind of situation rarely goes by itself. Almost invariably, it forms part of a complex which includes higher education, a more responsible job, better wages, and a standard of living and way of life which begin to approximate more closely that of a European. Over the years the rift within the African urban community has tended to widen and nowadays English has become, on occasion, the convenient symbol of the dominant cleavage within African society – a symbol therefore marked by growing ambivalence.

It follows from the preceding discussion that the vast majority of Copperbelt Africans employ only the vernacular. Many speak a number of different languages, for in general Africans display a remarkable facility in picking up the speech of other tribes and areas. The principal languages spoken are Bemba, Nyanja, Lovale, and Lozi, but many others are also heard. In linguistic classifications all of these are listed as belonging to Central Bantu, and they share many structural features in common, such as the well-known distribution of nouns into classes, each with its own distinctive concordial prefixes. But in other respects they differ among themselves as much as do English, French, and German. However, the problems of communication are not as acute as might appear at first sight, for the numerical preponderance of Bemba-speaking Africans on the Copperbelt has led to the fairly widespread acceptance there of this language.[3] Together with English, which is used only in the higher standards, Bemba is now the medium of instruction in Copperbelt African primary schools, and it is also generally used on those occasions when people of different tribes are gathered, as at church services[4] or public meetings, so that it has come to enjoy almost the status of a lingua franca there.[5] The linguistic data I collected in the field relate solely to Bemba.

Urban Bemba differs considerably from the traditional language of the villages. Non-Bemba who have learnt the language in the towns are not always punctilious in observing the strict grammatical forms, while among the Bemba themselves many of the nuances and finer points of the classical idiom have lost their relevance under urban conditions and are undoubtedly disappearing. I suspect, too, that a qualified linguist would also find evidence of considerable changes in phonetic structure and pronunciation (compare Comhaire-Sylvain 1949). The most obvious changes, however, are the innovations in words and phrases, and it is with these that I am concerned in the following discussion.

I have already noted how individual speakers frequently interlard their conversation with English words and expressions. In the example given above the speaker's remarks reflected a purely personal expression, something unique to himself. There are now, however, a large number of English words which have been adopted into Bemba and are now part of the language, at least as spoken in the towns. A couple of typical examples, where the English words are assimilated to Bantu phonemic structure and adapted to the appropriate noun class, are contained in the following verse from a popular song:

> Ubu nindeta mubili obe mama
> E *bulangeti* bwa kufimbana;
> Mpumi yobe
> E *kalashi* ndoleshamo

This I have brought, your body my love,
Is a *blanket* for covering myself;
Your face
Is the *glass* [i.e. mirror] I look into.[6]

In a paper on Swahili borrowings from English, Gower (1952)
notes correctly that instances of such borrowing are to be
sought in those spheres where contact with European culture
impinges most widely and affects large numbers of Africans,
and he lists examples which have derived from African
experience of hospitals, transport, sport, and service in the
army. But I have little doubt myself that the list could be
multiplied extensively. For, to the African, the town represents
a completely new kind of social environment which touches his
life at nearly every point. The political, economic, social, and
other institutions of the town provide a framework to which he
has to adjust his behaviour. Many of these institutions were
wholly unknown to tribal society, certainly in the form in which
they are now experienced, and loan words are required to fill the
gaps. So we have, for example, *amasukulu* (schools), *amachalichi*
(churches), and the like. Others did have their counterpart in
the tribal system, but the divergence of function and practice is
so marked that the vernacular provides no exact equivalent to
the modern form, and the English term is again adopted. Thus,
Bemba has the abstract noun *ubuteko* (government, from the
verb *ukuteka*, to rule), but this is distinguished from the
bureaucratic machinery of local and central government by the
use of the terms *Municipal* and *Kafulmende*, the agencies which
are responsible for so many of the rules and regulations which
control the lives of urban Africans. Similarly, there is a perfectly
good Bemba word for a court of law, *icilye*. This is also used
when referring to the African Urban courts, but the loan word
ikoti is frequently preferred, presumably because it suggests
better the European character of much of the procedure in these
courts where proceedings have to be initiated by the taking out
of a summons (*ukushita* [to purchase] *saimoni*), where the
parties are required to go into the box (*mbokoshi*), from which
they make a statement (*istatmenti*).

Above all, what distinguishes urban society from the way of
life of the villages is the need for paid employment. As in every
urban community there are those who are able to survive by
living on their wits or by sponging on kinsfolk (*amalofwa*,

'loafers'), but these are a minor exception to the general rule of wage-labour. Accordingly, we shall not be surprised to find a large number of loan words associated with occupation, for example, *bukalaliki* (office-work from the English word clerk); *bukalipenta* (carpentry); or *ukucita business* (to run a store). One may also note here terms like *ukufola* (to draw wages or earn,[7] which derives from the command 'fall in' used at army pay parades[8]), or *itiketi* (ticket, the period to be worked before one becomes entitled to draw pay). Finally, there is a vast array of items of Western material culture and technology which in the towns have become part and parcel of African daily experience. For obvious reasons these provide an enormously fertile source of loan words, ranging from household goods such as *ibeketi* (bucket) or *machisa* (matches) to motor-cars (*muotoka* or *limotoka*) and railway trains (sing. *istima*).

Most of the examples just given are cases of simple borrowing and adaptation of words from English and other languages in order to fill lacunae in the vernacular vocabulary. For the most part, these words refer to a new social environment, in a sense external to the African, but impinging upon him at every point. Thus, the choice of words here has been largely pragmatic: the words themselves are morally neutral in the sense that they express little of the values and attitudes which Africans hold in regard to life in the towns. Of greater sociological interest, therefore, are those linguistic innovations which reflect directly the new customs, institutions, and modes of thought through which the towns are marked off as possessing for Africans today a wholly distinctive way of life. This vocabulary consists in the creation of completely new vernacular terms, or the investing of foreign loan words with a significance unknown to the original, but often singularly appropriate for expressing the new categories of Copperbelt experience. The material I was able to collect on these new semantic creations is very far from complete: first, because it was gathered mainly in the course of casual conversations or in interviews directed to other matters; and, secondly, because the terms themselves are being added to or dropped continuously. However, the tendency is for the terms to proliferate around certain areas of experience which have particular interest for urban Africans, and I have been able to group them loosely under a number of convenient headings.

To begin with there is the town itself, for which a number of alternatives is available. The Copperbelt proper is *Ku mikoti* which derives via Fanagolo from the Zulu word *umgodi*, meaning 'a hole of considerable size' and, by extension, a mine-shaft; all line-of-rail towns are *Ku nyanji (Ku njanji)* from the Bemba word *nyanji*, a railway line.[9] *Kalale* (from Harare, a Southern Rhodesian place-name) was first applied indiscriminately to all the mines of Southern Rhodesia, which provided centres of employment for Northern Rhodesian Africans before the opening of the Copperbelt, but is now used to refer to the urban areas in general, as in the English word town, *itauni*, itself. However, these terms frequently express more than the idea of mere physical location. *Kalale* and *itauni* in particular suggest the ethos of urban life and in this sense are equivalent to the notion of 'civilised' or sophisticated. Thus, a young man who had spent some years working in Elizabethville in the Belgian Congo (now Zaire) and had now returned to the Copperbelt once remarked with some feeling: 'Ku Kongo ni ku *town*, kuno ni ku mushi' (In the Congo it's really 'civilised'; here it's just as backward as a village.)

In a context involving mere physical location Africans simply use the name conferred by the local authority when speaking of different parts of the African housing area, for example, section M or S in the Main Municipal location in Ndola, or the new part of the location recently opened up called Kabushi. In other contexts, however, new terms are freely invented which express each section's special character in African eyes. While I was at Ndola a new device which was intended to serve the dual function of providing an overhead shower and flushing the latrine had been introduced in one of the newer sections of the location. The system did not appear to work very satisfactorily, and householders complained strongly of the public indignity they had to suffer in carrying a large tin of water with them on each visit to the latrine. The term *Ntapila* (from the verb *ukutapa*, to draw water) was quickly coined for the section, though others preferred *ku mabeketi* ('the bucket section'). More often it is the quality or type of housing that provides the distinguishing criterion. One large section of the Main location at Ndola consisted of semi-detached one-roomed houses of very poor quality. They were invariably known as *wayalezi* (wireless [radio]) or *telefon* (telephone), since everything that went on within the house was immediately broadcast to one's neighbours. Again, a new suburb has gone up in the course of the past few years. The houses are much larger and much superior to anything in the adjoining Old location. Typical of the urban scene is the way certain residents of the new suburb have come to designate themselves as *fwe bamafourroomed* ('we people who have four-roomed houses') in contradistinction to those lesser breeds in the Old location, *Aba mu mabottle* ('those who live in bottles'), a reference to the rondavels which provided the earliest type of housing for Africans at Ndola, but which were now being rapidly pulled down and replaced. These and indeed most other houses in the Old location had only one room. There was little space for 'proper' furniture, even if the occupants had the means to buy it, and they generally present a bare appearance inside. Such houses are commonly known therefore as *ballroom*, from the exclamation one might make on entry: 'Kuti mwaba mu *ballroom*. Ng'oma shili kwi?' (You might be in the dance hall. Where are the drums so that we can dance?)

Semantic creation and innovation are at their richest in those areas of Copperbelt experience which diverge most sharply from traditional tribal custom and mores. Thus, an entirely new vocabulary has grown up around the distinctive pattern of relations between the sexes that has developed in the urban areas. The social status and role of women in particular shows marked changes, and these are plainly reflected in the new terminology. Thus, town life itself is epitomised in the person of the *town lady*, an expression which refers to an African woman who has become fully acquainted with urban customs and habits. One very popular song *Cupo* ('Marriage') refers to the difficulties of a young wife newly arrived from the village who was a source of embarrassment to her more sophisticated husband because she could not learn to serve tea properly when his friends came to visit - she would insist on putting peas into the teapot. Emphatically not a *town lady*!

Other terms specify more carefully the character of certain common Copperbelt types. Thus, *championi* or *muchampioni* generally refers to a young woman who dresses smartly in the modern fashion. The term itself, the English derivation of which is obvious, in fact relates to what was an extremely popular make of bicycle; its popular usage, however, appears to have originated in the context of ballroom dancing competitions, which have long been an established feature of African urban life. Apart from the skill of the dancers, great emphasis is laid on their immaculate grooming, the men wearing full evening dress and the women attractive evening gowns and long white gloves. But, like so much else relating to African life on the Copperbelt, the term is steeped in ambivalence, for, on the one hand, it suggests excellence and standards to be emulated, while on the other, it denotes sexual laxity. Hence, young husbands frequently object to their wives spending too much time in the company of other women, for it is thus that they learn *fyabuchampioni* ('loose ways') and develop into *runners*. In the eyes of 'respectable' married women *amachampioni* are equally suspect, for they do not know how to 'keep their own marriages' and are a constant threat to everyone else's.

Yet another, and somewhat similar category, is provided by the *bakapenta milomo*, or more usually just *bakapenta*. The expression means literally those who paint their lips, adopting the English verb to paint. The *kapenta* tends to be less sophisticated than the *championi*, but both terms are readily applied to young girls of easy virtue who hang around the Beer Halls and Bottle Stores in search of a good time. By extension, the word *kapenta* has also come to be applied to a tiny minnow-like fish (*mushipa*) which is used as a very cheap relish. It is so easy to prepare that a woman who has been occupying her day with a *boy-friend* instead of busying herself with the housework can readily dash along to the market and buy some *kapenta* to prepare for her husband when he comes back from work in the evening. On the other hand, such a meal can sometimes lead to awkward questions. A woman might tell her friend: 'Abalume bandi teti mbepikile ubwali pali *tukapenta* pantu twa cabecabe, kabili nabo balakalipa nga basanga uto njipike abati pali kuntu waciya' (I wouldn't cook my husband a meal with *kapenta* relish for they are just rubbish, and besides he would get angry and say 'so that's where you've been'!)

The word *ihuli*, from the Afrikaans *hoer* (whore), is also an accepted term in current use, though many Africans would deny that prostitution, in the sense of a purely commercial sexual transaction, exists among Copperbelt Africans. By this they mean that most sexual liaisons ordinarily have an element of reciprocity so that, they will explain, even the casual pick-up at the Beer Hall commonly develops into some kind of temporary union – even if it lasts only a matter of days – in which the man buys the food or gives presents and the woman cooks and cleans up the man's quarters. Most of these liaisons involve extra-marital relations for at least one of the parties, and the lover or mistress is designated by a whole host of terms, for example, *cibamu, cikule, madear,* or *dali,* the latter two of English derivation but with a different nuance. The expression *spare wheel* aptly describes the woman whom a husband finds it convenient to have in reserve, so to speak. Some men do not enter into a 'proper' marriage until quite late. If they are taxed about it they will quickly dispel any reflection that might seem to be cast on their manhood by explaining: 'I married late because I have travelled a lot in foreign countries like the Belgian Congo or Southern Rhodesia. Of course, I have had many *banakashi ba pleasure*', or again: 'I have never married, but you know I have had many *piece-work* women.'

Where extra-marital relations feature so prominently on the urban landscape it would be rather surprising if the art of love itself were linguistically ignored. *Amakiss* speaks for itself, but I think lacks the poetry of the verbal form *ukutomona,* which in rural Bemba has as one of its meanings 'to taste the first fruits'. Highly admired in a girlfriend is the ability to perform a *danse à ventre.* The woman who does not know how to 'dance' during intercourse, or as Copperbelt Africans would express it, *ushaishiba double clutch,* is regarded as pretty poor game since the act then gives the man little satisfaction. To impregnate a woman is to *womb* her, while there are also a number of colloquialisms for the act of intercourse itself, including the rather unusual verb form *to coit.* In a matrimonial dispute that came before the Tribal Elders at Ndola, one of the Elders whose command of Bemba was limited but who had a flair for metaphor spontaneously produced a new word for the sexual act: *ukushanta.* This was a reference to the shunting of goods trains that goes on every night at Ndola, which is the railhead. The innovation was loudly acclaimed by all present, and I would not be at all surprised to learn that the term had passed into common use.

Another major source of linguistic innovation centres on the institution of beer-drinking. Each town on the Copperbelt has its Beer Hall run by the local authority, the profits of which went towards providing African social welfare amenities. In addition, a vast amount of beer was brewed privately and, for the most part, illicitly. Home-brewed beer offers greater variety than the Beer Hall. As well as typical village brews such as *cipumu,* the millet beer of the Bemba known on the Copperbelt as *hookworm* because it is said to cause diarrhea, or *katata,* a

milder drink frequently referred to as *diesel* because of its
thickness, there is a wide assortment of other concoctions such
as *Seven Days, Pineapple*, or *Babitoni* (from Barberton, a
Transvaal town), many of which have been introduced from
Southern Rhodesia or South Africa. Such beers are often
preferred by really heavy drinkers, *bachakolwa* (from the verb
ukukolwa, to be drunk), because they are usually more potent
than anything to be obtained at the Beer Hall, and thus enable
one to get drunk more quickly and at less cost. On the other
hand, beer drinks in private houses are always likely to be
interrupted and broken up by a police raid if the brewer has not
taken the precaution of bribing the *kanyangu*.[10]

Despite the prevalence of private drinking, the Beer Hall
remains the indisputable centre of community life. It is the one
part of the whole town which Africans regard in some way as
unassailably and peculiarly their own. A large, open area laid
out in chalets, the Beer Hall is the Africans' common
rendezvous. Thus, far from being just a place where beer may
be taken legally, the Beer Hall has come to serve as the public
arena in which the struggle for prestige is ceaselessly waged.
Thus, the capacity of the *cakolwa* is greatly admired, but what
one drinks is also relevant. 'Kafir beer' – the Beer Hall brew – is
the poor man's drink bought by *bacibombebombe*, 'anyhow'
labourers (from a form of the Bemba verb *ukubomba*, to work,
meaning 'to do something any old how') and others. On the
other hand, the prestige which attaches to European bottled
beer is evident in the remark of a young woman once overheard
at the Beer Hall: 'Teti nsumine ukucito bucende pa mulandu wa
kumpela *disilo* [*diesel*] kwati ni Castle uyo banwa abasungu wa
mpya shingi' (Do you think I can sleep with you because of the
diesel you've given me as if it were Castle beer Europeans drink
that costs such a lot?) All those who can afford it, therefore,
buy European bottled beer, and always a quart in preference to
a pint.[11] The quart is generally known as *maka maka*, the
Nyanja word for 'particularly' or 'especially'. The expression
originated in the mine compounds where the 'wealthy' miners,
frequently referred to as *BaNdalama*, literally the 'moneyed
ones', would buy quarts exclusively. During my stay at Ndola
the term *maka maka CiMukume* ('especially Mukume's') was
coined and soon found widespread acceptance. This was a
reference to an African clerk of that name who was responsible
for allocating houses in the location. It was generally asserted

that he had a very profitable income from the bribes he received which enabled him to visit the Beer Hall every day where he would surround himself with pretty girls and down innumerable quarts of Castle beer to show he was a *top guy*. A cheap wine also sold at the Beer Hall was known derisively as *ngungayi*. It sometimes happened that a *sugar boy* (one who was born in, or had grown up in, town and so accustomed to the sweet things of life) or other person accustomed to buy bottle beer would be temporarily short of cash. He would then buy the cheaper *ngungayi*, but promptly pour it into an empty Castle beer bottle. Similarly, Castle beer may itself be poured into an empty brandy bottle so that others are deceived into thinking it was a real *big boy* ('genuine brandy'), the sale of which at this time was forbidden to Africans.

Nor does one go to the Beer Hall necessarily to drink. Leaders in the community, frequently known as *Bameetingi* will go to be seen by the people and to learn their problems; *bamambala* or *amacrook* will meet there to transact illicit dealings in diamonds etc., while many others go simply to meet their friends and for the entertainment. As mentioned earlier, the Beer Hall is the favourite haunt of the *bakapenta*, and in themselves these provide an attraction. As one young man once expressed it: 'You should know that people do not go to the Beer Hall just for beer alone, but to feed their eyes on the *flowers of the country*.' In order to attract attention, the *kapenta* will *ukupanga four*, that is sit with legs crossed and skirt raised so that young men nearby would be led to comment 'ali na *mastanding yambi yambi*', an expression which seems to imply long, straight legs just like those of a European woman.[12] If the *kapenta* wished to further the acquaintance she might then say: 'Nimkupela *Luna Park* isuma nganshi' (I have given you a real thrill, haven't I?) Not surprisingly, the combination of beer and provocative young women gives rise to innumerable fights and brawls in which newly acquired techniques are employed. 'Namuteya *Chicago* awa na panshi' ('I tripped him up') derives from the films, Chicago being associated with *amacowboy* and others given to fighting. *Ukuma bullet*, on the other hand, is to butt someone with the head, an effective way of knocking an opponent out with a single blow just as an animal is killed with one bullet from a gun.

One important source of linguistic innovation is provided by newspapers and magazines, especially in the sphere of politics.

Here a large number of English words and expressions have
been adopted, and are used in a vernacular context by the more
sophisticated Africans, though often with a significant change
of meaning. The term *amapolitics* itself has come into common
use, generally to express the heightened political awareness
that Africans have developed in recent years. For example,
when Chitimukulu, Paramount Chief of the Bemba, visited the
Copperbelt in 1956 he was received by Africans with little
enthusiasm and a good deal of hostility. Discussing this one
day with an educated but otherwise conservative Bemba, he
remarked, perhaps a trifle ruefully: '*Amapolitics* yafulisha . . .
umuntu uwacenjela ukwenda pakati' (There is so much politics
today . . . one has to be a very clever man to walk the middle
path.) Other terms are further removed from the English original
such as *left wings*, which simply means opposition; or *tactics*,
which means to find a line of argument that will convince
people. Current events are themselves reflected in a number of
expressions, though, again, not without some modification of
meaning. Thus, at the time of the Korean War the word *Korea*
itself was adopted into the language of the day to refer to
industrial strife, violence, and the strike weapon itself, though
for the last the English loan word *listraka* remained the more
usual. Similarly, leaders of the African National Congress
addressing public meetings would speak of the Cold War,
nkondo yatalala, when referring to some political action, such
as a *boycott*, which was to be carried out without violence.[13]

One development of particular interest that should be
mentioned at this point concerns the growth of a new vocabulary
of personal abuse, much of which has originated in a purely
political context. Terms such as *Uncle Tom, informer, Capricorn*
(see Epstein 1958: 174 fn), *Government tool*, etc. are in everyday
use and are not confined to the political elite. Thus, an ordinary
spectator at a football match at which Paramount Chief
Chitimukulu was present was heard to remark: 'Takwaba mu
calo mfumu yatumpa nge 'yi. Ishinankwe shonse shalingile mu
Congress yena iyo - *Government tool*!' (In the whole country
there is not a chief as stupid as this one. All his fellow chiefs
joined Congress, but not he - Government tool!) Similar notions
are expressed today in the use of such terms as *malinso* or
mbulu ne nsamba, the monitor lizard and the iguana, the
pertinence of which derive from folklore. The crocodile lays its
eggs on shore: but the land is not its real home - its home is in

the water. When the mother crocodile has hatched her eggs she trains her offspring so that they learn to follow her into the river. But there are some who have failed to follow her example, and so they have remained on the bank as lizards, out of their own proper environment. In the same way, all informers, all those who had joined the Capricorn Society, and so on, were *malinso* who had been left on the bank (that is, with the Europeans) and were not with their own people. The terms *malinso* and *mbulu ne nsamba* were commonly used by speakers at Congress meetings to refer to African police or detectives present on these occasions who, as the meeting began, would be invited to sharpen their pencils by way of challenging them to record everything they saw and heard. The same or similar terms would also be heard cast at a woman seen buying meat at the butcher shop during a Congress-organised boycott of the European-owned butcheries, or at another at the communal water tap whose husband was known to have left the Mine Workers Trade Union to join the Salaried Staff Association. In times of social tension the use of such terms served as a powerful sanction in stifling dissent and promoting social and ideological conformity.

We have now looked at *CiCopperbelti*,[14] the term by which Africans themselves now characterise the distinctive language of the towns, as it is used in a number of different social contexts. The picture of African urban culture that emerges in this way is, of course, a partial one; nevertheless, it mirrors vividly much that is characteristic of the new way of life of the towns: its humour and patience in the face of poverty and squalor; its uncertainties, ambivalence, and frequent intolerance; but, above all, its tremendous zest and gusto, its crude vigour and general restlessness. At the same time, I think we may detect running through the various categories of semantic creation I have listed a single common thread which provides a major clue to the understanding of African urban organisation. Thus, if we take the terms and expressions which are applied to the town itself and to its different parts, or those that are used in the context of beer-drinking and relations between the sexes, it will be seen that many of them involve, directly or indirectly, some evaluation in terms of prestige. Prestige, indeed, is a dominant concept in African urban thought: it remains now, therefore, to examine in closer detail some of the ways in which it is expressed.

The general notion of prestige itself is frequently conveyed by the terms *amastanding* or *ciheavy*, the English derivation of which requires no explanation. Thus, one would say *takwata* (it does not have) *amastanding* of a cheap brand of cigarettes. Or again, when I once inquired the meaning of a word in the Lamba language my informant said he did not know and added that anyway Lamba was not a language *lwa ciheavy*. At one time the English word 'gentleman' itself served as a common index of status (see, for example, Wilson 1941: 24), but today one is more likely to hear the expression *gentleman wa ciheavy* or even simply *umuheavy*. People who enjoy high repute in general are known as *bamashina*, literally 'those with names', while particular individuals will be *big shot, top guy*, etc. Thus, when a young Health Assistant employed by the Ndola Municipality was falsely charged with unlawful possession of a bicycle he demanded angrily of the policeman 'Mulensebanya, tamwaishiba ukuti ndi *top guy*' (you are disgracing me. Don't you know I am a person of rank?) At the other end of the scale, the notion of social distance is aptly conveyed by the adoption of the English word 'far', as in the expression 'Ine, nshifwaya ukulanda na *mafala*' ('I do not wish to speak with "far-ones"' that is, trash). Lack of sophistication and low social status generally are also suggested by the word *babuyasulo*, a compound of the Fanagolo *buya* (to come) and the Nyanja *dzulo* (yesterday). Synonymous with *kamushi* (a villager or country bumpkin), *babuyasulo* expresses the idea of the newcomer: crude, uneducated, and unacquainted with the ways of the town.

The importance of occupation in rating prestige is very evident in daily speech. I have already mentioned *bacibombe-bombe*, who are also known categorically as *amaleba* (labourers) while the expression *mwana leba* (son of a labourer or manual worker) is commonly used as a term of abuse, not least of all by women swearing at their ne'er-do-well husbands. Yet another term for casual and unskilled workers that has come into fashion is *bakapepala*. This derives from the practice on the mines whereby new employees work a short period without pay and receive only food rations, for which they have to produce a chit (*ipepala*, from the English word paper) daily at the Food Store. The office clerks there do not bother about their names, but simply call out 'Imwe *bakapepala* iseni mupoke ifyakulya fyenu' ('you chit-people, come and collect your food'). It should, perhaps, be noted here that the use of these terms is not confined to clerks or others enjoying high prestige; they are equally accepted and used of themselves by those whom the terms designate. Wealth is an important component of prestige in this context, but it is not necessarily the major one. Reference has already been made to miners, *bandalama* (the moneyed ones), but for all their ability to buy quarts of beer ordinary miners still remain *bachimba mabwe* (diggers of stones). The notion of the parvenu is perhaps best conveyed by the term *kaboi* (house-boy). Because of their close contact with Europeans, African domestic servants are regarded as having achieved some of the more superficial marks of Western 'culture', but in other respects are viewed as still unrefined and lacking in taste. An interesting illustration of this notion was provided for me by a young government clerk who had received a bursary to attend university in South Africa. There he had to learn European-style ballroom dancing to avoid the taunts of his new friends. Back home on the Copperbelt he had never learnt to dance because ballroom dancing was regarded as essentially *fya bukaboi*, the quintessence of the *kaboi* way of life.

In this chapter I have been concerned simply to illustrate some of the linguistic innovations that mark Africans' adjustment to modern urban life and conditions on the Copperbelt. Many, perhaps a majority, of those innovations I have called semantic creations centre on the concept of prestige, but the material I have presented is obviously inadequate for a more detailed analysis of the role of this principle in social organisation. But a few general observations may not be out of place. To begin with, it is apparent that there is scarcely a single aspect of social life or behaviour to which the notion of prestige does not extend. I have described how drinking, sexual prowess, occupation etc. provide measures of prestige, but these represent only a few of the criteria by which prestige is evaluated. I might have added physical appearance, as in the expression *ukukashika ni passport*, which stresses the value of a light complexion; or clothes, as in the term *simyamfule* (literally, 'switch off the light while I undress'), which refers to a cheap petticoat of such inferior quality that a girl would be ashamed to let her lover see it; or even membership of a particular tribe, as in the expression *Ba ku six o'clock*, a derogatory reference to the peoples of the far west of the country, the land of the setting sun and, by implication, of darkness. In short, the criteria of prestige are many and varied. Some obviously run together, such as the ability to speak English, white-collar occupation, well-furnished home, etc., and this has enabled Mitchell and myself (see Mitchell 1956a; Mitchell and Epstein 1959) to speak of the 'European way of life' as providing a scale in terms of which the urban African population is stratified. There is much in the present discussion to support this view, but the evidence also suggests that we need to be much more careful and precise in the use of a concept of 'Europeanisation', for as it stands it tends, I think, to oversimplify what is, in fact, a very complex process of selection. Secondly, given the existence of such prestige classes or categories, it must be noted that the criteria of prestige may vary considerably from one stratum to another, and from group to group. Hence, in speaking of the Europeans as a 'reference group' (Mitchell 1956b), we need to bear in mind that the 'European way of life' would have to include the behaviour of Whites living on the Copperbelt as it is perceived by Africans; patterns of behaviour as they are observed in Hollywood or the novels of Peter Cheyney (which seem to have inspired a number of items in the Copperbelt argot); and even aspects of the life of American Blacks as it is transmitted through popular African magazines published in South Africa. Finally, while the 'European way of life' provides a valuable model of African social stratification in terms of structure, the very diversity of the criteria of prestige introduces great flexibility into the system. Such diversity allows of many different combinations and permutations which often make 'class placement' extraordinarily difficult in practice. In terms of social process, therefore, the variety of factors that may be employed in evaluating prestige serves to promote a continuous and unremitting struggle in which different and increasingly refined criteria may be variously invoked to advance one's claims to status, and leads to a bewildering assortment of rivalries, allegiances, and cross-cutting ties, both within and between social groups and categories.

7

The Millennium and the Self: Jehovah's Witnesses on the Copperbelt in the 1950s

Introduction

For an anthropologist at work on the Copperbelt in the 1950s, even one for whom 'religion' was quite peripheral to his research interests, it would have been difficult to remain unaware of Jehovah's Witnesses - or Watchtower, as the movement was still more commonly known in this part of Central Africa - as one of the most distinctive groups within African urban society (see also Mitchell 1956b: 5). As Dorothea Lehmann, co-author of the study *Christians of the Copperbelt* (1961) has observed, no other church within the country has caused so much controversy in the past or now received so much publicity. Whereas most of the other Christian denominations represented in the towns were struggling to keep a grip on their flock, Watchtower alone appeared to be gaining ground, the number of its adherents continuing to rise at an impressive rate.[1] For some time, indeed, this had been a development of major concern to the other churches from which so many of the converts to Jehovah's Witnesses were said to have come; tension was particularly strong between the Witnesses and the Roman Catholics, reflected from time to time in minor incidents between individuals or groups of protagonists and on one occasion in a dramatic confrontation at Mufulira, news of which spread rapidly throughout the other Copperbelt towns.

But what drew my own attention to the movement was not just the alleged evangelical fervour of its members, nor their undoubted achievements in winning converts, it was also their stance on a variety of social and political questions. For example, at a time when trade unionism was beginning to take root among the African labour force, and to record its first successes, Watchtower alone stood aloof. William Comrie, a British trade union official, brought out to Northern Rhodesia to help in establishing African trade unions, reported that the major

resistance came from Witnesses (Hooker 1965: 105); underlying
this response were attitudes and assumptions I was to encounter
later in my own fieldwork. Much of this research was to be
carried out at a time when the African National Congress had
also won widespread support throughout the country for its
campaign against the setting up of a Federation in Central
Africa. For most Africans, the proposals for Federation appeared
as a move to entrench the Europeans in their position of social,
economic, and political dominance, and therefore to be resisted.
But this, too, was a situation in which Witnesses refused to
become involved. The question that immediately intrigued me
was how to account for this development. What was the appeal
of Watchtower and the nature of its hold? However, as I began
to learn more about the movement, I quickly discovered that
the problem was more complicated than my first formulation of
it allowed or indicated. What complicated matters was the
historical dimension. For I soon learnt that in earlier days the
expression Watchtower - or, in its Africanised form, *WaChitaw-
ala* - was associated with a millenarian movement whose
prophets preached an apocalyptic message that was often so
distinctly radical in tone that it was quickly branded by
government officials and other Europeans as seditious. Against
this historical background, how was one to account for their
subsequent apolitical stance and seeming disengagement from
the world? In the earlier period the two movements were often
confused, not only by people on the spot but even by scholarly
commentators (see Hooker 1965). But, even if it was now
possible to see them as distinct, there were still clear historical
links between the two, suggesting that there were questions to
be asked not only about change but also about continuity.

These, then, are some of the issues to which this chapter
addresses itself. In the following section I sketch something of
the historical background, noting in particular certain contrasts
between the Watchtower movement of earlier days and the
Jehovah's Witnesses whom I observed in the 1950s. I then pass
on to consider the approach of the Witnesses to the issues of
evangelism and recruitment, which leads directly into a
discussion of the composition and social attributes of the
membership. While, from one point of view, becoming a Witness
involves an act of individual choice, it also becomes quickly
apparent that membership is not randomly distributed throughout the population at large; Witnesses not only tend to share

certain social characteristics they are also disproportionately represented among the various ethnic groups that compose the African urban population. In seeking to account for the particular appeal of the Society to this membership, I have examined the ideology and values embodied in its doctrine and organisation, and tried to show how, in a rapidly changing social environment, these have been important in helping many individuals to develop a new-found and more congenial sense of self.

Watchtower: the two strands

Although, as I have already indicated, Watchtower has relatively long and complex roots in south Central Africa, it is not necessary for present purposes to trace that history here in any detail.[2] However, it may be helpful by way of leading into the discussion to pursue the contrasts between the earlier and later periods in the growth of Watchtower by focusing on a few central features.[3] In this section, therefore, I touch briefly on some aspects of doctrine as well as of local organisation and leadership. Finally, a word will need to be said about the situation in rural and urban areas.

At the heart of the Watchtower creed were certain doctrines which were enunciated and propagated by Pastor Charles Russell, an American evangelist who founded the Watch Tower Bible and Tract Society in the latter part of the nineteenth century. The message was based upon detailed study of the Bible, but emphasising in particular its millenarian and apocalyptic elements: the present phase of world history was soon to pass to be succeeded by the institution of the Heavenly Kingdom. But before mankind could experience the glorious happiness of the new earth, it had to face the terrible ordeal of Armageddon, when Satan and his hordes of demons would contest the supremacy of the world. Locked into this titanic struggle were, on the one side, the principalities and powers, the men of wealth and influence who controlled governments, economic systems, and, not least, the established churches. On the other side, was the figure of Christ, who, it was held, had returned invisibly to earth in 1874 to prepare the way for the elimination of evil from the world and the establishment of a righteous new system of human existence. The task of adherents in these circumstances was to witness to God's existence, His loving nature and plans for the world, as well as to dedicate their lives to spreading the word of the millennium and opening the way to their own salvation and that of others by calling on them to repent their way of life.

By the early years of this century the message had found its way to Africa. Joseph Booth, a rather remarkable missionary figure originally from England, had introduced Watchtower literature into Nyasaland in 1906, and the later Chilembwe Rising there of 1915 was attributed by the colonial authorities to the diffusion of half-understood ideas about the millennial significance of 1914 (see, for example, Shepperson 1953, 1963; the *locus classicus* on Chilembwe himself is Shepperson and Price 1958). Making use of Watchtower literature which they were able to acquire from Booth, and later others, in Cape Town, a number of Africans (foremost among whom was Elliot Kamwana) began to preach the millennial doctrine and to acquire followers. Within a relatively short space of time the movement had spread from Nyasaland into both Southern and Northern Rhodesia. In this process of diffusion, however, the message took on a distinctive African colouring, adapting itself, moreover, to particular local conditions. One example is provided by the case of Tomo Nyirenda (see Cross 1977; Ranger 1975). Originally from Nyasaland, Nyirenda was arrested early in 1925 preaching among the Lala people in the Serenje District of Northern Rhodesia. He is reported to have taught that those who were baptised would never die, that the aged would again be young, and believers would see their forefathers; that the white man would be driven away, but their womenfolk would remain to be enslaved and carry loads, and European property would be divided among the believers; that taxation would cease, food would fall from heaven, and great wealth would be brought by Americans. In this particular instance Watchtower teaching was associated with a witchcraft eradication movement. Indeed, Nyirenda, more commonly referred to locally as Mwana Lesa, Son of God, was later executed for his part in the killing of large numbers of people who were held to have been witches. It is hardly surprising in the circumstances that the European representatives of the Society in Cape Town should have been quick to disavow any connection between themselves and the developments taking place further north. Yet what also needs to be stressed, as emerges clearly from Ranger's (1975: 52) account, is that the Watch Tower Bible and Tract Society provided the main source of Nyirenda's ideas; the central message remained biblical millenarianism based on texts drawn from the official Watch Tower literature which he carried with him as he moved through Lala country.

Another prophet who adapted the Russellite doctrine to 'Africanist' purposes was Jeremiah Gondwe, whose preaching in the late 1920s in the Ndola District gained him much prestige among the local Lamba people. After being convicted for sedition, Gondwe was jailed and then deported to his own home district, but eventually he returned and obtained permission to establish his own village, Tunduma, composed exclusively of his own Watchtower followers who were drawn, interestingly, from a number of different ethnic groups, including Luba from the northern Katanga (Cross 1970). When Cross visited Gondwe in 1969 he found a flourishing community; one, moreover, that had remained steadfastly independent of Jehovah's Witnesses.[4] At the time of my own fieldwork on the Copperbelt in the 1950s, Jehovah's Witnesses – the name officially adopted by the Watch Tower Bible and Tract Society in 1931 – continued to be known among Africans as Watchtower, but the radicalism that had earlier given the Watchtower concept of the millennium its distinctive 'Africanist' tinge had virtually disappeared, and the message was now almost totally indistinguishable from what was taught in other communities of Witnesses throughout the world.

What has just been said about doctrine also serves to highlight some of the contrasts in regard to organisation and leadership between the earlier and later periods. As already indicated, from the very outset those who preached the Watchtower gospel depended upon, and made use of, the literature that was available through the mail or was otherwise transmitted from Cape Town. However, relations between what had become an official branch of the Watch Tower Bible and Tract Society in South Africa and local groups in Northern Rhodesia were always ambiguous and equivocal. So, for example, Pastor Russell's immediate reaction to news of the Chilembwe Rising had been to sever all links with the 'unofficial' movement in Central Africa; on various subsequent occasions, as in the case of Mwana Lesa just mentioned, officials of the Society in Cape Town were prompt to deny any connection between itself and the African Watchtower groups to the north. In spite of this, they continued to be prepared to send literature to all those who claimed to be interested. As for the Africans

themselves, while they found it advantageous to maintain links
of a kind with Cape Town, it was also plain that they were not
prepared to accept European control: all the indications were
that Watchtower would develop as an independent African
church. But at this stage the movement lacked any coherent
organisation. Individual preachers, the best known and most
influential of them known as prophets, gathered around them
smaller or larger bands of followers who formed locally
autonomous congregations, though leaders were in touch and
seem to have gathered from time to time in Southern Rhodesia.
It was this very looseness of organisation which allowed or
encouraged the diversity in regard to message and form the
movement took in different parts of Northern Rhodesia.

This situation stands in marked contrast to the one which
has prevailed since the end of the Second World War:
Watchtower adherents, particularly those in the urban areas,
were absorbed into Jehovah's Witnesses and in this way
integrated into a global organisation that was highly centralised
and left little scope for local or congregational initiative. There
is a very real sense in which, where Jehovah's Witnesses as a
group are concerned, the organisation is the message, a point I
shall seek to elaborate on later.

In drawing the contrast between the earlier and later periods,
one also needs to look at the situation in the rural and urban
areas. The first evidence of Watchtower activity in Northern
Rhodesia appeared in the north-east part of the country, which
had experienced severe disturbance arising from the campaign
against the German forces in the First World War (Cross 1970,
1977), and from there it spread gradually to many parts of the
country, reaching a peak of millennial expectancy in the mid-
1920s. And, although congregations were in time to be found in
many of the urban centres, the movement seems to have made
the greatest headway in the rural areas and, as I shall discuss
later, in certain areas in particular. One point that is of
considerable interest is that in some parts of the country, at
least, Watchtower ideas had clear implications for social and
economic organisation. Church and community organisation
were based on a rural economy, and some local congregations
seem to have been entirely self-supporting. For example, on the
Luapula cassava gardens and finger-millet crops were cultivated,
hoed and harvested on a communal basis, while relish was

obtained by the sale of surplus garden produce or from Watchtower fishermen (Quick 1940). All of this seems a far cry from the individualism and *petit bourgeois* ethic of the Jehovah's Witnesses as described by Norman Long (1968) for Lala villagers in the early 1960s. The raw new mining camps and other townships of the Copperbelt might well have seemed to provide a ready-made audience for Watchtower's radical message, with its emphasis on White oppression, particularly with the onset of the Depression during 1931 which led quickly to the closing down of mines and other enterprises and unemployment for many African workers. Indeed, local administrators of the day did speak of a 'certain amount of irresponsible teaching and preaching by insufficiently educated and self-appointed evangelists', but they also noted that this had found little, if any, acceptance and had produced no disturbances and little enthusiasm (NRG 1931). But there was a noticeable change in official attitudes as the effects of the Depression began to bite deeper: when, in 1935, the Copperbelt experienced its first serious riots and numbers of Africans were killed, the Commission of Inquiry set up to look into the matter found Watchtower activities 'an important predisposing cause of the recent disturbances'.

In the course of his thoroughgoing account of the movement, Cross (1973) has re-examined carefully the part played by Watchtower in the 1935 riots. He concludes that Watchtower adherents generally took no part in the actual strikes which sparked off the further disorders, but he also acknowledges that the apocalyptic ideas which Watchtower preachers had been spreading in the compounds were important in creating an atmosphere of excitement and unrest that helped the strike to catch on in several areas. But, however these events are interpreted, it becomes plain that they represented a watershed in the development of the movement. For years the colonial government had vacillated over what policy it should adopt. Now it opted for recognition in the hope that closer supervision by European staff would bring the movement under control. The visit of de Jager,[5] a representative of the Society from Cape Town, and the subsequent permission given to set up an office in Lusaka, marked the turning point. By the end of 1935 a number of Watchtower congregations had emerged in the towns of Northern Rhodesia which were fast becoming branches of the

far-flung body that had recently taken to itself the name of
Jehovah's Witnesses. The initial organisation of these congregations took place under the leadership of Africans who, in
some cases at least, continued to draw on their experience of the
independent Watchtower movement. Moreover, since the name
Watchtower continued to be used by Africans, as indeed it still
is (Cesara 1982), it is hardly surprising that a certain confusion
remained both for adherents and outsiders, as to who was
Watchtower, who was Witness, or that the radical anti-
European preaching associated with the movement in earlier
days was still occasionally to be heard. When the Second World
War broke out the Witnesses again came in for official
disapproval because of their refusal to participate in the war
effort, but afterwards and throughout the 1950s 'quietism' and
seeming disengagement from the world had replaced the earlier
agitated stance.

Evangelism and recruitment

For many Africans on the Copperbelt, that Christianity should
contain within itself many different churches posed no more of
a problem than the fact that they themselves belonged to so
many different tribes. More significant, so far as the churches
were concerned, was what they had in common: that they all
prayed to God.[6] And if, in response to questioning, they did
refer to differences, they would do so not in terms of doctrine or
dogma but in regard to mode or style of prayer. Pursuing this
local perception offers not only a convenient lead into a
discussion of Jehovah's Witnesses but also a way of bringing
out quickly what seems distinctive in their approach. Lehmann
(1961: 232) has given a short, but instructive, account of services
she attended at Nchanga, part of which is worth citing here:

> The public services or meetings had the very simple design
> of instructing classes rather than worship. . . . There is no
> set order of service, the simple prayers are extempore and
> limited to the conventional petitions for understanding
> Jehovah's will and for perseverance in the way of the
> righteous. The main purpose of the meeting is clear. It is
> not worship, but indoctrination.

Since Dr Lehmann was herself a missionary of more orthodox
persuasion, some might question whether her account can be
accepted as wholly impartial. On its basic points, however, the

view she presents is completely in line with what the instruction manual which Witnesses themselves use itself proclaims:

Active service, not ritual, comprises their worship. They must preach. Each Witness is a minister. One not preaching is not one of Jehovah's Witnesses. Their preaching results in salvation to themselves and others.

The view expressed here is deeply rooted in doctrine, the full significance of which emerges clearly in a central address given at a district assembly held in the Luapula Valley in 1950.

Armageddon is surely coming. That is what we are here to concentrate on and so there is no point in being interested in worldly things. If there were a great wall of water fifty feet high coming down the Luapula, what should we do? Should we try to stop it by building a dam five feet high against it? No, we should warn the people to be out of the way. Thus we can show mercy not by trying to stop Armageddon but by warning others of its approach, by preaching from house to house (Cunnison 1951: 460).

Jehovah's Witnesses is an evangelical movement that demands that each of its adherents must be an activist.

The point at issue here has been skilfully developed and documented by Beckford (1975) in a notable sociological study of Jehovah's Witnesses in Britain. The improvement in the Society's fortunes, he argues, were not to be accounted for only in terms of growing anxiety about developments in the world at large and an associated rise of interest in matters religious; it also reflected changes in the group's organisation under the regimen of Judge Rutherford, and the heightened effectiveness of its work that followed (Beckford 1975: 40). Individual preaching with the aim of conversion had been there from the very onset. But under Rutherford's presidency various reforms were instituted which paved the way for a more highly centralised organisation. The underlying rationale has been assessed by Beckford. Rutherford's concern to gain control over local Elders and thereby whole companies was not dictated principally by considerations of doctrinal purity, as has frequently been the case with other religious movements, but was largely rooted in the desire to achieve ever higher levels of evangelical 'output' by Jehovah's Witnesses. In Rutherford's view, this demanded unremitting striving to satisfy quotas for hours by individuals in door-to-door campaigns (Beckford 1975: 32).

These concepts applied universally and were put into effect with the same skill and dedication on the Copperbelt as elsewhere. Lehmann's account is again of interest. When she was about to begin her study at Nchanga, she approached some of the Witnesses there in order to explain the purpose of her inquiry and to win their co-operation in the study. After meeting initial reluctance, she was at length invited to one of their houses. She found a group of young men and women busy preparing for their work the next Sunday. They were packing the monthly issue of *The Watchtower* (in its Bemba translation) and each copy was checked against the card index. Wall maps showed the figures of membership and number of visits planned for each month of the year, with those actually achieved filled in for comparison (Taylor and Lehmann 1961: 228).

The same methodical approach and attention to detail were seen in regard to preaching, the central obligation acknowledged by every committed Witness. At the regular gatherings of the congregation, apart from the discourse around a biblical text, the major focus was on instruction: in how to approach people in their homes or on the path; how to deal with different kinds of argument and response; on the preparation necessary before one could go out preaching, in the art of public speaking; and so on. But it was on the occasion of the larger gatherings, the circuit and district assemblies or the annual Memorial, that the Witnesses' mastery of organisational skills and logistics was most clearly exemplified.[7] The assemblies that I myself attended displayed the same features as those reported by Lehmann and Cunnison; in fact, certain points of local detail apart, so far as matters of organisation and character are concerned, an assembly of Witnesses on the Copperbelt was not likely to differ greatly from one in London or a city of the American Mid-West (see, for example, Pike 1954; Whalen 1962). Cunnison's account brings out those aspects that are of most interest for present purposes. The assembly itself was 'slick', he tells us, a choice of term that, whether intentionally or not, conveys something of the professionalism associated with American-style organisation.

> Everything was controlled and orderly. There were ushers to show people to their places. Gates were closed after starting-time. There was a lost and found department. The slightest noise of voices could be controlled by the wave of

a hand or by the blowing of a whistle. . . . Everything happened at the advertised time.

But if the cultural idiom harks back to Brooklyn, we should also be careful to note that the running of the assembly itself was in African hands. In this regard, as Taylor and Lehmann (1961) correctly observe, although supervised and guided by a mere handful of American missionaries, Jehovah's Witnesses in Northern Rhodesia were so organised as to have all the 'feel' of a purely African movement.

The assumptions which underline the approach to organisation reflect the 'rationalism' which Witnesses like to think characterises their religion. It finds its expression in a variety of ways, as Beckford (1975: 201-3) discusses perceptively, and no more clearly than in their view of conversion. Not for Witnesses the cardinal expectation of other evangelical movements that God would work on the hearts of men to convert them (Wilson 1973: 28); still less that conversion should follow, as appears to be the case in some other modern African religious movements, successful treatment of actual sickness or misfortune (see, for example, Peel 1968). So, for example, when once in the course of a lengthy conversation with Mr Arnott, the American missionary based in Luanshya, I asked what aspect of their teaching he considered made the strongest appeal to Africans he had no hesitation in replying: 'We appeal to their understanding. We ask them to reason. . . . Our beliefs can be discussed, and we can provide evidence for them. . . .' Conversion emerges from this point of view not as a sudden and powerful emotional experience but rather as an intellectual process that goes on throughout a lengthy period of instruction and training – a view that also came across in the accounts given by many of our respondents recalling how they came to leave the church to which they had previously belonged to join Watchtower. They would describe how they had been approached by Watchtower evangelists and gradually came to see that in the other churches the Bible was not taught satisfactorily or clearly. The approach of these other churches, moreover, was authoritarian; questioning on matters of doctrine that one found puzzling was discouraged. The point that was made repeatedly by those with whom we talked was that whereas in other churches it would have been regarded as reprehensible to ask a question in the course of a service, Witnesses were encouraged to do precisely that.[8] In this way, and by regular attendance at study classes, one came gradually to read the Bible with fuller understanding.

The *modus operandi* developed by Jehovah's Witnesses thus goes a long way towards explaining the success of the movement in recruiting new members, as Beckford argued (compare Taylor and Lehmann 1961: 232). Witnesses who spent time regularly in Bible study and were thoroughly versed in text and exegesis clearly enjoyed a great advantage over anyone who was prepared to accept argument on their terms. And, given that every Witness was required to be active (as, in fact, considerable numbers of them were), it should occasion no surprise that they succeeded in drawing so many converts. Yet the matter is surely more complex than this. For if recruitment were simply a question of command of techniques of persuasion, and a commitment to put them regularly to use, one would expect an examination of Jehovah's Witnesses' membership to show a fairly random distribution throughout the various groups and categories making up the African population of the Copperbelt. This, then, is an appropriate point to turn to the question of who joined Watchtower?; or, equally revealing, who did not?

The pattern of membership

However successful a social movement, it is unlikely to draw into the fold everyone within the population exposed to its message. Seeking to establish whether there are sections of the population to whom the message appears to make a particular appeal, and noting some of their social characteristics, would therefore seem to provide a useful first step towards clarifying its nature. Accordingly, in this section I look at the social composition of Jehovah's Witnesses on the Copperbelt in terms of education, occupation, and ethnic affiliation.

To begin with, it may be noted that to be an effective Witness one had to be literate: study of the Bible was central, but one also had to read the magazine *The Watchtower* and other publications in order to take part fully in study classes and other activities. This is not to say, however, that all who joined were already literate. This was far from being the case, and it was to meet the needs of the many illiterate 'hearers' or neophytes that Watchtower congregations organised their own reading classes. Writing was also stressed, evidenced in the way those attending a meeting would turn up armed with note-book and pencil to record references to a text cited in an address or discourse. But, if there is an emphasis on the attainment of certain educational skills, it is also important to ask what meaning attaches to education in this context. For it is plain that no great value was placed on formal schooling as such. A comment encountered frequently in the Society's literature, and recited repeatedly at assemblies, was that the Apostles of the New Testament, who provide the model for contemporary Witnesses, did not possess school certificates, still less degrees from a theological seminary. Jehovah's Witnesses, it was said, pursued an alternative educational scheme of values that was not secular, but spiritual. It is worth glancing, therefore, at the level of schooling attained by Watchtower adherents as against members of other churches. Data on the point, drawn from Taylor and Lehmann (1961: 233-4) and the Copperbelt social survey conducted in the same period by Clyde Mitchell, are set out in Table 7.1. The two sets of figures differ in detail, particularly as they bear on the position of the Roman Catholics, but they are in overall agreement in showing the groups occupying the same positions relative to one another.[10] Jehovah's Witnesses have the highest proportion of their numbers to reach only the sub-standards, followed by the Roman Catholics, and the CCAR; Jehovah's Witnesses also have by far the smallest proportion of those who had achieved a Standard 4 or higher grade of education, again followed by the Roman Catholics and CCAR. Some of the reasons for these differences, and their significance for the problem under discussion, will be taken up later when there has been an opportunity to identify some of the other processes at work.

That level of schooling should have a close bearing on the occupational profile would seem fairly obvious, but ideological factors may also have to be taken into account. Testing out in a Zambian context some of Weber's ideas on the relations of religion, economy, and society, Long's study of changing patterns of economic activity in the Serenje District is of particular interest here. The connection between attitudes towards work, choice of occupation, and so on and the teachings of Jehovah's Witnesses emerges quite clearly. For Witnesses everywhere it is a tenet of the faith, ascribed to the teaching of Isaiah, that the world would be rebuilt by God's chosen people. Accordingly, by acquiring such skills as bricklaying, carpentry, and tailoring, or by using improved methods of cultivation, the Witnesses of Kapepa Parish believed they were raising their

Table 7.1 Level of schooling attained by members of
Jehovah's Witnesses and other churches

Church		Sub-standards	Standard 4 and over
		%	%
Jehovah's Witnesses	Lehmann	60	10
	Mitchell	65	6
Roman Catholics	Lehmann	46	26
	Mitchell	58	11
CCAR[9]	Lehmann	35	39
	Mitchell	38	25

standards of living, both materially and spiritually, preparing
themselves in the process for the new life and the tasks ahead
for which it would call (Long 1968: 210). Similar ideas were
encountered on the Copperbelt, but as the data presented in
Table 7.2[11] show, the occupational profile does not in the main
vary very strikingly or significantly from one group to another.
The simple fact is, of course, that in the conditions of the day
very few jobs requiring skill or the exercise of responsibility
were available to Africans. Not surprisingly, therefore, as Long
himself points out, many Witnesses who left their villages for
the Copperbelt found when they got there that there was fierce
competition for the more skilled jobs they felt they were
qualified to get, and so often they had to resign themselves to
taking poorly paid, unskilled employment.[12]

Yet if the overall picture is one of uniformity between the
different groups, there are also suggestions of difference which
deserve to be noted. In this 'White settler' society trade and
commerce were dominated by Europeans and Asians, but a
category of African businessmen, made up of storekeepers in
the Municipal locations, itinerant traders, or 'hawkers' dealing
mainly in second-hand clothing, petty commodity producers
and the like, was gradually beginning to make its appearance.
Generally speaking, self-employed Africans were discouraged
from renting houses in the main housing areas or locations
which were under Municipal supervision and control. There
were, however, small, relatively autonomous African townships
that lay outside the boundaries of the different Copperbelt

Table 7.2 Occupation and church membership

Occupation	Jehovah's Witnesses %	IA	Roman Catholics %	IA	CCAR %	IA	Dutch Reformed Church %	IA
Domestic	26.3	1.50	15.6	1.11	12.0	1.04	24.1	1.40
Unskilled	43.5	1.13	49.0	1.01	39.8	0.89	35.7	2.02
Traders	2.0	1.48	1.4	1.08	1.1	0.85	0.4	1.71
Supervisory	5.3	1.22	3.7	1.15	4.0	0.95	5.0	1.18
Semi-skilled	7.5	1.23	9.1	0.97	8.0	1.28	7.9	1.15
Skilled	11.4	1.21	11.6	1.24	15.3	1.80	14.3	1.55
White-collar	1.2	0.45	1.8	0.67	14.7	5.80	5.4	2.03
	97.2		99.2		94.9		92.8	

towns where, so I was frequently told, concentrations of Jehovah's Witnesses earning a living as traders were chiefly to be found.[13] What emerges more clearly from the table, however, is the relatively small numbers of Witnesses in white-collar employment, confirming the impression from general fieldwork that, with rare and, indeed, outstanding exceptions, Witnesses were not to be found among the ranks of the new African urban elite.

The simple fact is, then, that the vast majority of Witnesses, as with the members of the other churches, were to be found among the mass of largely unskilled and poorly paid urban workers. But such 'lumping' on quantitative grounds does not do justice to Witnesses' own perceptions of the situation, in particular to their aspirations and the life-style in which they seek to give them expression. A remark of one of Long's informants helps to make the point neatly: 'Those among us who now practise as carpenters and bricklayers will continue to do so in the New Kingdom, while those who are unskilled will remain as labourers.' In religious terms they were an 'elect', numbered among the few who had chosen the path of salvation; in social terms they were no less a distinctive group, in their own eyes set apart from the mass of their fellow unskilled African workers by their more cultivated way of life, and recognised as such by the latter for their sobriety, industry, and pursuit of respectability. For Witnesses on the Copperbelt the ideology appeared to be finely attuned to a seemingly new-found sense of self.

But before pursuing this theme further, there is one other aspect touching the social composition of Watchtower adherents that needs to be considered. This is the question of ethnicity. 'Tribalism' as it operated at this time on the Copperbelt can be regarded from one point of view as being concerned with categories of interaction in certain social contexts; from another, it may be seen as offering a system of conceptual categories for ordering and explaining the data of social life. How it worked may be illustrated simply. I was chatting once with a man I knew well, a much-respected storekeeper in the Ndola location, and the conversation turned at length to the subject of Watchtower. Those who became Witnesses, my collocutor remarked spontaneously, were mostly uneducated. He then proceeded to define the membership not in occupational terms nor in terms of social class, but in relation to ethnic group: they were Kaonde, Lamba, Lenje, he said. This suggestion of a connection between ethnic affiliation and adherence to Watch-tower was supported by other of my material. However, data drawn from Clyde Mitchell's Copperbelt social survey, set out in Table 7.3, provides an opportunity to test the association on a much larger and more representative sample.[14]

It is clear from Table 7.3 that Witnesses are to be found in a wide variety of ethnic groups throughout the country, but what is equally apparent is that their distribution among the various groups differs strikingly. It can be seen that if the popular stereotype reflected in the comments of my informant just cited does not adequately represent the facts, it is nevertheless not entirely without substance. The figures for the Lamba and their neighbours of the central region are by far the highest – almost 50 per cent of the total – followed by the Luapula peoples of the northern region who constitute some 20 per cent; the figures for the eastern and western groups are very low. But these figures do not tell the whole story. Where ethnic groups often differ considerably in size, simple tallies can be misleading. For a fuller understanding of the situation we also need to know the degree to which Jehovah's Witnesses are represented proportion-ally within the different ethnic groups. This information is set out in Table 7.4. Figure 7.1 recasts this material using an index of association.

What is the significance of this data? The issues are complex,

Table 7.3 Membership of Jehovah's Witnesses on the Copperbelt by ethnic group

Ethnic group	Males	%	Females	%	Sub-totals
1. Northern					
Aushi	475	5.91	253	4.91	
Ng'umbo	194	2.41	62	1.20	
Lunda (Kazembe)	337	4.20	270	5.25	
Chishinga	479	5.97	262	5.09	
Tabwa	258	3.21	123	2.39	20.60
Bemba	651	8.11	376	7.31	7.80
Mambwe	63	0.78	70	1.36	
Inamwanga	150	1.87	86	1.67	
Lunga	256	3.19	95	1.85	5.47
2. Central					
Bisa	582	7.25	409	7.95	7.52
Lala	608	7.57	310	6.02	
Lamba	899	11.20	868	16.87	
Lenje	291	3.62	354	6.88	
Kaonde	961	11.97	708	13.76	
Lima	237	2.95	177	3.44	
Swaka	237	2.95	299	5.81	45.18
3. Eastern					
Ngoni	11	0.14	11	0.21	
Cewa	116	1.44	42	0.82	
Nsenga	200	2.49	63	1.22	
Kunda	61	0.76	22	0.43	3.99
4. Western					
Lozi	11	0.14	—	—	0.08
Lovale	32	0.40	26	0.50	
Chokwe	52	0.65	20	0.39	
Luchazi	93	1.16	39	0.76	
Ndembu	93	1.16	16	0.31	2.82
Others	677	8.41	182	3.54	6.52
TOTALS	8024	99.91	5145	99.94	99.98

Table 7.4 Representation of Jehovah's Witnesses in various ethnic groups

Ethnic group	% Female	% Male	% Male and Female combined	% by groupings of ethnic groups
Aushi	18.1	20.0	19.3	
Ng'umbo	5.1	10.7	8.5	
Chishinga	21.8	24.3	23.3	
Lunda (Kazembe)	28.2	24.1	25.8	19.2
Bemba	6.7	7.8	7.4	7.4
Mambwe	24.0	12.9	20.9	
Inamwanga	15.1	15.4	15.3	18.1
Lala	24.2	28.5	26.9	
Lamba	32.9	32.6	32.7	
Lenje	39.8	32.5	36.1	
Kaonde	35.6	26.0	29.3	31.2
Ngoni	0.5	—	0.4	
Cewa	4.6	6.6	5.9	
Nsenga	5.1	8.2	7.6	
Kunda	3.7	9.3	6.3	5.0
Lozi	—	1.8	1.3	
Lovale	5.4	2.4	3.2	
Ndembu	3.0	6.3	5.4	4.3

and some at least of the questions they raise go far beyond the scope of the present chapter. One point, however, that is of immediate interest, is that the groups for whom the association between membership of Jehovah's Witness and ethnic affiliation is most pronounced are precisely those in whose areas the earlier radical Watchtower movement had flourished. This raises a number of questions which for the moment I simply note, deferring more detailed discussion to a later stage of the analysis. In the first place, there is the question of continuity as between the earlier Watchtower movement and the contemporary Society of Jehovah's Witnesses. A second, and related matter, concerns the problem of ethnic ranking on the Copperbelt. As discussion elsewhere (see, for example, Mitchell 1956b; Epstein

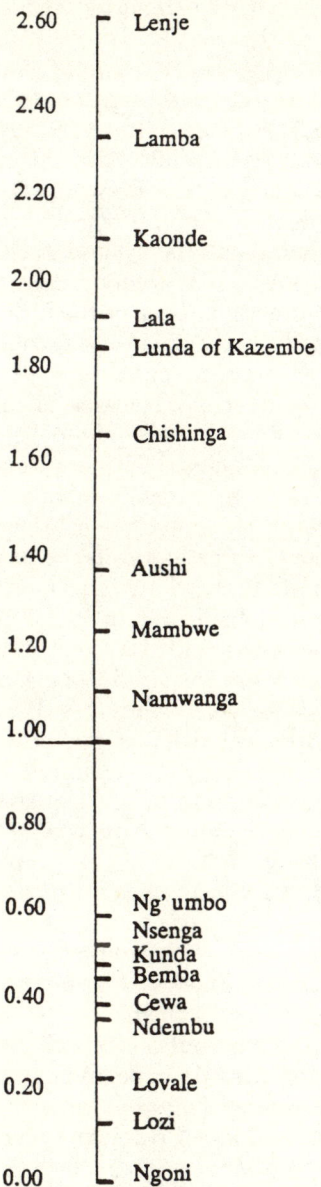

2.60 — Lenje

2.40

— Lamba

2.20

— Kaonde

2.00

— Lala
— Lunda of Kazembe
1.80

— Chishinga
1.60

1.40 — Aushi

— Mambwe
1.20

— Namwanga
1.00

0.80

0.60 — Ng' umbo
— Nsenga
— Kunda
— Bemba
0.40 — Cewa
— Ndembu

0.20 — Lovale

— Lozi

0.00 — Ngoni

Figure 7.1. Copperbelt membership of Jehovah's Witnesses by ethnic group using index of association

1978) has shown, a fairly clear-cut pattern of ethnic ranking had developed there: at the top were the centralised, once militarily dominant groups – the Bemba, Ngoni, and the Lozi; at the other end of the prestige continuum were those groups from the far west of the country often collectively referred to pejoratively by others as Kalwena. While the pattern obviously owed something to perceptions that drew on the past, it also has to be understood as reflecting processes at work within the contemporary urban-industrial system itself: ethnic groups held in high regard tended to be predominant in those occupations that carried high prestige; those at the bottom of the scale were poorly represented in these positions and were numerically strongest in the poorest paid jobs (Epstein 1978: 132). Membership of Jehovah's Witnesses is interesting from this point of view. Certain of the Luapula peoples apart, who in the urban context were associated with the Bemba, Witnesses were not to be found in large numbers among those ethnic groups that ranked high on the prestige scale nor, as already noted, were they commonly to be found in the more highly evaluated jobs. But neither did they belong to groups at the bottom of the ethnic ladder; as for jobs, in aspiration, if not in actuality, they aimed at the level of the skilled worker or 'artisan'. Both of the matters just touched on will need to be considered again later. For if it is the case that Jehovah's Witnesses were drawn predominantly from a particular segment of the population, then it is first necessary to examine the sources of the movement's appeal to those people. Since what the Witnesses sought primarily to communicate was a 'message', it would seem logical to focus, at least initially, on some of the central ideas embodied in the Society's doctrine and teaching.

Ideology, values, and self-image

The teachings of the Witnesses offer not only a highly complex theology but also a view of the historical process that claims to explain not just the past but also offers a key to the unfolding of contemporary events. My concern here, however, is not with this body of doctrine as such, but rather with its impact on a particular population, and I dwell therefore on only certain of its central ideas and values, particularly those encountered in the Central African context as they were expounded at local meetings and assemblies or enunciated by one's respondents.

Reference has already been made at a couple of points to

Armageddon, that convulsive struggle between the forces of good and evil that will mark the passing of the old world and usher in the New Kingdom. The Kingdom itself is not understood in symbolic or even mystical terms, but concretely. For it is held that a remnant of humanity, including among them many who are presently still living, will pass through Armageddon and will go on living in happiness forever: the Kingdom is on earth, but an earth that has been cleansed and where total harmony prevails. All one's attention, therefore, should be concentrated on, and energies directed towards, preparing for the new life which is imminent. These ideas have to be understood in conjunction with the Witnesses' concept of salvation, a concept which, as Beckford (1975: 110) has observed, is more tangible than that of other Christian conceptions of salvation, placing more emphasis on purely personal benefits. One of our respondents once summed up his understanding of the core doctrine as follows:

> The main teaching in our church, as I know it, is to let many people hear the work of God and do His work. Those who do not do His work will be sent to hell on the Day of Judgment when Jesus Christ will come to judge the dead and the living. Righteous people (*abololoke*) will be saved and will live in a world of everlasting life (*mweo wa muyayaya*).[15]

Baptism was important as a mark of commitment, though in itself still only a step in the right direction for, as Long (1968: 208) has observed, being a Witness is a process, not a state: membership demanded that one become 'more mature in the knowledge of the Bible and acquire the ability to teach others'. This is what is primarily entailed in doing God's work, but ministry also required the development of various personal qualities as well as a heightened spirituality. The official publications of the Society listed many regulations which the dedicated Witness was obliged to observe in his personal life. But where so much emphasis was placed on setting one's sights on the New Kingdom, it is not difficult to see how 'earthly things' came to serve as a general principle shaping attitudes on a variety of attitudes or governing the response to some novel set of circumstances. As an example of the latter, there was the occasion when, calling at a house in his section, my research assistant found there an agent of an insurance company. At this time insurance for Africans was something quite new, and the agent was seeking to stimulate the interest of the householder and his wife so as to attend a meeting where the matter would be more fully explained. The wife appeared to be initially attracted to the idea, but in the end they decided against going to the meeting: 'The Society does not allow us to participate because all these are "earthly things".'

But it was in the public domain, where political and economic relationships were involved, that 'earthly things' tended most frequently to be invoked and to influence behaviour. In approaching this issue, it is helpful to recall the radical note in the message of the earlier Watchtower, with its sometimes quite explicit theme of role-reversal between Black and White. The inequities and abuses of the social system which some knowledgeable contemporary observers claimed had fuelled the movement in the 1930s (see, for example, Moore 1942; Quick 1940) were no less in evidence twenty years later, and African anxieties and resentments were indeed intensified as the movement for the closer association of the Rhodesias and Nyasaland gathered momentum (see Chapter 8). There was, however, one major point of difference between the two periods: by the 1950s Africans had developed their own political and labour organisations through which they could hope to play a part in the shaping of events. In what follows, reaction to the boycott of European and Indian-owned stores organised in Ndola by the African National Congress offers a point of entry to the discussion of Jehovah's Witnesses' attitudes towards, and relations with, these different bodies.

The boycott, viewed by Congress as a means of rallying African support in the aftermath of Federation, played on legitimate African grievances about the way they were treated in the shops. Something of the response of Witnesses to it emerged at a circuit assembly I happened to attend at Ndola. A young man had been called to the platform to recount an 'Experience', a regular feature of these gatherings to which I will return later. He did this with great skill and humour, evidently amusing the audience who laughed quite freely at his sallies. His 'Experience' centred on the fact that he had gone into a shop at the height of the boycott. The European who served him expressed surprise, asking what sort of person he was that he should enter a shop he knew his fellow Africans were boycotting. He replied that all of these things were of this world, they were not of the government of God, for the time of the establishment of His Kingdom had not yet come, and he could pay no attention to such matters; he would shop if he wanted to. His account was greeted with loud applause.

Such an episode exemplifies neatly the principle that Witnesses should not allow themselves to become involved in political action; organisations (*filonganino*), it was said, could not lead to the Promised Land.[16] Yet it would be a mistake to proceed to infer that Witnesses were indifferent to what went on around them. Numbers of them, in fact, did attend some of the meetings in the Ndola location called in connection with the boycott; at one such gathering their presence was acknowledged by the Congress leader when he cited the Bible and declared that it was the wickedness of African 'informers' that was responsible for delaying the coming of Jesus. Presumably those Witnesses who were drawn to the meeting shared the same interest in the matter as other African customers. For other Witnesses, however, the interest may have been more specifically economic. As Lehmann (Taylor and Lehmann 1961: 168) points out, Congress had a particular appeal to independent African traders, many of whom, particularly in the freehold townships such as Twapiya, seem to have been Jehovah's Witnesses. Certainly, a number of the latter whom we encountered, while they did not actually belong to Congress, quite spontaneously indicated their support for the boycott.

For many Witnesses, indeed, it was as though a clear line could be - and was - drawn between economic and political activities and interests. The point was made most explicitly in regard to trade unions. I discussed the matter at length on one occasion with Oliva Kabungo, without question the most prominent African Witness on the Copperbelt, whose home was in Twapiya. He explained that this issue had come to the forefront of Witnesses' attention when, a few years earlier, the first steps were being taken to introduce trade unionism to Africans. After consulting with Mr Arnott, the two of them had toured the Copperbelt together explaining the position to their members. The Society, he pointed out, was not opposed to its members joining a union. Mr Arnott had said unions were not political bodies, and everyone was entitled to seek better pay and housing conditions. If there was a strike, Kabungo continued, as a result of which wages were raised, was that not a good thing? There was nothing to prevent a Witness being a member. If he did not like to take part in meetings, he could still pay his membership dues. In principle, then, as Mr Arnott himself was to confirm for me, the Society had no declared policy in the matter of union membership; it was something that was left entirely to the individual. It is all the more interesting, therefore, that so many Witnesses refused to join unions; while this was something that union secretaries were sometimes heard to deplore, employers would applaud the fact that Witnesses refused to join their fellows in demands for higher pay and would continue to work in the event of a strike.

How is this response to be accounted for? In some cases, at least, it seems clear that there was a misunderstanding of the official position. Thus, one man, a 'boss boy' on the Roan Antelope mine at Luanshya for five years, described himself as still a 'hearer', his friends coming to his house nearly every evening to instruct him in the teachings of the Society. But he doubted if he would ever become a full member because that would mean having to leave the African Mine Workers Union. 'But I will never leave the Union, because it has done a lot for me', he concluded. Kabungo himself, and others with whom I spoke, pointed to other motives. In the beginning, it was said, union leaders were going around forcing everyone to join. Witnesses became suspicious and felt that 'there was something behind it'. Then again for a long time government had been hostile to Jehovah's Witnesses. Linked with this was the fact that in the past union meetings had often ended in fights. Witnesses wanted to have nothing to do with activities of this kind; they feared that if they attended meetings and became involved in brawls they might be blamed for starting them.

But for whatever reasons, what seems plain is that the concept of 'earthly things' was widely interpreted to imply a ban on participation in any kind of association; it did not, however, imply indifference to one's own material conditions. One of our respondents, a Kaonde, employed as a manual labourer, once expressed it this way: what trade unions asked for was fine - more pay, better housing and working conditions - but to go on strike because one's demands were not met was sinful. That is why, he said, Witnesses did not join unions. But what of the pursuit of money, he was asked, did this not also display an improper concern with 'earthly things'? He had no difficulty in rejecting this line of argument. The pursuit of money was not wrong in itself, he replied; what was wrong was seeking it by evil means. It was a bad thing to stop worshipping God when one was rich or to use money in a sinful way like running after women or spending it on other things that led one to forget God. 'Things like beer. For when you drink a lot, you get into things like fighting, insulting people, and such like. Once you are rich and use your money rightly, there is nothing bad.'

Reference has been made to the importance of organisation in accounting for the Witnesses' remarkable evangelical success. From one point of view, organisation appears simply as a particular set of arrangements designed to achieve certain ends. But organisations which are addressed to human purposes are apt to involve something more: they embody, or give expression to, certain ideas and values. These may be formulated explicitly as part of the doctrine, but their meaning may also be reinforced by the pattern of activities of which the actors themselves are not consciously aware or which they are unable to articulate. In these terms, the Society of Jehovah's Witnesses immediately appears to the outside observer as a highly centralised global organisation in which the smallest units, local congregations, are locked by way of a complex hierarchical structure into the head office located in Brooklyn, New York. To Witnesses themselves the matter appears quite otherwise: they speak of themselves as belonging to a non-hierarchical, egalitarian Society.

This ideological stance is best appreciated if we focus on certain features of the organisation as it operates at the local level. The basic unit everywhere is the congregation defined as a group of Jehovah's Witnesses in a certain locality who meet regularly for worship and Bible study and unitedly preach the gospel in the field. In all congregations there are a number of appointments to be filled by persons referred to as 'servants' or 'overseers': these and their assistants attend to the running of the various aspects of the congregation's activities. Within the Society there are also individuals known as 'pioneers'; in Northern Rhodesia at the time of my fieldwork they numbered about a hundred altogether; assuming special responsibilities, they operated mostly in areas where local organisation was still not fully developed and the people were still held to be in need of guidance. In Northern Rhodesia, too, there were also at this time a handful of trained missionaries from overseas. These positions, it should be stressed, carry no privileges; they do not

constitute a structure of rank. From the point of view of
Witnesses, all members become dedicated servants and there
can be no higher position than that of servant of God.

Of central importance in all these regards is the concept of
ministry already touched upon. The distinction between clergy
and laity found in other churches is quite unacceptable to
Witnesses, who see in it yet another mark of the apostasy of
orthodox Christianity; in their view, all members are ministers.
In these circumstances the minister cannot be elevated above
the congregation as in other churches; the only 'elevation' that
Witnesses acknowledge relates to increased responsibility. No-
one, it will be recalled, could be a fully committed Witness who
did not go out and preach the gospel. For some, perhaps, this
might in itself appear as elevating, but the more crucial point to
note is the responsibility of ministry, the demands that ministry
laid upon the individual. To engage in preaching required
intensive preparation in terms of Bible study as well as
practising the various techniques to be employed in conducting
one's ministry in which one had been trained; there were no less
the demands of the spirit - 'a man must not be proud. He must
be filled with feelings of humility. He was not a true minister
unless his work was for the glory of God alone.'

The idea of equality found its expression chiefly in the fact
that all were ministers. It was in this way, for example, that
Witnesses could claim that whereas other churches preached
equality, they alone actually practised it. In the context of the
Copperbelt, there were two areas of social life where this claim
became particularly meaningful: the first was in regard to
ethnicity; the second related to gender relations.

I have mentioned earlier the pattern of ethnic ranking that
had developed on the Copperbelt, and Jehovah's Witnesses
were as familiar with the stereotypes on which the system
rested as others, particularly since they were so often the butt
of them. By stressing equality, Witnesses were, as it were, in a
position to 'deny' ethnic differences and the stigma that ethnic
affiliation sometimes carried (see Siegel 1989; Epstein 1978:
128). As one man, himself a Bemba and a recent convert from
Catholicism, once remarked: 'In this church we do not say that
this man is Ngoni or that one Bemba . . . we are all simply
brothers and sisters.'

'Brothers and sisters' was, indeed, a favourite phrase, and it
serves here to draw attention to the important question of the

position of women within the Society. This requires a
preliminary word about the view of the family its teachings
sought to encourage. As Mr Arnott once explained to me, they
had to build up a sense of the family unit. In their view, the
family was the fundamental unit of society, divinely sanctioned.
It was in certain regards, however, a strongly traditional view
that left no doubt that the husband was head of the household
and that his wife must defer to him. Yet in other respects it is
plain that the teachings of the Society did serve to promote a
pattern of relations within the household that represented a
sharp break with the traditional African viewpoint, as well as
presenting a strong contrast with what had been achieved by
other Christian denominations.[17] So, for example, whereas in
other congregations men and women continued to sit apart in
line with the customary separation of the sexes, Witnesses
gathered at their services in family groups, made up of father,
mother, and children. Husbands and wives were also encouraged
to read and study the Bible together, and Lehmann (Taylor and
Lehmann 1961: 112) has commented how women would take
their place in the meeting and in discussion without embarrassment. But, without question, the most striking expression of
change in the status of women who became Witnesses was
represented in their freedom to participate equally with men in
fieldwork, namely, going out to preach the gospel. In earlier
days the Watchtower movement had frequently been charged
by its opponents with encouraging *bwafwano* or wife-exchange
and other sexual improprieties, echoes of which were still to be
heard many years later in the common assertion that most men
became Witnesses in order to have access to pretty women,
while women themselves were similarly lured by the opportunities fieldwork and preaching provided for illicit liaisons. Those
who made these statements would often cite particular cases,
but the emotive tone in which they were generally voiced
carried a strong suggestion of a powerful stereotype at work.
For the outside observer at any rate, it was difficult to resist
the conclusion that underlying the expression of such views
were the anxieties of men and women who had come to feel
threatened by the equality of status which female Witnesses
appeared to have acquired and which they feared other women
might be tempted to claim.[18] However, it also needs to be said
that equality of status in this context implied more than the
freedom of women to be away from their homes and to move

around the location, important though this was. Another
element of transformation, no less significant, was also at work
in that women, customarily obliged to defer to men, especially
in public, and thus ordinarily reluctant to speak in mixed
company, now acquired as Witnesses a voice of their own.
Participating in meetings as well as in fieldwork, they found
themselves developing the same debating skills and arts of
persuasion as their 'brothers'.[19]

In his study of Jehovah's Witnesses in the Serenje District,
the close affinity he found between the religious value
orientation and the social characteristics of the members led
Long (1968: 217) to see how the Watchtower ethic served to
legitimise and provide religious sanctions for the mode of life,
achievements, and status aspirations of adherents of this rural
community. What Long was chiefly interested in was the way
membership of Jehovah's Witnesses went hand-in-hand with
the adoption of new socio-economic roles and the development
of entrepreneurial and innovative attitudes. Something of these
same processes was to be seen at work on the Copperbelt, but
what I believe comes through more clearly from the present
account is the way the ideas and values we have just been
discussing may be seen as contributing importantly to the
building up of a new sense of self among Witnesses there. As we
have seen, a new category of African businessman was gradually
coming into being, and on the Copperbelt, as the Weberian
thesis would lead one to expect, many of them appear to have
been Jehovah's Witnesses. But their numbers were still small,
as were the numbers of those in junior white-collar jobs, which
commanded the highest prestige within the African community.
Given the low level of schooling attained by Witnesses, very
few of them were to be found in this latter category, and the
vast majority, like the overwhelming majority of all Africans in
the towns, had to be content with employment in a range of
unskilled or semi-skilled and poorly paid jobs. But, however
lowly their actual position was within the occupational structure,
the doctrine of the Witnesses encouraged in them aspirations
and a style of life that set them apart from the mass of their
fellow Africans; the status and sense of worth they were so
blatantly denied in the secular system could thus find ample
expression in their religious life.

How, then, was this new sense of self achieved? What I hope
to have shown in this section is how certain ideas and values

embodied in the doctrine and organisation of Jehovah's Witnesses served to nourish a sense of self-esteem where other areas of the social system worked rather to inhibit it. Lehmann's comment cited earlier, that the Witnesses were so organised in Northern Rhodesia as to have all the 'feel' of a purely African movement, points to one important dimension of the process. The rise of African trade unions, the African National Congress, and certain other bodies did point to a major expansion in the area of African autonomy, but office in these bodies had become the preserve of the new intelligentsia. But Witnesses, who were precluded from such positions in these bodies by their lack of formal education, could themselves find in the Society a strong sense of running their own affairs. In practising their religion they were indeed encouraged to develop the same literary, rhetorical, and bureaucratic skills as members of the more prestigious white-collar elite. As we have seen, in mastering these skills, they had come to display a truly impressive capacity for organisation.

But this was not the only way in which being a Witness helped to foster a more positive personal identity. In pursuing this matter further I suggest that we should look a little more closely at the ordering of services and assemblies, where we will discover a variety of ways in which the individual is made a focus of attention. To begin with, a large-scale meeting often provided an opportunity to introduce recent converts; at the same time 'conductors' would be publicly praised for their continued good work. At the end of the service, many would gather round the new members, shaking their hands and making them welcome to the 'brotherhood'.[20] But it is the method of instruction, which provided the central purpose of so many of these gatherings, that holds most interest. Teaching proceeded by question and answer. A question might be asked as to the meaning of a certain phrase; anyone who knew the answer raised his or her hand and was invited from the platform to give it. Or, consider the part of the programme given over to 'Student Talks': a student would be given a text on which to preach and perhaps ten minutes in which to deliver his or her discourse. At the end, the speaker would be criticised by a senior Witness both for the substance of the talk as well as for the manner in which it had been delivered. While, on the one hand, this might appear to be somewhat unnerving; on the other, it also meant that the student was being accorded serious attention in public, perhaps for the first time in one's life. Then there were what were called 'Experiences'. A number of individuals would be called to the platform in turn to recite some personal experience he or she had encountered as a Witness. In the example cited earlier, I believe that even in my unfurbished account, the speaker's sense of being a distinctive personality, something, indeed, of his smugness, comes across quite clearly. And when at the end he left the platform to loud applause, it was impossible to mistake his smirk of self-satisfaction. Finally, we may note how, following instruction and training, the neophyte, now qualified to be a minister, may himself be called upon to give the central address or offer a discourse at such a meeting. Of this same situation in England, Stevenson (1967: 67), himself a former Witness, has written: 'As a result of such training, I have known men who entered Ministry school scarcely able to read or write, who are now able to speak with compelling eloquence.' In Central Africa, where at this time the ability to address and sway an audience was usually the sole prerogative of the new educated urban elite, the acquisition of such skills must be regarded as no less ego-syntonic than elsewhere. I have noted earlier how Witnesses when characterising their religion like to point to its 'rationality' and Beckford (1975: 201) indeed uses the term 'rationalistic' to describe the movement's dominant 'cultural style', deprecating mystery and affect while explicitly lauding certainty and reason. From one point of view, this is undoubtedly so. On the Copperbelt, Watchtower made its appeal cognitively through its emphasis on literacy, on study and exegesis, and in its claims to provide a key to the understandings of the ills and evils of the contemporary world. Yet the affective dimension also needs to be taken into account. For, both explicitly and implicitly, through its forms of organisation and the methods of instruction it had developed and practised, Jehovah's Witnesses also made a powerful emotional appeal to those who enjoyed little standing in the secular social system by opening up to them various ways in which they could affirm their own sense of worthiness and find meaning in their lives.

Conclusion

I described at the outset how my attention was first drawn to the Witnesses by their high social visibility and the remarkable evangelical success they appeared to enjoy. The matter seemed to merit further inquiry and some attempt to account for their seeming ability to attract new members in such large numbers. But, as my inquiries proceeded, I came to appreciate that the issue was rather more complex than I had at first supposed. In particular, I learnt that the Witnesses were, at least in a historical sense, the successors to an earlier movement known as Watchtower, which, from small beginnings in Nyasaland before the First World War, spread fairly rapidly thereafter to Southern and Northern Rhodesia. The rise of Watchtower, with its radical and often explicitly anti-White teachings, has been variously interpreted by later scholars. To Lanternari (1963), for example, it was to be classed with other millennial cults as a religion of the oppressed; Rotberg (1965), however, offering a much more detailed account, treats it rather as a movement of protest, the reaction of a conquered people who, in their powerlessness, 'cloaked their rejection of colonialism in religious garb'. From this latter perspective, Watchtower thus appears as providing the first glimmerings of a nascent African nationalism. The earlier Watchtower movement undoubtedly drew on the literature made available by the Watch Tower Bible and Tract Society, forerunner of the present Jehovah's Witnesses, and its prophets preached a message that at least in its main outlines derived from the teachings of Pastor Russell. Yet in the 1950s, when a secular African nationalist movement had emerged in Northern Rhodesia, the Witnesses stood apart from their struggle; like their brethren elsewhere, they had adopted a stance of disengagement. There is a seeming discrepancy here which points to change as an important dimension of the problem. At the same time, in so far as Jehovah's Witnesses in Central Africa had their historical roots in the earlier Watchtower, questions are also raised about continuity between the two movements. The two issues are intimately interwoven, but for convenience of exposition I take each in turn.

The problem of change in this context is particularly complex because we have to deal with two fields of relationship, each moving independently under its own dynamic, yet also interlinked: on the one hand, there were the developments going on within the Watch Tower Bible and Tract Society itself, the movement founded by Pastor Russell which became Jehovah's Witnesses under the very different regimen of Judge Rutherford; on the other hand, there were the complex processes at work within the colonial society of Northern Rhodesia. Earlier in the chapter I spoke of the two strands in Watchtower, drawing attention in this way to the sharp contrasts that existed between the earlier Watchtower and the later Jehovah's Witnesses. These differences were accentuated by the way in which representatives of the Society in Cape Town would quickly take steps to dissociate themselves from the Watchtower movement further to the north when, from time to time, some dramatic episode brought the latter under public scrutiny. But if such incidents can be momentarily discounted, and full account taken of the historical situation, the differences perhaps will not appear quite so extreme. So, for example, the sharp contrast suggested at the outset between the loosely knit, almost amorphous Watchtower of earlier days and the highly centralised and tightly controlled Witnesses of the 1950s needs to be considerably softened. In its own earlier days the Society was democratically run and each local congregation enjoyed a considerable measure of autonomy; it was only in Rutherford's day that the concept of theocracy, with its highly centralised system geared to higher levels of evangelical productivity, came to prevail. Then, again, in regard to doctrine, the tone in which the Society's message was originally delivered was much more strident than it was later to become. Much of it, moreover, had direct relevance to Africa. In the Russellian critique, for example, colonies were not only the creation of the worldly capitalist states, it was also in these areas that the missions of the established churches chiefly operated. Such anti-colonialism was grist to the mill of early Watchtower preachers, who, remote and unsupervised, could give the message an emphasis of their own. But by the 1950s, in Africa as elsewhere, the message of the Witnesses had itself acquired a softer tone, as the earlier antagonism to earthly institutions gave way to a more constructive emphasis on preparing for the New Kingdom. In line with this development, the movement, still known in Northern Rhodesia as Watchtower, had settled into quiescent respectability: among Africans at least, it had simply become a church among other churches, a point once underlined for me by Mr Arnott when he mentioned that he had just received a reply from government favouring his application to be allowed to solemnise marriages. 'The climate of ignorance has been removed', he explained, 'as with the passage of time Government had come to see that Jehovah's Witnesses was in fact a responsible body.'

The period we have been considering was also one of profound change within Northern Rhodesia, change, moreover, that was proceeding at an increasingly accelerated tempo. In the years following the First World War, when Watchtower had its early beginnings in Northern Rhodesia, although migrant labour was already established as part of the modern African way of life, the country remained essentially rural in its orientation. Consequently, even into the late 1920s and early 1930s when the Copperbelt had sprung into being, it was, as Cross has emphasised in his various analyses, in the rural areas that Watchtower gathered its main support and found its most creative expression; the concerns of the movement were with the redemption of local society whose ills could be attributed to the incursions of the Whites. By the 1950s the picture had become a much more complex one: with the growth of the Copperbelt, Africans had become much more integrated into a modern industrial society. As part of this process, they had become more socially differentiated as their economic and other interests diversified. The conflicts that wracked the society were still primarily between Black and White, but they could no longer be formulated in quite such simple dichotomous terms; in a variety of contexts Blacks were also in competition with, and thus opposed to, other Blacks. The fuller significance of this will become clearer when I return shortly to the question of the ethnic affiliation of those who supported the earlier Watchtower or became at a later date Jehovah's Witnesses. For the moment we may simply note that it would hardly be surprising if such momentous changes in the structure of society were not accompanied by significant shifts in religious attitudes.

These shifts were crystallised when in the mid-1930s members of the Watchtower movement were absorbed into congregations of Jehovah's Witnesses, now integrated into the Society's global organisation and under the supervision of its official representatives. Yet if this development marked a distinct break with the past, by the very nature of the historical link between the two movements, as I have indicated, questions are also raised about continuity. Continuity found expression in a number of ways. To begin with, as noted previously, there was the continuing employment among Africans of the term

Watchtower for both movements; the usage may have been encouraged by the fact that the main monthly magazine of the Society was called *The Watchtower*,[21] but it must also be seen as a pointer to a certain ambiguity. Then, again, there were numbers of Jehovah's Witnesses who, some years before, had also been Watchtower adherents. In some cases at least there seems to have been some blurring of the lines between the two groups. Thus one man, a circuit servant in the Ndola area who had himself joined Watchtower in the early 1930s, told me of the problems posed by some Witnesses who still followed Gondwe's teachings (see p. 123). And, indeed, echoes of the earlier doctrine were still apparently to be heard from time to time in the preaching of some Witnesses in the various compounds around the town.[22] Echoes of it were also to be found in the notion sometimes encountered among Witnesses that the power of the Europeans lay in their possession of the Bible, the secret parts of which they had withheld from the Africans. Among non-Witnesses, the link with the past found expression most frequently in reference to *bwafwano* (wife-lending) and other allegations of sexual looseness mentioned earlier.

But these are perhaps peripheral matters, the loose ends of a complex historical process, and it is in regard to social composition that the issue of continuity poses the most interesting problems for analysis. For the point that emerged clearly from our earlier discussion was not simply that there was an association between ethnic affiliation and contemporary membership of Jehovah's Witnesses, it was also that the groups for whom the association was strongest were precisely those in whose areas the earlier Watchtower had flourished. A number of difficulties stand in the way of any immediate attempt at an adequate explanation of this situation. In the first place, detailed information on the rise of the Watchtower movement in the different parts of the country is still often lacking, so that there is no sure basis for understanding why it took root in one area and not in another. A second issue of crucial importance concerns the process of conversion, and here again, unfortunately, there are many questions for which as yet we have no answers, and where the need for further research is plainly indicated. For example, of Witnesses in town, what proportion became converts in their rural homes, what in the urban areas? And at what stage in the life-cycle did conversion take place? From the comments of many of our respondents, it was plain that for someone growing up in a rural area where the Society was already strongly entrenched becoming a Witness was likely to be less a matter of deep personal conviction, an individual response to the message of a 'publisher', than an expression of social conformity. That is to say, so far as many rural districts were concerned, Jehovah's Witnesses had become very much like those churches which had achieved dominance in other districts and which many people came to join as a matter of course. The picture for the towns is even less clear. Studies of Jehovah's Witnesses elsewhere suggest that recruitment through the network of family, kinsfolk, and friends is quite common and, given the importance of kinship and ethnicity on the Copperbelt, this was likely to have been no less the case there. But what is really needed is knowledge of the pattern of approach among those spreading the gospel. Did those who set out to deliver their message call at houses on a random basis so that in this way members of many different ethnic groups were likely to fall within the net? Or did they call mainly upon people of their own or related ethnic groups with whom they shared a common language and from whom perhaps they could expect a more sympathetic response? Only by finding answers to questions of these kinds can we hope to establish the pattern of acceptance and rebuff encountered by Witnesses and thus to achieve a closer understanding of how, and to what extent, the pattern of ethnic composition was being perpetuated.

But if the issue of continuity in regard to social composition raises a number of questions that cannot satisfactorily be resolved at this stage, examining the ethnic affiliations of Jehovah's Witnesses at the time I was in the field not only serves to pose some interesting historical problems but also helps to shed some light on the contemporary nature of the Witnesses' appeal. Seen from the perspective of the Copperbelt, the essential point can be made in the form of a blunt contrast. On the one hand, the Witnesses, like the Watchtower movement in earlier days, made little or no headway among groups like the Bemba, Ngoni, or Lozi. On the other hand, there were the areas where the earlier Watchtower flourished, and from which the contemporary Witnesses continued to draw much of their support: the central regions of the country, home of such peoples as the Lala, Lamba, Kaonde, and Lenje; the Luapula Valley, inhabited by such groups as the Lunda of Kazembe and the

Chishinga; and perhaps some parts to the east, occupied by
such ethnic groups as the Nsenga and Kunda.[23]

At first glance, then, with the exception of the Lunda of
Kazembe, the contrast would appear to be between a number of
centralised and once-powerful African states, and various loosely
organised (and in pre-colonial days militarily weak) peoples.
However, such a dichotomous model would not account for the
position in the far west of the country, where neither
Watchtower nor Witnesses appear to have had much impact,
despite the absence there of powerful monarchs. A broader view
of the situation is therefore required, one which takes full
account of the new context created by the imposition of colonial
rule. Of particular importance here is the historical process by
which the colonial presence was established over the country as
a whole. This story is too long and too complex to be recalled
here; for present purposes the main point concerns the way in
which the different missionary bodies entered the country and
established their respective spheres of influence (see Rotberg
1965). In this way, to state the matter very baldly, Bemba
country became dominated at the centre by the Roman Catholic
White Fathers and at the peripheries by the London Missionary
Society and the Church of Scotland; the Lozi came under the
powerful and lasting influence of the Paris Evangelical
Missionary Society, while the Dutch Reformed Church came
from Nyasaland, on the invitation of Mpezeni, to establish their
mission in the Ngoni capital. The central and western parts of
the country were the last to come under missionary influence,
and these were mostly small and relatively poor organisations
(the accompanying map, Figure 7.2 shows how support for
Watchtower/Jehovah's Witnesses fits in with this pattern of
distribution). Comparison of these different areas in terms of
the numbers of schools and the kinds of schooling provided
would make the point quickly (see, on this score, the table
presented in Taylor and Lehmann 1961: 23). What begins to
emerge, then, is a fairly general picture, the main outlines of
which had been laid down before the onset of colonial rule, but
which the whole of the colonial experience served to perpetuate
and, indeed, to accentuate. In the period preceding the onset of
colonial rule, certain strong tribal groups had come to the
forefront, dominating their immediate and weaker neighbours;
in the days of *pax britannica* these groups developed closer
links with the administration with such benefits as these

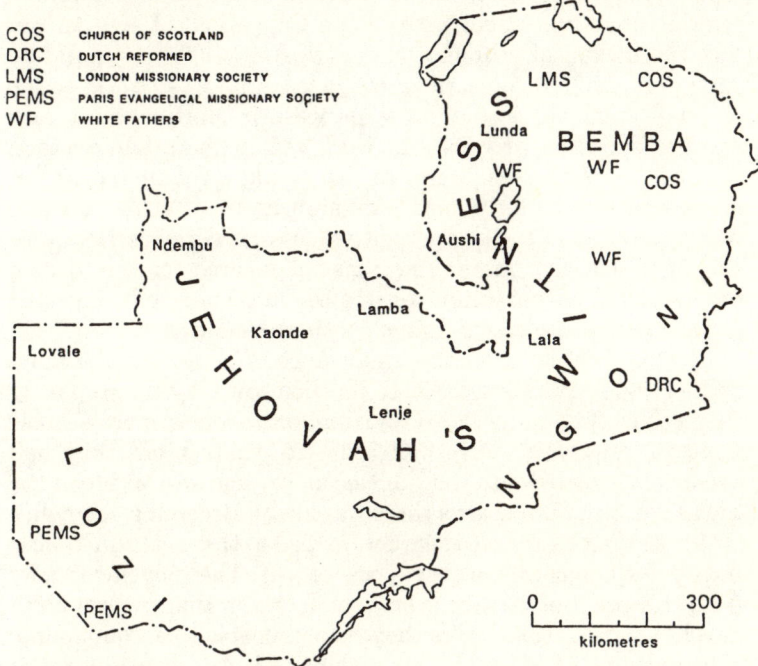

COS   CHURCH OF SCOTLAND
DRC   DUTCH REFORMED
LMS   LONDON MISSIONARY SOCIETY
PEMS   PARIS EVANGELICAL MISSIONARY SOCIETY
WF   WHITE FATHERS

Figure 7.2. Distribution of missionary societies in Zambia
during the colonial period

brought; such stronger groups also served as a magnet to the
major missionary societies, as I have just described.

In these more centralised polities, I suggest, the chiefs, who
still retained much of their traditional authority, and the
missionaries, in regular and close touch with the villagers, were
well placed to contain the threat when the Watchtower
movement began making rapid headway in other parts of the
countryside.[24] Yet later still, the opening up of the Copperbelt
served further to strengthen the link between ethnic group and
mission affiliation, for, as Africans were increasingly drawn
there for work, those who got the better paid jobs were obviously
the better schooled. Thus, by the time of my research, the
occupational distribution of the African labour force disclosed a
pattern in which there was a fairly clear-cut association between
type of job, ethnic affiliation, and church membership. Mitchell

(1956b) had quite early drawn attention to the system of ethnic ranking that had developed on the Copperbelt. Later, in my own discussion of ethnicity there (Epstein 1978), I sought to show that while the system of ethnic ranking was cast in terms of traditional values, military prowess in particular, it also expressed certain processes at work within the urban system. Jehovah's Witnesses were to be found predominantly in occupations that did not call for high levels of schooling and which in terms of the Copperbelt values of the day carried little prestige. In the main they also appeared to be drawn predominantly from ethnic groups which tended to be grouped at the lower end of the prestige continuum as well.

In their emphasis on the importance of acquiring the more skilled jobs, Witnesses were, in their own eyes, preparing themselves for life in the New Kingdom; from a more secular point of view, they were indicating to what extent they had become integrated into the wage economy and way of life of the towns, though their status there was lowly. Becoming Jehovah's Witnesses, as I suggested earlier, helped in these circumstances to provide them with a new sense of self. The movement may from this point of view be seen as adaptive in that by providing psychological satisfactions they helped people to accommodate to conditions of life over which they had little control. Yet it should also be said that since their ideological stance involved a denial of stark social realities the adjustment could only be partial. With their stress on cleanliness and keeping themselves unsullied from contact with defiling, earthly things, Witnesses developed strong group-boundaries which served to separate them from non-Witnesses. The strong sense of in-group solidarity generated by intensive intra-Witness interaction and the sense of being an 'elect' were reinforced by an unmistakable note of paranoia that was a leitmotif of many assemblies: 'And ye shall be hated of all nations for my Name's sake.'

At the time of my fieldwork, as has been observed, Witnesses were no longer viewed as seditious as Watchtower had been in the past; on the contrary, as seen from the perspective of the Witnesses themselves, prepared to co-operate with government, they received in turn its understanding and support.[25] In his account of Cargo Cults in Melanesia, Peter Worsley (1957: 256) notes how such millenarian movements, radical and anti-White in their beginnings, turn in the end to becoming passive sects. At first glance, this formulation would seem to sum up neatly the history of Watchtower/Jehovah's Witnesses in Northern Rhodesia. Further reflection, however, suggests that at least in the case of Jehovah's Witnesses, it would miss a fundamental ambiguity in their ideology. For, when all is said and done, the doctrine of the Witnesses remains millenarian, and has a built-in bias against all forms of earthly authority, even if at times, as during the period of the 1950s in Central Africa, this aspect of the teaching was not emphasised. As Gershom Scholem (1973: 12), in his masterly account of Sabbatai Sevi, the mystical Messiah of seventeenth-century Europe, has remarked: 'Utopianism not only arouses hopes and expectations; it also threatens existing traditional patterns. . . . Every Utopia that is more than an abstract formula has a revolutionary sting.' Potentially, at least, from this point of view, the two strands of Watchtower, to which I pointed earlier, were still there. From this perspective, it can hardly be regarded as a matter of accident that in post-independent Malawi Jehovah's Witnesses should have been banned and that in Zambia they have frequently come in for governmental censure and attack (Assimeng 1970).

8

Response to Social Crisis: Aspects of Oral Aggression in Central Africa

One very important difference between open and closed thinking obviously lies in the completeness of the information available. All thinking must start from some information, and both the scientist and the artist are, in a sense, trying to complete something, either by filling gaps or by extending the limits that the information allows. The scientific thinker in a closed system is searching for something that is 'there', or should be, in the system. The open experimenter is in the position of somebody who must use whatever tools may be available for adding to some structure that is not finished. He is trying to find something but does not know yet what it is.

Young (1971: 257)

Anthropological-style fieldwork, with its immersion of the researcher in the life of the people whose ways he is studying, is commonly regarded as a distinctive feature of the discipline as well as one of its major strengths. In the growth of the subject fieldwork and theory are thus seen as working in tandem; the former providing a means of testing ideas formulated in the study in what is an ongoing process of mutual interaction. But this is an over-simple view, which does not take adequate account of the circumstances in which fieldwork is ordinarily undertaken and so fails to note what I have come to see as a built-in dilemma of the discipline. Traditionally, fieldwork has taken the researcher to some remote part of the globe where he will be expected to spend at least a year. Thus, for financial, or for other no less pressing, reasons many anthropologists will have the opportunity for no more than a single spell of fieldwork, usually undertaken at the outset of one's career, and there are few who are able to contemplate a speedy return to the area of their first research. It is likely to happen, then, that the anthropologist only becomes alive to some of the interesting problems posed by his data long after he has left the field and too late discovers that he lacks the information needed for the kind of analysis he now wishes to make. Alternatively, he may become aware of certain problems while still in the field but, because his training did not provide him with adequate conceptual tools for the task in hand, is unable to pursue the matter satisfactorily on the spot.

The present chapter reflects something of my own experience on both these scores which, I suspect, many others will be able to recognise, at least in certain respects, as their own. Quite early on in my second spell of fieldwork on the Copperbelt I encountered certain events of a rather bizarre and puzzling kind that occurred in the context of attempts then being made to bring about a Central African Federation of the two Rhodesias and Nyasaland. It seemed plain to me at the time that the episodes I discuss later raised important questions about the role of affect in human social behaviour, but it was not until much later that I came to see how certain notions derived from psychoanalytic theory might help to shed light on this material. It follows, therefore, that the analysis I have sought to develop here is more conjectural than I could have wished.

But my problem also raised a methodological issue of a rather different kind. In terms of the prevailing paradigm of the day, at least for those brought up within the tradition of British social anthropology, and a theoretical position which even today commands substantial support, affect was a field of inquiry that was held to lie beyond the competence and legitimate interests of the social anthropologist. Emotion, that is to say, was a matter for the psychologist or the psychoanalyst, into whose domains the anthropologist was cautioned not to stray. At the most, if he felt obliged to take cognisance of such matters, he was advised, in Gluckman's terms, to adopt a stance of 'deliberate naivety'. As Gluckman himself expressed it, the anthropologist is interested in the fact that emotion is evoked and not in the specific quality of its constituents. Rephrased in slightly different terms, an anthropologist need take account of emotion only in its gross character; he does not have to concern himself with 'the precise sources of unconscious feeling and wishing' (Gluckman 1964: 239). In this chapter, as will shortly become apparent, I have plainly violated these precepts by concerning myself very much with the sources of unconscious feeling. My justification for overstepping the 'limits of naivety' in this way is that I could see no other way of coming to grips with the problem posed by my data. But what I also hope in the end to have shown is that when full account is taken of the emotional dimension of behaviour many features of social life we have observed, at first sight seemingly so remote from one another and appearing to belong to quite unrelated social contexts, turn out to be intimately linked. In a word, by refusing to attend to intra-psychic processes, the anthropologist sets obstacles in the way of discerning connections between phenomena of the kind in which, as an anthropologist, he claims to be most interested (compare Fortes 1980).

These, then, are some of the assumptions that underlie and have guided the analysis offered here. Yet it should not be imagined that I arrived at them easily or that their relevance to the problem I was struggling with was immediately apparent. To the contrary, 'by indirections find directions out' more aptly sums up the manner of my progress. It is for this reason that I have eschewed here an orthodox mode of presentation, where, in effect, it is the conclusions which structure the layout of a paper or article, in favour of one that sets out the sequence of steps by which the argument came to unfold. This will mean traversing a good deal of ground in a way that, even to a sympathetic reader, may appear quite unsystematic and even arbitrary. To ease the reader's task, therefore, I sketch in here an outline of the chapter's framework. As already noted, certain bizarre events encountered in the context of an attempt to establish a Federation in what was then, in the mid-1950s, British Central Africa, furnish me with the central problem of the chapter. However, it is the concepts of injury and liability in the customary law of the traditional societies of Zambia that provide the point of entry to the discussion. Although at first glance seemingly remote from the issues which principally concern me here, it was in pursuing their analysis that I came upon a first clue to the understanding of those puzzling episodes to which I have just referred. For, as will presently be seen, the case-material presented in the following section offers a number of examples of oral aggression: in coming to grips with this and other perplexing features of the data, I set out how I was led to see the possibility that certain assumptions that appear to underlie the legal doctrine concerning injury and liability in these societies, an aspect of what we may call their ethos, are rooted in unconscious mental processes. In the light of these considerations I then move to a discussion of the campaign for Federation itself. This requires some analysis of the overall political and social background to the issue, but my main concern here is in coming to understand how Africans perceived the situation and what underlay the nature of their response to it. The hypothesis advanced is that much of the behaviour that had struck one as so puzzling reflected certain of the intra-psychic conflicts of early infancy among Africans of this region, conflicts which continued to colour many of their adult social relationships and which were particularly apt to be revived in circumstances of crisis or acute stress. The evidence bearing on this supposition is then examined in a section dealing with the character of the childhood experience in these parts of Africa. The final section of the chapter attempts to knit together the manifold strands of the argument, and to develop some of its methodological implications. But let me at this point begin by setting out some of the raw material, and my analysis of it, from which this whole train of thought stemmed.

The concept of 'wholeness'

My initial discussion of the concepts of injury and liability in African customary law was based upon cases I had recorded in the course of my studies of the Urban courts (Epstein 1969). Many of these were concerned with assault, the most obvious and elementary instance of injury in the sense that it involves the direct application of physical violence by one person to the body of another. The case I now present was of this kind, involving a man and his wife, both Bemba. The gist of the complaint, brought by the woman, was that she had been assaulted by her husband, once on a public path when returning from a beer drink, and a second time when he had seized her violently and bitten off a piece of her ear and swallowed it. When the husband came to make his statement he said that the trouble was his wife had an excessive love of fornication. In Livingstone she had committed adultery twice, and in Ndola twice again. Once, when he had gone by himself on a visit to Livingstone, he had left his wife in the care of her brother at the Farms, an area a short distance out of Ndola, but she had decided to move back to the location where they lived. On his return from that trip he found his wife naked in the path fighting with a man. They exchanged words and then, all of them being drunk, they began to fight. On the second occasion they were again drunk, and he had bitten her ear because, he said, she had refused to listen to what he told her. She behaved like a goat, the husband remarked finally, and could not resist adultery when he was away for a short time. The couple were then examined on their statements by the court. Part of the questioning ran as follows:

Court	(to complainant): 'On the occasion when you were fighting and he "broke" your ear, were you drunk?'
Wife:	'No, not in the slightest.'
Court:	'And the other time, where were you coming from?'
Wife:	'We were coming from the Farms.'
Court:	'And you were all drunk?'
Wife:	'Yes, we were completely drunk.'
Court:	'Was there any man to whom you had given beer?'
Wife:	'No, none at all.'
Court:	'How long have you been together with your husband?'
Wife:	'It is now seven years.'
Court	(to defendant): 'Where were you married?'
Husband:	'Here on the line of rail [i.e. in town].'
Court:	'How many times has your wife committed adultery?'
Husband:	'On four occasions' [i.e. with four different men].
Court:	'Is your wife then a cross-cousin?'
Husband:	'No, there is no relationship.'
Court:	'How is it then that you did not divorce her and marry another?'
Husband:	'I hoped perhaps that one day she would give up her ways.'
Court:	'Well, since it appears that you like your wife, what have you to say about this case?'
Husband:	'She herself knows the answer to that.'
Court:	'All right. Now when you want to "instruct" your wife, is it your custom to bite her ears?'
Husband:	'Well, I bit her ear because I got so angry.'
Court:	'And you say that you still want your wife.'
Husband:	'Yes, that is so, and no lie.'
Court:	'When you committed the offence, were you drunk?'

Husband: 'Yes, we were all very drunk indeed.'

Court: 'Well, what is the reason for all this?'

Husband: 'It's that she went and slept with other men when she ran away from her brother's house at the Farms.'

Court: 'How many times have you assaulted her?'

Husband: 'Twice.'

Court: 'Did you do wrong in "breaking" her ear?'

Husband: 'Yes, as for that I was completely in the wrong indeed.'

The defendant had earlier agreed that he had no witnesses to speak in his support. His wife, however, was accompanied by a brother, who was invited to make a statement before the court. He confirmed the husband's testimony, saying that his sister seemed to think only of drinking and running after other men. He himself had nothing ill to say of his brother-in-law. The fact that his sister had her ear bitten off was her own fault entirely since she always refused to listen to what she was told. At length the court passed to judgement:

As to all this, you, Kantwa, we find that you have a case for 'breaking' your wife's ear and swallowing it. Therefore the court finds that you should pay £5. You will take £3 and give it to your wife; the rest will go to the court. Furthermore, we feel that you ought to divorce her otherwise you will kill her one day with your beatings. As for you, girl, we see that you have no child. This is because you love only fornication. So that the fact that you have had your ear bitten off is your own fault entirely. You must cease this habit of committing adultery as though you were a dog that knows nothing of *mucinshi*, respect.

The facts in issue in this case were never really in dispute. The husband admitted the main charges against him, and he also agreed that what he had done was wrong. Yet a good deal of time was devoted to the hearing, and it is clear from the judgement that the court had some sympathy for the husband, whom it considered to have suffered considerable aggravation. The judges said, in effect, that the woman was on the way to becoming a whore, if she were not one already, and in a sense she got what she deserved. Yet if this is so, we may wonder why she should have been awarded what was by the Copperbelt standards of the day a fairly substantial sum of money. In many matrimonial disputes the court would order a sum of 10s or a chicken to be handed over to the aggrieved party. This was not so much a payment of compensation as an earnest of goodwill designed to open up the way to a full reconciliation - 'to cool the heart' as Africans would put it. In the present case, however, far from seeking to reconcile the parties, the court actually advised a divorce. Thus, the award to the woman has to be seen as reparation for damages received. The question then arises whether assaulting one's wife is an offence for which the husband is always liable, irrespective of the blame that may attach to the wife's prior conduct. The answer would appear to be clearly not, for a husband's beating of his wife was recognised as an appropriate way of asserting his authority in the household, and anyone who intervened in such a marital squabble was himself likely to be found at fault. On the other hand, if the court's concern was aroused by the gravity of the injury that the wife had sustained, why did it not simply treat the matter as a penal offence and impose a fine on the husband or sentence him to a term of imprisonment? It certainly does not follow that because the African judges in the Urban court handled the matter rather differently from the way in which it would probably have been dealt with by a European magistrate, they were muddle-headed or confused. On the contrary, I believe they were thoroughly consistent in their thinking, and that their finding flowed from certain assumptions about the nature of the human person which are deep-rooted in indigenous philosophy and culture.

A clue to the nature of these assumptions is contained in the court's reprimand of the woman that she should cease behaving like a dog that knows nothing of *mucinshi*. The phrasing emphasised the repugnance in the court's eyes of the woman's behaviour, but the contradistinction of humans and animals recurs so frequently in the judgements delivered in these courts as to suggest that something more fundamental is involved than mere rhetoric. Thus, in another case we find the court admonishing a man who sought a divorce because his wife complained of his frequent adulteries: 'You fellow, you are a lunatic, you have no sense (*taukwata mano*). It is time you came to learn that a man of sense ought not to roam about as though he were a wild animal of the bush.' Implicit in the comments of the judges on these occasions is the view that man is bound by certain canons of conduct that are regarded as axiomatic. Man enjoys the gift of reason or intelligence (*amano*, in Bemba). He knows, therefore, that in his behaviour he must display proper manners and respect; in so far as one does not measure up to these expectations one's humanity (*ubuntu*) is diminished. But a further attribute of the person is also involved here. This is conveyed in the Bemba word -*tuntulu*. This is an adjective meaning whole, complete, in good health, but it also carries overtones of wider import where it stands for life itself. The association of wholeness with life was brought home to me one day when I was discussing with Bemba hereditary councillors the connection in Bemba thought between the east and life, on the one hand, and the west and death, on the other. One of the councillors present had especially important ritual duties to perform on the death of the Paramount Chief Chitimukulu, and whenever he visited the tribal capital he was required to stay in a section to the west of the village. He was being playfully chided by some of his fellow *Bakabilo* who were required to stay to the east, one of whom at length remarked: 'You are a prince of the dead, but we are princes of the living (*ifwe tuli batuntulu*).' The life-principle then is a sacred value which finds its embodiment in the whole human person, who must not, therefore, be diminished (compare Tempels 1959). This basic postulate, it seems to me, accounts for the overriding concern the courts display in regard to physical violence to the person, and leads to the principle that one is liable in damages for any act which has as a direct consequence the diminishing of another's person, even though the act itself was prompted or provoked by that other's prior wrong.

In the paper in which I originally set out this line of analysis, I felt it necessary to substantiate what might otherwise have seemed a rather fanciful argument by discussing in detail a second, and perhaps even stronger, case. On this occasion a man was ordered to pay compensation to another, two of whose teeth he had knocked out, even though he had resorted to violence in order to protect his daughter against a threatened rape. In this instance, wholeness as an attribute of the person was given quite explicit expression by the judges of the Urban court: like life itself, it is a gift of God. Two further points are worth noting here: first, the way in which the court kept reiterating the gravity of the assailant's offence in knocking out the other's teeth as though it were tantamount to homicide; secondly, that in both cases the offending act, like the act of homicide itself, leads to consequences which are irreversible. Under tribal conditions at least a person who has lost an ear or some of his teeth can never be made whole again. The final words of the judgement in the second case express this point neatly: 'Since you knocked out two of John's teeth he is unable to chew meat and other hard foods. You have spoiled the "wealth" which was given to him by God. If a pot breaks can it be mended?'[1] In short, the lesson of these cases is that he who resorts to violence, even in defence of his legitimate interests, does so at his peril, since the consequence of his act may well be the maiming, or most heinous of all, the complete physical destruction of another person.

Within the limited aims of my earlier article I felt that I had made a contribution towards advancing our understanding of the notions of injury and liability in certain African legal systems. Moreover, by introducing the assumption of whole-ness, I also felt that I was able to account for a number of other features of practice and legal doctrine in these systems which previously had not appeared to be directly connected, as well as to explain why certain offences, disclosed by the same set of facts, were quite differently regarded by Africans and Europeans. At the same time, I recognised that the argument, if it was valid, posed some further knotty problems. Why, for example, should these cultures have developed the concept of wholeness? What was it in their way of life, that is to say, that had generated the concern about the integrity of the person, at least in this particular form? In pursuing these problems I was led to reflect on a number of others which puzzled me and, indeed, gave rise to increasingly gnawing doubts whether I had done any more than construct an elegant but otherwise quite spurious argument.

A striking feature of so many of the cases I recorded in the Urban courts, including the two cited here, was the repeated emphasis by the judges in their remarks to the litigants on the need 'to live together in peace'. Violence was always deplored, even where it had been sparked off by another's provocation. Sociologically speaking, there is nothing in this that seems to call for special comment. The tribal groups with which I was concerned were in the main centralised polities: there was usually some degree of central administration, and the exercise of power and authority was controlled institutionally, often through a very elaborate system of political offices. In such systems the application of physical violence becomes a monopoly of the state: not only does the state deny the individual the right to take the law into his own hands, save perhaps in certain specified circumstances, but it also arrogates to itself the right to inflict physical punishment for certain classes of offence. Yet these considerations do not satisfactorily account for the emphasis in Central African courts on the redressive as much as the penal aspects of law, or the fact that African judges display as much concern with the nature of the damages sustained as with wrongful acts as such. Furthermore, I was constantly struck by the way in which Urban court members reacted to a situation of violence, actual or potential, in what seemed to me an exaggerated fashion, as when an assault was repeatedly referred to as though tantamount to homicide or where a divorce was granted simply because one of the parties insisted on it on the grounds that if husband and wife were compelled to stay together only hatred would result, and in the end somebody might even be killed (compare Epstein 1953: 67). Such exaggerations hint, however faintly, that all is not as it appears on the surface, just as, in a psychoanalytic session, the exaggerations of the person under treatment alert the analyst to some source of conflict in his patient's psyche.

There was, moreover, another aspect of the problem, which I had not touched upon in the original paper and which now bothered me considerably. I refer here to the whole theme of bodily mutilation in the culture of the Bemba, one of the major tribes of the region and a group which has come to be a dominant force in the new life of the towns. Codrington, the first Administrator of North-eastern Rhodesia, introduces the matter in his report for the two years ending in March 1890 (quoted in Gann 1964: 91):

> The cruelty hitherto practised by the Awemba, not only towards captive tribes, but towards free-born men of their own tribe, is incredible. The number of mutilated persons is enormous. In nearly every village are to be seen men and women whose eyes have been gouged out; the removal of one eye and one hand is hardly worthy of remark. Men and women are seen whose ears, nose, and lips have been sliced off and both hands amputated. The cutting off of the breasts of women has been extensively practised as a

punishment for adultery but . . . some of the victims of these atrocities were mere children. . . . Indeed these mutilations were inflicted with the utmost callousness.

Codrington's account has been amply confirmed and expanded by Audrey Richards, the leading ethnographic authority on the Bemba, who carried out her researches in Bembaland in the mid-1930s. Richards has referred on a number of occasions to the complex attitude combining admiration and fear which the Bemba subject has for his chief, and it is plain from her accounts that the fear was well grounded, for she shows that killing or physical mutilation was practised in a number of traditional contexts. The singers of the royal praise-songs, for example, were old, usually blind, men. Some of them had had their eyes gouged out, it was said, to prevent them deserting the court of one chief for that of another (Codrington in Gann 1964; Richards 1963: 27). In this same account, Richards refers to the large numbers who would flee the tribal capital following the death of a monarch to avoid the butchery associated with these occasions; even as recently as my own visits to Bemba country in the early 1950s the tale was being told of how, despite all the vigilance of the administration, a number of individuals had been killed so that they could be buried with a recently deceased Chitimukulu in the sacred grove at ShiMwalule. Of more direct concern for our discussion, however, are the punishments that were meted out for various offences in pre-colonial days. Thus, the story is told of the great chief Mwamba Cipoya that once he was so enraged at the discovery that one of his wives had committed adultery that he at once ordered the whole company of her fellows, about twelve of them, to be burnt alive together with all the young men of the section of the village to which the adulterer belonged (Richards 1963: 29). In other cases, principally it would seem where the chief perceived some affront to his majesty, he might order the offender's hands or nose to be cut off or his eyes to be plucked out.

In a personal communication on the general issue, Richards mentions that the praise-songs of the Chitimukulu, the title borne by Bemba monarchs, seem to go out of their way to glory in cruelty, and certain of the evidence just cited would certainly seem to justify that impression. But what also needs to be stressed here is that I am not reporting just the subjective reaction of the anthropologist herself. It was also a judgement that was shared by the Bemba, too, as some of her informants made abundantly plain when they explained to her that their senior chiefs, members of the Bena Ngandu or Crocodile clan, were so named because they were 'like crocodiles that seize hold of the common people and tear them to bits with their teeth' (Richards 1940a: 106). There is surely a glaring discrepancy between this view of traditional tribal authority and the picture presented a little earlier of a legal system concerned to affirm and preserve the integrity of the human person. How is the discrepancy to be explained? A number of possibilities suggest themselves. First, that my earlier analysis was elegant, perhaps, but otherwise simply wrong, even though the source of error is not evident to me. Second, that the argument was valid in general terms, but my findings, far from bearing on traditional modes of legal thinking, merely reflected the changed circumstances of the day, particularly in the towns, a factor for which the analysis had not allowed. However, there is a third possibility: that the contradiction is more apparent than real, the expression rather of two perspectives on the same reality, the key to the understanding of which was still missing.

As I continued to mull the matter over, I was at length reminded of a chance experience which, although at first blush appeared to have singularly little relevance to the problem bothering me, in fact soon seemed to offer a first glimmering of a way out of the dilemma. Some years before, while on the staff at the University of Manchester, I had received an invitation from Professor Heron, then Director of the Institute of Social Research, University of Zambia, to carry out a series of interviews with a group of Zambians who were at the time on a local government training course in Dublin. It was hoped that my inquiries would lay the ground for later follow-up studies back in Zambia. I was given a completely free hand as to the form the interviews should take, so, in addition to covering various routine matters, I decided to include an item that would elicit the respondents' views on some aspects of social status and prestige. I employed a variation on the idea of the 'balloon debate' familiar to me from my schooldays. In such a debate the participants represent certain well-known personalities (scientists, writers, film actors, etc.) who happen to be together in a balloon. When the balloon runs into trouble it is agreed that one of the company should be cast overboard in order that the others be saved. Thus, the 'debate' takes the form of a series of speeches in which each speaker seeks to justify his existence;

the audience acts as adjudicator and decides who shall make the supreme sacrifice. In the Dublin 'experiment' the 'balloon situation' was presented to the respondents, but instead of being asked to make speeches, each was given a sheet of paper on which was set out a randomised list of social positions occupied by Africans in Zambia and was asked to rank them in terms of 'dispensability'. The members of the group were mature men, mostly in their late twenties or early thirties, and they had been most co-operative throughout the interviews. Previous experience, moreover, had indicated that Africans responded well to this kind of pen-and-paper test (for example, Mitchell and Epstein 1959). The results, therefore, were all the more unexpected and puzzling. When the sheets were finally returned to me I found that some had not completed the schedule, and of these nearly all had appended a word of explanation. All men, they said, were worthy of life, and none is entitled to order the sacrifice of another.

It was intriguing to discover these respondents offering, as a way of explaining their refusal or inability to complete the schedule, an affirmation of the life-principle as a sacred value which I mentioned earlier. And, although the point is difficult to substantiate, their uninvited comments nevertheless suggested to me that the individuals in question felt compelled to deny that they could kill even in fantasy. Applying this notion to the other material I have presented, I was led to speculate that the people with whom I was concerned experienced powerful aggressive impulses which they found difficult to handle and of which they were somehow afraid. This was still little more than an ill-formulated hunch, and I began to sense that if I were to pursue the matter further along these lines I would need a much closer acquaintance with psychoanalytic theory and concepts than I at that time possessed.

Some time later, when I had the privilege of spending some time as a visitor at Anna Freud's Clinic in London, I had the opportunity to present some of my case-material from the Urban courts to one of the seminars there. A member of this group, Dr Alex Holder, immediately noted that the cases in question centred on acts of oral aggression, a point which at that stage I had not recognised and to which, therefore, I could have attached no significance. Dr Holder, however, found it of interest because, apparently, assaults involving biting, as distinct from hitting and kicking, are relatively infrequent in Western society.

He did not enlarge on the point, but in the context of my reading at the time his comment served to trigger off a whole new chain of thought. It suggested, for example, that for a group like the Bemba, experiences in early infancy had generated some unresolved conflict rooted in what Freudians call the oral phase of psychosexual development and which later found expression in certain characteristic ways in the behaviour of many adults. This speculation in turn produced a flood of associations in which a great deal of assorted material, long-since buried away in my field notes and the recesses of my mind, began to emerge into consciousness and, seemingly, to fall into place. This, then, is an appropriate point to turn to those events, alluded to in my introductory remarks, that I encountered in the course of my fieldwork in 1953-4. Throughout this period, the issue that was agitating the whole country was the question of the establishment of a Central African Federation embracing Northern Rhodesia, Southern Rhodesia, and Nyasaland. By the beginning of 1953, following the Carlton House Conference in London, it had become clear that the die was cast and that Federation would become a reality in spite of the opposition of Africans in the two northern Protectorates. It is no part of my task to discuss this large and complex matter in any detail here, but there are certain aspects of the Africans' response which have a direct bearing on my present theme. I will consider these, and lay the beginnings of an attempt to account for them, in the following section.

Federation: the African response

The question of a closer political association between the territories of British Central Africa had been under consideration for many years. Throughout the 1930s the White settlers of Southern Rhodesia had repeatedly voiced their demands for amalgamation, coupled at times with the claim for full autonomy of the enlarged territory. The movement received a temporary setback when the Bledisloe Commission, reporting in 1939, concluded that the time was not ripe. A prime factor underlying this view was 'the striking unanimity, in the Northern Territories, of the native opposition to amalgamation' which the Commission felt 'could not be ignored'. After the Second World War the settlers, under the leadership of Sir Godfrey Huggins (later Lord Malvern) in Southern Rhodesia and Roy Welensky (later Sir Roy) in Northern Rhodesia, returned to the attack.

The world had seen many changes in the meanwhile, not least in Britain's position within it; in the new political climate the Conservative Party in power in Britain was now prepared to be not merely more responsive but supportive. Favouring Federation as the appropriate form of closer association of the three territories, official arguments stressed the advantages for economic development and advancement in other fields. African opposition, based on the recognition that any such move would lead to the entrenchment of White domination, remained a stumbling-block. At first, the proponents of the scheme adopted the comforting view that, provided adequate safeguards were designed and included to protect African interests, the Africans would quickly see its advantages and come to accept the situation (Cmd. 8233: 1951). When, over the next couple of years, this expectation was not borne out, and African opposition hardened, other arguments came to be invoked. Opposition was not so widespread as some people made out, and many Africans were only prevented from speaking out in favour of Federation because of intimidation; alternatively, although there were not a great many Africans who supported the scheme, this was because they did not understand it.

Admittedly, there were factors present which made it difficult for Europeans, particularly visiting politicians from Britain, to assess African public opinion in the matter, even if they were prepared to be receptive. Among those who came to see for himself, for example, was Clem Attlee, then Leader of the Opposition Labour Party in the British Parliament, not a man, as Welensky (1964: 58) has remarked, to be swayed by sentimentality. In the course of his tour through the country, Attlee paid a visit to a Lenje village, of which Peter Fraenkel (1959: 166–8) has provided an illuminating account. Some of the exchanges he reports are worth reproducing.

'Sir', said the chief, 'I and my people are against this thing. We do not want it. We do not want to hear about it. We have been happy and we do not want any change.'

'I see', nodded Attlee, 'but what are your reasons?'

'We will lose our land if this thing comes. We are against it . . .'

'But according to my reading of the constitutional proposals African land-rights are entrenched firmly.'

'Maybe, maybe. But we do not want this Federation. We are afraid.'

The encounter produced no meeting of minds. One can sense in Fraenkel's account the growing exasperation of Attlee and his party. He had come to hear 'rational' argument, to join, if need be, in political debate; instead he was confronted with a withdrawn and frightened people whose fears, in his eyes, were groundless. But the fact of fear was real none the less; the Federation issue had aroused among Africans throughout the country confusion, uncertainty, and anxiety. Among large sections of the population the prevailing mood was of resentment, sullenness, and suspicion, as I was quickly to discover on my return to Northern Rhodesia for a second spell of fieldwork at the beginning of 1953.

I proceeded at once to Bemba country. At the village of Chief Munkonge, with whom I had stayed for a short period a couple of years earlier, I received a heart-warming and enthusiastic welcome. The reception was quite different when shortly afterwards I moved to another village in the chief's area, where I was not previously known. Instead of the general friendliness which I had encountered everywhere on my previous visit to the district, I now found the behaviour of the villagers markedly constrained. They were withdrawn and showed a reluctance to answer what seemed to me the most innocuous questions. Thinking of ways to improve my rapport, I went off one day to Munkonge's village and returned with two calabashes of beer. It was a time of the year when beer is scarce. Even so, the beer drink was a dismal failure. Instead of the spontaneity that usually marks these occasions in a village, there was only some desultory conversation, initiated by myself, punctuated by pauses of heavy silence. At length, I retired defeated to sulk, like Achilles, in my tent. It was my assistant and general factotum, a young man from another part of Bemba country, who reported to me shortly afterwards the villagers' fear that the beer was poisoned.

Had this just been an isolated incident I might simply have shrugged it off, particularly since my relations with the villagers soon rapidly improved. However, when a little later I moved to the Copperbelt, I learnt of the rumours that had been, and still were, circulating over the entire countryside, and even further afield, that cast the matter in quite a different light. Some of the stories seem to have been directly sparked off by certain remarks made by Welensky in the course of a major debate on Federation in the Northern Rhodesia Legislature in July 1952.

The speech received wide publicity, and parts of it were soon to be cited frequently in highly garbled form. In the relevant passage of the speech what Welensky said was:

> If they [the Africans] do not come with us, and I do not mean it as a threat, if they do not come with us they will meet with the same fate which came to the Indians in the USA, they disappeared. We have got to become part of the industrial civilization that the western world insists on. If we do not do that, we will disappear.

Had Welensky been a more tactful man, he would surely have sought to express his meaning in more carefully chosen words. Certainly, it is difficult to imagine that he would have spoken as he did had he foreseen the interpretation that Africans were to put upon his words. For, despite his own disavowal, to the Africans they were indeed a threat, a clear statement of intent: to wipe them out as the Whites in America had wiped out the American Indian.

Shortly afterwards, it was noted on the Copperbelt that the sale of sugar had dropped suddenly. Rumour had it that the Europeans had poisoned it, and that Roy Welensky had ordered a massacre. The stories spread quickly to Broken Hill, Lusaka, and Livingstone. The matter came fully into the open when, early in December 1952, the local press reported that two Africans in the Department of Information had been charged with secretly duplicating a leaflet that was likely to cause fear and alarm to the public and to disturb the public peace. The leaflet said that on 28 October the 'House of Laws' in London had decided to put poisoned sugar on sale to Africans, through the native trading stores. The effect of taking the sugar, according to the leaflet, was that in the case of women their children would be born dead, and in the case of men they would be rendered impotent.

A later variant on the same theme is also reported by Fraenkel (1959: 199). A low-grade meat had recently come on the market, labelled 'For African Comsumption'. The story this time was that this was human meat, poisoned to break down opposition to Federation. One District Commissioner on the Copperbelt sought to dispel the absurdity by holding a public meat-eating demonstration in which he himself participated. Had he been a little more familiar with 'witchcraft thinking', he might have recognised that all he had demonstrated was his own possession of 'medicine' sufficiently strong to resist the poison. The fear was unabated.

A further development which conveys vividly something of the nightmarish atmosphere of the period was a resurgence of the belief in *banyama*, or vampire-men. Once again, *banyama* were stalking the land, seizing their victims at night, injecting them so that they became docile, then taking them off to some remote place, there to suck their blood and feast on their flesh. In a modern variant, the victims were held to lose their will-power and were converted into becoming supporters of Federation. As Fraenkel observes (1959: 209), unlike the vampires of European legend, *banyama* were not dead men who returned to walk the land, they were living persons. Anyone could be a *munyama*, a European or an African, one's next-door neighbour or someone hitherto held in high public regard or esteem. Many ugly incidents were reported, and for a time as night fell many terrified Africans took to their houses and barred the doors. The *banyama* outbreak expressed perfectly the breakdown of trust in social relations.

I find it a matter of interest that, Fraenkel's book apart, academic texts I have consulted that cover this period of Central African history have little, if anything, to say of these events. Thus, Rotberg (1966), for example, whose book on the rise of nationalism in Central Africa devotes a lengthy chapter to the 'battle over Federation' but passes over in complete silence the incidents outlined here. How are we to account for these omissions? Part of the answer would seem to lie in the way the issues are approached. In the case of a historian like Rotberg, who builds up his account chiefly around the records of memoranda, meetings and conferences, and the speeches of politicians, the struggle that developed around Federation is seen as a confrontation of two ideas: paramountcy and partnership. From such a standpoint the events to which I have drawn attention are of peripheral significance. From another point of view, however, the data might be more aptly described as inconvenient in the sense that the behaviour they disclosed could not be readily accommodated within the conventional rubrics of history or the social sciences of the day. But, whatever the reasons, the fact that they have been ignored must at least raise the question how far an analysis that purports to explain the African response to Federation can be accepted as adequate

that does not take full account of the plainly emotional
components in the situation. Of course, for many local
Europeans there was a simple explanation for all this bizarre
behaviour: the more sophisticated and unscrupulous African
politicians propagated, if they did not invent, these canards the
better to manipulate their more primitive and gullible brethren.
The possibility of some degree of conscious manipulation cannot
be dismissed, but even if it is conceded certain questions still
remain. We would need to know not only why the stories found
such ready acceptance but why they came in the particular
guise of fantasy that they did. For myself, Fraenkel (1959: 207)
appears to offer a more fruitful approach when, summing up his
own discussion, he remarks that the form that African
opposition took and the morbid intensity of their fears seem to
have struck some deep root. It is the nature of this root, I
suggest, that needs to be explored.

In Freudian perspective the behaviour just reported indicates
reactions that are akin to panic. This occurs, according to
Fenichel (1946: 43), when the expectation of danger, instead of
producing a purposeful fear that might be used to avoid a
traumatic state, in fact precipitates such a state. This response
is evoked not merely by the nature of the objective threat but
also by the way in which the threat is perceived, and in analytic
theory the prototype of such perception is likely to have been
laid down in early childhood. The line of argument I shall try to
develop here has been well stated by Erikson in his study of
Gandhi. Remarking how the Mahatma's assessment of, and
response to, political situations was regularly coloured by certain
experiences of his childhood, Erikson (1969: 221) goes on to
comment:

> In a psycho-historical context it seems important to hold
> to the dictum that such an emergence or breakthrough of
> the past into the present always depends upon two factors,
> namely the undiminished actuality of the past [in this case,
> the father-son-thief theme] and something in the actuality
> of the present which literally 'recalls' that past in the very
> convergence of infantile and adult themes.

In the issue of Federation and the African response to it, we
have, I believe, such a convergence of infantile and adult themes.
Some of the evidence I have presented seems to point clearly in
the direction of castration fears, but the references to orality are
no less plain and suggest even more archaic conflicts than those

classically associated with the phallic phase of development. In fact, as modern psychoanalytic theory recognises, the stages postulated by the model of libidinal development cannot always be neatly separated from one another in actual cases, a point which, as I discuss below, assumes particular importance in the African context. Accordingly, the hypothesis that I now wish to consider is this: that the Federation issue produced on Africans an impact akin to trauma which reactivated intra-physic conflicts that had once centred on the earlier stages of libidinal development. My task will be to try and explain why Africans' opposition to Federation took the particular form it did.

As I have just noted, trauma is usually conceived of as the product of the interaction of external and internal factors. A feeling of helplessness is the hallmark of a traumatic situation, but whereas earlier formulations of the concept phrased this in 'economic' terms, that is in terms of an over-taxing of the 'stimulus' barrier, more recent discussion (see, for example, Krystal 1971) sees stimuli as traumatic not by virtue of their physical intensity but by their meaning and the affects they evoke. From this point of view, it becomes important to examine the external or 'reality' situation created by the proposals to establish a Central African Federation as it was perceived by the Africans themselves. What is of crucial importance in this regard is the extent to which they saw it as being within their power to influence events.

We have seen that already in 1939 the Bledisloe Commission came out against amalgamation chiefly because of African opposition in Northern Rhodesia and Nyasaland. The opposition at that time principally took the form of verbal testimony and memoranda submitted to the Commission by various individuals and groups; it took no politically organised form. A decade later, the position in regard to African political representation had changed in certain important respects. The Native Authorities, which had for so long functioned as the main governmental instrument of local administration, were being reorganised in order to attract younger and more educated men into 'tribal' government, and at the same time to enable the local authorities to undertake a wider range of responsibilities. Meanwhile, the administration had also embarked on a policy of giving Africans wider representation by introducing a chain of councils, at different administrative levels: councils at lower levels came to serve as electoral colleges for those at a higher level. Eventually, there was at the apex of this hierarchy the African Representative Council. These various councils were all consultative bodies with an assigned role in the machinery of government, but they lacked any effective executive power. Not surprisingly, therefore, Africans, particularly in the towns, had begun to form their own groups outside the official framework. Welfare societies had been an early feature of the Northern Rhodesian urban scene (Epstein 1958: 47), and these formed themselves into a Federation of African Welfare Societies in 1946. This body held a number of conferences in Lusaka, the capital, and at one of these, in 1948, decided to disband and reconstitute itself as the Northern Rhodesia African Congress (NRAC). By this time the political future of the region was again being hotly debated and many Africans, alarmed at the proposals being canvassed, began to feel that something stronger was called for than the moderate line being pursued by Godwin Lewanika, the first President of the NRAC. In 1951, following publication of the White Paper on the Closer Association of the Central African Territories, Lewanika was replaced by Harry Nkumbula, a schoolmaster on the Copperbelt who had recently returned from a period of study at the London School of Economics, and the Northern Rhodesia African National Congress came into being.

The overriding purpose of this body was to mobilise African opposition to Federation. From his headquarters, now switched from the Copperbelt to Lusaka, Nkumbula set out to build up Congress organisation. For a time there was a scurry of activity. Leading Congress figures toured the country, addressing gatherings of chiefs and villagers, forming branches, and collecting funds to send delegations to London to argue the African case there. Some while later a Supreme Action Committee was set up with nine members, five of them from the African trade union movement. Its main task was to plan 'mass action', including, if necessary, a total stoppage of African labour. But none of this really amounted to anything, and as time passed it became increasingly plain that all the Congress's efforts were doomed to failure; in retrospect, it is difficult to see how in the circumstances of the day it could have been otherwise. Among the Congress leadership few displayed any real talent for organisation. That Congress enjoyed widespread support throughout the country cannot be questioned, but the co-ordination of a nationwide network of branches necessary to transform it into an effective political body simply did not exist; membership was uncertain, communication between branches was haphazard in the extreme, and planned activity was at best sporadic. Then there were the internal divisions, to be readily exploited by those inclined to do so. The tribal chiefs were in a particularly vulnerable position, and while a number openly gave their support to Congress, others were persuaded that their own interests, and those of their people, were best served in continuing loyalty to the administration (see, for example, Watson 1958). The presence of other cleavages was brutally exposed when, in April 1953, in a final desperate effort to stem the tide, Congress called on the African people to stay away from work for two days of national prayer. This, it was hoped, would demonstrate unequivocally not only African solidarity in their opposition to Federation but also that that unity was embodied in the African National Congress. The affair turned out to be a complete fiasco. In Lusaka, where a high proportion of the African population was in government employment, only a handful of civil servants obeyed the call, while on the Copperbelt the African Mine Workers Trade Union, the most powerful body of its kind in the whole country, failed to co-operate and the strike was completely ignored in all the mine townships save one.

None of this is to assert that the attempt to resist Federation by resorting to political methods was 'unrealistic'. Nor am I seeking to argue that all the effort that went into the anti-Federation campaign was no more than an exercise in futility; it was in many ways an invaluable experience, some of the lessons of which were quickly learnt and soon put to effective use. My point is rather that in the conditions of the day, given, on the one hand, the feebleness of African organisation and, on the other, the determination of the colonial government to brook no opposition, the Africans were powerless to resist. The Zukas affair probably marked a watershed in the campaign. Zukas, a young civil engineer whose parents had come to Northern Rhodesia as Jewish refugees from Lithuania and made their home in Luanshya, had openly and actively associated himself with the African cause and become a member of Congress. Accused of being a communist, he was seen by Europeans as controlling and manipulating Congress for his own nefarious ends (Rotberg 1966: 240). Eventually he was

arrested and, after a brief trial, served a period in prison until
he was finally deported to England in December 1952. Following
the trial there appears to have been a decline in support for
Congress on the Copperbelt (Epstein 1958: 181). A mood of
increasing disillusion and despondency had set in among the
Africans; it had become apparent to many that they were
trapped in a situation over which they had no control. The
recurring cry to be heard at this time was that they had been
betrayed by an administration to which above all they had felt
entitled to look for protection.

In the psychoanalytic view a diminished capacity for
controlling one's environment is often a precipitating factor in
the onset of trauma. A further point of interest is that the
traumatic state itself is in turn frequently marked by regressive
behaviour, that is behaviour more characteristic of an earlier
phase of psychic development. Certain of the material reported
earlier appears to fall into this class. However, in order to
understand more clearly the character of the African response,
we need to consider another and wider aspect of the external
reality we have just been discussing. I refer here to the nature
of the colonial situation itself.

The colonial experience has not everywhere been uniform; the
presence of many different variables has given it a distinctive
cast in different parts of the globe. But when full allowance has
been made for the diversity, there remain certain nuclear or
recurring features which serve to define the phenomenon.
Mannoni (1956: 18) asserts that a colonial situation is created,
so to speak, the very instant a White man, even if he is alone,
appears in the midst of a tribe, even if it is independent, so long
as he is thought to be rich or powerful or even merely immune
to the local sources of magic, and so long as he derives from his
position, even though only in his most secret self, a feeling of
his own superiority. One senses in these remarks a deliberate
exaggeration, but at least they direct attention to a point of
fundamental importance: that we are dealing with a situation of
dominance; one group, hitherto independent, has become
subordinate to another. From this fact certain consequences are
likely to flow. All power now rests in colonial hands and,
although there may be variation in the degree to which
traditional authorities are incorporated in the new machinery of
government, there is always some loss of indigenous autonomy.
Thus, once a population comes under alien rule important

changes occur in the pre-existing structure of the political arena in particular and of social relationships in general. Inequality, lack of reciprocity, and social distance represent important aspects of the new structure that develops; another, and closely related one, is the coming into being of a new scheme of relationships of dependence. By dependence I refer here to the bond, akin to and in a sense reproducing that between parent and child, that develops between the indigenous subjects and their alien masters. This bond assumes particular symbolic importance where, as in the case of Northern Rhodesia or Nyasaland, the colonial territory acquires the constitutional status of a Protectorate. Hence, despite the vast social gulf that is, at least initially, perceived on both sides to separate them, the response of the vanquished is not simply to submit passively to the colonials' overwhelming command of power. As Mannoni (1956: 80ff.) points out, the dependence relationship has a strong bilateral component. On the one hand, it gives rise to claims on the part of the subjects, for whom it is also a source of protection and psychological security; on the other hand, it confirms the rulers in their view of their own superiority over the indigenes whom they come to look upon as their wards. An interesting aspect of the relationship is the development of a measure of identification of the governed with their governors: the former come to adopt many of the criteria of their rulers in evaluating themselves, their institutions, and their behaviour, a feature which helps to account, for example, for the frequently reported tendency of Africans to imitate the Europeans. In particular, they come to perceive their governors as father-surrogates, powerful figures to be propitiated, respected, and obeyed, but who are at the same time seen as having assumed responsibility for protecting and providing for the needs of those in their care. Dependence then is founded upon trust, to which nothing can be more inimical than the threat of abandonment. Accordingly, as Mannoni (1956: 136, 162) observes, any snapping of the bonds of dependence is likely to be accompanied by an appalling feeling of desolation, reviving old memories of abandonment and leading to an outburst of hostility or other expression of aggression.[2]

Applying these notions in the Northern Rhodesian context, let me now consider how they entered into, and help account for, the African response to the Federation issue. Once the initial phase of pacification was over, social life throughout most of the country continued relatively undisturbed. Mining for zinc and vanadium began at Broken Hill in the early years of this century, but industrialisation did not really get under way until the opening up of the Copperbelt in the late 1920s and early 1930s; otherwise there was little economic development. Directed change was introduced by the missionary rather than the administrator, who usually sought to utilise as much as possible of the indigenous system in the task of maintaining law and order. The character of the regime thus remained fairly stable for many years, and has been succinctly epitomised in the remark of John Barnes (1955: 178) that 'under paternalism the White administrator was cast in the role of school prefect, while his Black subjects were members of the lower grades who never grew up.'

The attitudes of dependence associated with the phase of paternalism touch almost every aspect of social life and behaviour, but for present purposes their most interesting expression is to be found in the early debates of the African Provincial and Representative Councils. The following is a fairly typical example taken from a speech in the African Representative Council opposing the proposals for 'representative government' that had been put forward by Unofficial Members of the Legislative Council (that is, by representatives of settler interests) in 1948:

> And now we have got these proposals. I have heard about them from many Europeans. They say that this present Government is too slow, and it would be much better if responsible government took over. Well, we Africans saw a great change when the Imperial Government took over from the British South Africa Company. We have been given a lot of schools in the villages, we have been told how to use our lands, and if we continue with this Government, we shall get better and better, and that is what we want. But we don't want to grow and suddenly think that we are big people. We know when you have a little child, it takes him quite a long time before he can walk. We are quite satisfied with this Government, and we shall grow little by little, because our great hope is for tomorrow, because we hope that tomorrow we may be people. (ARCP 1948: 14)

The image of the African as a child who still needs the care and guidance of 'our father, the Government', is one that recurs constantly throughout these early sessions. Nor was it invoked only in relation to government officials and administrative officers. Sir Stewart Gore-Browne, a wealthy landowner in the Chinsali District and perhaps the country's most prominent settler, was well known to Africans throughout the country whom he had served as nominated representative of their interests in the Legislative Council since 1938. His support for the proposals for responsible government alarmed African opinion, and a discussion followed in the African Representative Council. The following extract conveys well the general tone of the debate, when a motion of continued confidence in Gore-Browne was easily carried:

> I want this Council not to forget this word *Chipembele* [rhinoceros: Gore-Browne's African nickname]. Ever since this Council started, the leadership was taken by our *Chipembele*, and we always have had confidence in him. Today we still say that we want our *Chipembele*. . . . When it was difficult for us to get things on the railway line we got them through him. There are places where an African could not go, but we got things done through him. He is our father, and we are his children, and if he made a mistake, well it is a small thing in our hearts and we want him to continue in our work because we know that he will never make a mistake again. I therefore say that if I am angry with my father, it is for me, the child, to go and apologise, even if I know that my father is wrong. (ARCP 1948: 54–5)

But such expressions of trust by Africans in their governors and European representatives were soon to become increasingly rare. As one set of constitutional proposals followed another, and conference succeeded conference, there was a growing sense of insecurity among Africans, which found its reflection in the harsher tones that marked many later debates in these councils. Delegates now spoke of their lost confidence in the government, and of having been deserted by it. As Gabriel Musumbulwa, a spokesman from the Copperbelt, once put it: 'For some time we realized the British Government was our trustee. I do not believe that, today' (WPPCP 1950: 13). What fears lay behind this sense of having been abandoned?

The Africans had many reasons for rejecting any closer association with Southern Rhodesia: there was the whole question of their treatment in the countries of White settlement; of discrimination in all spheres of social life; and the constant harassment and affronts to their dignity sanctioned by law and convention – in a word, everything that they associated with the expression 'White domination'. But more specifically there was one factor that stood out unquestionably among all others: the overriding fear that Federation would mean the loss of their land. As Gann (1964: 407) says, 'the land-fear in fact became a real obsession with many Africans, despite the fact that there was little land hunger, apart from a few areas like the Tonga country, whilst only a small proportion of the territory's surface had been alienated to white men' (compare Fraenkel 1959: 169).

It should be emphasised at once that African fears for the loss of their land were, as they saw the matter, strongly based in reality; the fears, that is, were 'rational' fears. Africans from Northern Rhodesia had been working in the Union of South Africa and in Southern Rhodesia for many years, and were familiar with conditions in these countries. They knew in particular that in the latter the largest areas of the best land had come under European control, whereas in Northern Rhodesia most of the land was held as Native Reserve or Native Trust Land.[3] However, as in other parts of the world where land had not yet become just another commodity, land is invested with a value that goes far beyond its worth simply as an economic resource. The land becomes in these societies the focus of a deep-seated emotional attachment, so that in a situation of crisis, such as the Federation issue presented, land may become a powerful symbol of national identity. Such at any rate was the case here. To quote Gann (1964) again: 'land became a symbol for African rights and hopes, a symbol all the more powerful because so many industrial and white-collar workers too were still relying on the security of their tribal land rights for the dreaded days of old age and unemployment'. But I believe we are justified in pressing this line of argument a good deal further, and I suggest that the symbol also drew its potency from deeper sources of unconscious imagery. This would help to explain why fear spilt over and shaded into so intense an anxiety state.

In African thought, as indeed elsewhere, there is a close association between the ideas of land and mother: the land is Mother Earth who nurtures her children and gives them sustenance and comfort. Pursuing this imagery further, then, the view I am advancing is that the Federation issue represented to Africans, at an unconscious level, the conviction that the administration, the 'father' to whom they normally looked for protection, was now threatening to remove the mother from them, thus repeating the situation in childhood when the father had taken the child's place with her. In psychoanalytic theory, the hostility that this would arouse towards the father would serve to account for the appearance in this context of castration fears. Yet I have also suggested that the matter seems to have touched an even more 'archaic' level of the psyche in that anxiety also takes on an oral cast. Where, then, does orality come into the picture?

A point which might at first sight seem strange, but which has in fact been reported for a number of areas, is that colonial figures of authority are often perceived by their subjects not only as father-surrogates, but as mother-figures, too. Thus, Mannoni (1956: 62) reports that the words *Ray 'aman' dReny*, which literally mean 'the father and also the mother', the parental couple, are also the terms the Malagasy uses to address personages he deems worthy of respect – the administrator or the Governor, for instance – and with whom he would be happy to establish a strong bond of dependence. In the same way, we find this composite image expressed in indigenous contexts in Northern Rhodesia in the attitude towards chiefly authority among the Lozi, of whom Gluckman (1955: 19) writes: 'A chief is regarded as the parent of his people: he is called "father and mother".' The maternal aspect of the chiefly role is also stressed by the Ndembu (Turner 1964: 23) and the Bemba. According to Richards (1968: 32), chiefs are adjured at their installation, among other things, to look after their people and 'nurse them as is done to a child or a sick person'. Transposed to the field of Black-White relations, I once had a striking expression of this split image of authority from an African on the Copperbelt who was expounding to me the unequal treatment received by Europeans and Africans. 'The DC [District Commissioner] has two breasts', he said – it was the duty of the administration to care for and love all of her children equally!

I believe that this view of authority as a maternal no less than a paternal figure assumes importance in understanding the behavioural concomitants of the sense of betrayal that Africans experienced as it became increasingly evident that Federation was to be imposed on them against their will. I shall seek later to show that this particular response repeats an aspect of the early relationship of the child to its mother. For the moment, however, I want to digress briefly in order to consider how the theme of betrayal occurs in other areas of social life, above all in the field of marital and sexual relations.

Numerous field studies attest to the fragility of marriage among many of the peoples of this part of Africa, but most of these deal with the problem in its sociological aspects and say little of the psychological dimension. Presenting the evidence on marital relations in a way that allows the reader to test its objectivity presents considerable difficulties, particularly within the limited compass of a chapter of the present kind. For the Copperbelt, where most of my own fieldwork was conducted over a period of about five years, it is possible to offer a number of quantitative measures of marital instability, as indeed Mitchell (1957) has done, though even here it needs to be recognised that, because of conditions in the towns, such findings are likely to be subject to a high margin of error. But what kind of reliable index can be offered to document, say, the incidence of adultery? Nor is the problem simply one of measuring the extent to which extra-marital relations occur; it is rather to convey something of the quality of marital relations which such behaviour reveals. This is a task I have attempted at length elsewhere (Epstein 1981). Even so, I would feel much less confidence in my own assessment of the situation were it not for the fact that my findings coincide very closely with those of Hortense Powdermaker, based on her independent observations on the Copperbelt during 1953.

According to Powdermaker (1962: 152), distrust and jealousy, openly expressed, were the major themes of marriage: suspicions seemed to be endless, and recriminations between spouses were constant. It is, of course, certain that conditions in the towns, with their heterogeneous and highly mobile populations, their rapidly changing mores, and other factors, have a considerable impact on the indigenous institution of marriage. As against this, all the evidence of accumulated rural studies (for example, Mitchell 1956a; Marwick 1965; Turner 1957) suggests that while circumstances in the towns may have served to exacerbate the situation they cannot in themselves be held to have generated the discords and tensions of contemporary African marriage. That distrust was no less a feature of the traditional pattern is well conveyed in the Ngoni maxim 'Never confide in your wife, for tomorrow you may divorce her' (Barnes 1951: 116; compare Gluckman 1950: 179). Again, in support of her statement that doubts of each spouse's fidelity were common, Powdermaker (1962: 164) reports that 'if a woman stopped to talk to a man for a few minutes on the road, it was assumed that they were arranging an assignation. If she was late coming from the market, or had a few shillings that she could not account for, she was suspected of adultery. A man was suspected if he accepted food from a woman, outside the bounds of ordinary hospitality, or if he came home late.' I can confirm that these are not just casual impressions based on isolated incidents which happened to catch the ethnographer's attention; they are, in fact, presumptions of African customary law, frequently invoked as a basis for decision in matrimonial cases in rural and urban courts throughout the country (Gluckman 1955; Epstein 1954). In many instances the suspicions were thoroughly justified. As I have noted in an earlier chapter, the opportunities which the Copperbelt offered for casual *affaires* were in some respects regarded as among the more amiable aspects of urban life. On the other hand, as Powdermaker observes, it is interesting that although extra-marital relations were 'normal', they were not emotionally accepted, as they are in some societies where they are customary. She concludes her discussion with the comment: 'It was as if these Africans yearned unendingly for a faithful mate, but were compulsively unfaithful.'

One is reminded in all this of a case reported by Karl Abraham (1968: 470), where the patient, who had married a considerable time after a depressive attack, was constantly looking forward, without the slightest cause, to his wife's infidelity as to a self-evident occurrence. Once, as he was talking about a man, somewhat younger than himself who was living in the same building, his first association was 'My wife will have an *affaire* with him and betray me.' In much the same way many men and women on the Copperbelt appear constantly to expect, and to fear, that their spouse will be unfaithful, whether there are genuine grounds for suspicion or not. In the case cited by Abraham, analysis showed that the patient's mother had been 'unfaithful' to him and had transferred her favours to his younger brother. Abraham comments: 'In each symptom of his various depressive periods he faithfully repeated all those feelings of hatred, rage, and resignation, of being abandoned and without hope, which had gone to colour the primal parathymia of his early childhood.'

Pursuing this clue, it is time now to turn to a discussion of African childhood to try to discover how certain situations come to be perceived in particular ways and produce characteristic responses of the kind I have been describing. For the reasons mentioned at the very outset, when I was myself in the field I did not make the detailed and systematic observations necessary to sustain the kind of analysis that now seems desirable. Though the account that follows is necessarily tentative, it is not entirely speculative for I have been able to make use of the data and psychoanalytic interpretations presented by Ritchie (1943) in his short monograph *The African as Suckling and Adult*, as well as the observations on child-rearing reported in the ethnographic literature of the region, most notably Audrey Richards's on the Bemba. Even so, the many lacunae in the phenomenological record will be readily apparent.

Ritchie (p. 11) remarks of the infant born in the rural areas of this part of Africa that for the first year or so his life closely approaches that which he enjoyed in his mother's womb. He is referring to the fact that in his earliest period of life the child is hardly ever separated from the mother, even for a moment. In former times among groups such as the Bemba the mother carried her baby around during the day strapped to her back by a bark-cloth; today the traditional *mpapa* has given way to a piece of cloth purchased at the local store, but the end is the same: the infant still jogs continuously to the rhythm of the mother's movements. At night he sleeps in her arms or by her side. Indulgence is a term that, with suitable qualification as we shall see, can appropriately be used to describe the mother's behaviour towards the child throughout this period. There is no temporal regularity whatsoever in the feeding of the infant. He is given the breast as often and as soon as he wants it, and the mother will interrupt whatever she is doing in order to satisfy the baby's wish to suck. Commenting on this situation, Richards (1932: 42) observes that the mother is a perpetually indulgent presence who can be controlled with gestures and cries. She adds that this must influence profoundly the child's first attitudes towards those around him and she remarks, following Piaget, how the 'conduct of people towards it gradually gives the baby the habit of command' – what psychoanalysts would describe as the source of its sense of omnipotence.

At first Richards attributed this domination of the mother to the way in which the infant initially experiences her, that is chiefly through the immediate satisfaction of its demands on her for food (1932: 43). In her later and more detailed study (1939) she modified her position in a way that foreshadows the findings of more-recent research on the mother–child bond (see, for example, Bowlby 1969), reporting the Bemba view that the breasts give comfort rather than nourishment alone. Consonant with this view is the feeding of infants from the third or fourth week with a thin milk gruel. Richards (1939: 69) reports that the gruel is literally rammed down the baby's throat in spite of its protests. By three or four months the infant has become entirely used to the gruel, and by eight or nine months is being given to eat by himself small lumps of *bwali*, a 'porridge' usually made of finger-millet, and the staple diet of these people.

But despite this early introduction to gruel and then to solids, the infant continues to be given the breast on demand, a process that carried on into the second or third year and sometimes even longer. Throughout this time the child remains in the closest physical contact with the mother, and indeed enjoys her attention almost exclusively. Among many Bantu-speaking groups the husband is obliged to refrain from sexual relations with his wife while she is still feeding a child at the breast: it is held not only to be shameful but very dangerous for her to become pregnant again before her first baby has been successfully weaned. Weaning thus coincides, in these societies, with the resumption of normal conjugal relations between parents, a twofold experience which Ritchie refers to as 'about the severest blow the African ever suffers, one from which he hardly ever recovers completely'.

The position among the Bemba and other related groups differs to some extent from that just described. Like the southern Bantu, the Bemba hold that a woman should not conceive while she still has a child at the breast; in their view full intercourse followed by conception at this time would seriously affect the health of a child who had to be hurriedly weaned to make way for a successor. At first, then, following the birth of a baby, the husband is denied all access to his wife. Later, at around four months, a special rite, 'the taking of the child' (*ukupoko mwana*), is performed by the parents, after which coitus interruptus is permitted. Even so, there are a number of ways in which weaning would appear to represent for the child a radical break from anything in his earlier experience. First, what is involved is not just a simple refusal of the breast where formerly this was given on demand. Richards (1932: 49) states that disciplinary measures are evidently taken to dissuade the baby from suckling. Bemba women told her that they squeezed the juice of the *mulombwa* tree on their breasts. This is a red juice which, they said, frightens the child because it looks like blood. Richards also reports having observed mothers slapping their children for coming back to the breast when they should have been weaned at two or three years old. Secondly, once the child has been weaned it is no longer permitted to sleep in its parents' hut, and goes to stay with the maternal grandmother or other older kinswoman in the village. Thus, among the Bemba, too, weaning involves a double rejection: refusal of the breast is accompanied by the supplanting of the child, who hitherto had almost completely monopolised the mother's attention, by the father.

What are the child's reactions to this situation? As Erikson (1968: 82) has remarked of such circumstances, one cannot know what happens in the mind of a baby. On the other hand, as he indicates, direct observation of infants as well as much clinical evidence lead the psychoanalyst to expect that such a sharp switch in the child's relations with the mother would be accompanied by an experience of 'total' rage. And so it appears to be here, for Ritchie (p. 12) speaks of the surging up in the child of the most violent resentment and hatred for those responsible for his changed position. But no less important than the fact of hostility is the way the child handles and distributes it, and the extent to which what Erikson would call the original mutuality of parent and child is retained, impaired, or possible redirected.

We appear to have here, then, the familiar ingredients of the Oedipus complex.[4] But, of course, even if it is assumed that the Oedipal situation is a constant of human experience, this implies no uniformity of outcome and, indeed, as with other distinctive human characteristics, each individual case is likely to be in some respects unique. Many factors contribute to producing this variability, among them socio-cultural ones such as the structure of familial relations.

Although Freud himself frequently recognised this point, nevertheless it remains true that his model of the child's world, followed in much psychoanalytic writing, is essentially a representation of the nuclear family of parents and children within the physical setting of the home as a self-contained unit. This is perhaps an understandable, but none the less highly ethnocentric and even class-bound view. Certainly, the experience of an African child is as remote as can be imagined from that of, say, Little Hans, the subject of one of Freud's best-known case-studies, whose spontaneous contacts with other children appear to have been restricted to those made on his trips to the country in the summer holidays.[5] The African child is brought up in a tiny village community;[6] from earliest babyhood he is accustomed to the company of others. He will be fondled and dandled by other women in the presence of the mother. Later, when he is able to move around on his own, he will pass freely from one hut in the village to another, accepting titbits of food when they are offered, in some cases helping himself without even asking. Most of the adults with whom he is in regular touch he will count as kin, for whom in time he will learn the appropriate terms that are embodied in the classificatory system of kinship terminology, which emphasises for him the fact that within the group he has a number of parent-surrogates. At the same time he also comes early to participate in what is almost a separate children's world with its own distinctive sub-culture. Before he is able to walk, he will be introduced to the children's play group by an older sister, herself still a mere child, who carries him around on her back. Thereafter, he associates more and more with other children, but rarely moving far beyond the range of adult surveillance.

In his discussion of the case of Little Hans, Freud describes the conflict set up in the boy's mind by the arrival of his sister. While Hans was in the country and able to play with the children there, he found a sufficient outlet for his affections. But on his return to Vienna he was once more alone, and the conflict was revived and intensified. In the same way, it seems reasonable to suppose that the constant companionship of his peers which the African child enjoys does much to mitigate the shocks associated with weaning which might otherwise be too great to absorb. For a child growing up in this kind of society, one would expect that his object-relations would tend to be diffused rather than concentrated. A strong identification with one's fellows is encouraged which becomes the foundation for the development in adult life of that characteristic sociability on the part of the African so frequently remarked upon in the literature, and so vividly reflected in some of the earlier chapters. On the other hand, one must be careful not to push the argument too far. As Bowlby (1969: 308) has pointed out, it is a mistake to suppose that a young child diffuses his attachment over many figures in such a way that he gets along with no strong attachment to any one of them, and consequently without missing any particular missing person when that person is away. On the contrary, Bowlby continues, the evidence at present available supports the hypothesis that there is a strong bias for attachment behaviour to become directed mainly towards one particular person and for a child to become strongly possessive of that person. I believe that in the African context discussed here there are good grounds for claiming that this person is in most cases the mother, and that the bond thus created persists throughout life. But before taking this point further, there is another feature of the social environment that needs to be considered.

The classical model of the Oedipus complex tends to present the father as a powerful and threatening figure; in the child's mind it is usually the father who carries the threat of castration, and who therefore arouses fear. The model reflects a situation in which the father is clearly the head of the family, and exercises authority in all of its affairs, including disciplining the children. The societies with which we are concerned, however, are mostly matrilineal in their mode of social organisation, and the social position of husband/father differs in a number of important respects from that assumed by the psychoanalytic model. In the first place, each individual belongs to the lineage and clan of his mother, not his father. In particular, it is the mother's brother, not the father, who carries responsibility for, and exercises control over, his sister's children. In this kind of system, the parties to a marriage remain members of different social groups and, even though a high degree of sacralisation emphasises the importance of the marital bond, the conflicting pulls upon them are often so great that divorce is frequent. Where matriliny is accompanied by the practice of uxorilocal residence after marriage, as it is in many societies of the region, the position of the husband is weakened even further, for at least initially he will be a stranger in a village dominated by his wife's matrilineal kin, and many years may have to elapse before he is permitted to take her and her children to a village of his own choosing. All of this is quite clearly reflected in the overt attitudes and patterns of behaviour that mark the individual's relations with his mother's brother on the one hand, and his father on the other. To the former one gives respect: he is a man to be feared, and one can best avoid trouble by steering as clear of him as circumstances allow. By contrast, with the latter one can be more free and relaxed; between father and child there is often a profound bond of affection which lasts throughout life.

I am, of course, describing these relationships in terms of institutionalised modes of behaviour and attitudes; these express social norms. However, such norms offer little basis for firm conclusions about the unconscious factors that may enter into these relationships. In particular, it is an error to suppose, as Malinowski did in describing a very similar situation among the Trobrianders, that because a given relationship appears to be tension-free, as far as overt indications go, that there is in fact no unconscious hostility.[7] What seems more likely in these circumstances is that there is unconscious hostility towards the father, but that it is repressed; at the same time, given the nature of the authority system, it can find ready expression in easily disguised form by being redirected towards the mother's brother.

The Central African material appears to lend some support for this view. Although Ritchie does not consider explicitly the situation among groups practising matriliny, he claims to have carried out analyses with individuals of many different tribes, and his general account of the child's attitude towards the father is quite unequivocal. He points out that African men usually bear a generous share of attending to their 2- and 3-year-old children. So, before weaning, if it has been very late, the father has been the child's faithful servant and therefore an object of love, though not to anything like the same degree as the mother. But now, after weaning, says Ritchie, he appears as a thief and a bully, who has stolen the child's most precious possession, his mother. According to Ritchie, the infant firmly believes at first that his father takes his mother so that he can enjoy being suckled by her. Ritchie adds: 'This idea emerges in analysis of Africans with almost monotonous regularity; so frequently in my experience that I venture to regard it as general, absent only in certain exceptional cases' (p. 13).

But of no less concern than the perception of the father is the child's unconscious attitude towards the mother. As Bowlby

(1952: 11), puts it, the infant has enjoyed from birth 'a warm, intimate and continuous relationship with the mother in which both find satisfaction and enjoyment' - at first glance ideal conditions for the development of a firm and secure attachment. But, in fact, what one discovers very quickly is that the relationship with the mother is also marked by an intense ambivalence. As Ritchie describes it, as long as his mother was his faithful slave, ministering to his needs and desires, he loved her. Now, following weaning and separation, he sees her as a faithless renegade, and she becomes the object of his hatred. In particular, the breast that had once been the source of all good, but is now beyond reach, becomes transformed in fantasy into something bad, a prime target for revenge.

Ritchie's view of the Africans' persisting ambivalence is thus tied firmly to the trauma of weaning. Since this coincides with the removal of the child from the parental hut, and the resumption of full sexual relations between the parents, this might seem to suggest that the development of the child's personality is suddenly set upon a new course by the Oedipal experience. That would be an unlikely position to adopt, for psychoanalysts are accustomed to assume that each phase of maturation is reached following on a long and complex process of ontogenetic growth in which each of the preceding stages contributes in turn to shaping the form taken by the succeeding one - here the phallic phase. From this perspective it becomes important to ask whether we can not detect precursors of the attitudes adduced in yet earlier experiences. In a short paper in which he touches briefly on the mother–child bond in Samoa, Freeman (1974: 116) describes a child of about four months who on becoming hungry would respond to the mother's approach in an irate manner. Sometimes he would angrily reject his mother's breast when it was offered to him; later still, after his attachment to his mother had become fully established, he would, on occasion, lash out at her violently when the sustenance he expected was delayed or refused. Freeman cites a personal communication from Bowlby which suggests that such behaviour may serve an adaptive function. If this is so, behaviour of this kind is likely to be widespread, even universal, a reflexive response to a particular situation that ordinarily leaves no permament mark on the personality. To account, therefore, for a persisting unconscious antagonism towards the mother of the kind reported in this chapter we need to look to other factors.

There is one feature of African child-rearing practice which immediately commands attention here. This is the fact that the child continues to be given the breast long after the eruption of the teeth. To the possible significance of this psychoanalytic theory offers some clues. Thus, psychoanalysts have frequently noted how in the child's relations with the object world erotic and destructive elements are so intimately bound up with each other that it is difficult in any given reaction to disentangle them. Hence, as Anna Freud (1949: 40) puts it: 'We find it natural that the young infant's first emotional attachment, in the beginning to the mother's breast, later to the mother's person, shows the same characteristic qualities of aggressive, insatiable greed that we know from his attitude towards food.' In fact, analytic theory postulates a twofold division of the oral stage: an earlier pre-ambivalent one, in which only pleasurable sucking is sought; and a later one, referred to as the oral sadistic phase. The latter is distinguished by biting in addition to sucking; it is an aggressive phase marked by fears that aggression will dismember the loved object. Where a fixation develops at this stage it is likely to give rise to melancholic states and fantasies of restitution or re-establishment of the breast which has been attacked and injured by the infant's own aggression in biting, and which is not only 'bad' because it is damaged, but also because it might retaliate (see, for example, Pickford 1954: 68-9).

These views, it seems to me, help to shed a good deal of light not only on the African child's relations with the mother but also, as I shall discuss shortly, on certain aspects of his adult behaviour. A protracted period of suckling, prolonged beyond the eruption of the teeth, is likely to involve painful biting, accompanied by rejection of the breast and perhaps even mild slapping, and may be expected to intensify the conflicts ordinarily associated with the oral sadistic phase. These in turn would enter into and influence the Oedipal situation. At this point, however, it is important to sound a note of caution. The processes I have been describing for Central Africa are, after all, to be found quite commonly in other tribal societies, yet all may differ too where personality is concerned. The point would seem to be, as Devereux (1969: 73-4) has stressed, that it is important to avoid the mistake of assuming that where certain child-rearing practices are followed by particular consequences in one society, they will necessarily be followed by similar consequences in another in which the same child-rearing practices are to be observed. Far from seeing these practices as operating in some mechanically causal way, they themselves have to be understood within their particular cultural context or universe of meaning. To this one might add that full weight also needs to be given to the role of the natural environment in the total interactive process of personality formation.

On this latter score, it seems worth mentioning the possible relevance of the occurrence over large areas of this region of Africa of regular periods of food shortage. Thus, according to Richards (1939: 35), the most pronounced feature of the Bemba dietary is its alternation between hunger and plenty, a fact which she associates with the presence of only one staple crop, and that in an area where rainfall allows only one season of cultivation a year. Richards reports that children who seem to munch extras all day long in the plentiful season (April to October) are reduced during the 'hunger months' to a single dish late in the day, and that they tend to play listlessly. 'Usually more good-tempered than the average English baby, they whimper at the latest provocation.'

Richards does not say how this situation affects infants. In the course of my own stay in Bemba cillages I recall being wakened in the middle of the night by the persistent crying of babies. At the time I was mildly puzzled by this because, as we have seen, the infant is given the breast as soon as it begins to cry and ordinarily this has the effect of pacifying it quickly. When I inquired about the matter in the morning I would be told that it was because the baby was hungry. This suggests a number of possibilities: that deficiencies in the mother's own diet affects her supply of milk, or its quality, and/or her own behavioural response to the infant. The effect on the still unsatisfied infant, however, would be the same: to trigger its animus against the mother. It hardly needs to be added that in the light of present knowledge these views can only be offered as the most tentative of hypotheses for which as yet there is little or no firm evidence.[8] Should they turn out to have substance, they would lend further weight to the argument that in the societies with which we are concerned here the pattern of unconscious aggression against the mother, and specifically against the breasts, may be laid down in early infancy. This would carry through and lend a peculiar intensity to the second oral stage, which is ordinarily marked by high ambivalence, and in the end have an important bearing on the outcome of the phallic stage.

What emerges, then, from this discussion is that the picture presented initially of seemingly complete maternal indulgence has to be modified somewhat. In this particular environment, that is to say, a degree of privation is likely to be the general experience of infancy, however lavish otherwise mothers are in their love and attention towards their children. This, as I have just said, is likely to produce an intense ambivalence in the mother–child relationship and, I have suggested, at a later stage gives the Oedipal situation its distinctive cast. Or, restating it in slightly different terms, the Oedipal phase revives with particular intensity the more archaic conflicts centred on the painful ambivalence towards the mother. 'Castration fears', then, relate not only to the father but to the mother, too, who is viewed as punishing the child for the hostile impulses he harbours towards her. On the other hand, as Ritchie puts it, the love for her is not destroyed and cannot be.

> It is founded on need, and he is still very dependent on her and knows it is she who provides him with most of the necessities and the pleasures of life. For a very short time hate does indeed dominate the picture and love is relegated to the unconscious – or more probably it goes no deeper than the preconscious. But the will to hold on to life and enjoy it ordinarily asserts itself, and now hate is repressed and love rules on the surface. (p. 13)[9]

It is the aspect of love which is enshrined in such Bemba proverbs as *umushi ushili noko e kupula milimo* (in the village where you lack a mother begging is your work), or *Sankata, noko acilipo, noko wa mubiyo tekapilwa pa luino* (rejoice that your mother is still with you, the mother of your friend won't allow her food-rack to be touched). Nor is it surprising in these circumstances, as Richards (1939: 69) points out, that the act of suckling has become symbolic of the mother's generosity in Bemba oral literature as well as daily speech. Such notions carry over into the religious domain, too. Thus, Richards (1934: 271) has noted how the important position of the *namfumu* (the royal princesses) was reflected in a cult of the dead mothers of the chiefs. She goes on to point out that at some of the chiefs' villages there was a house kept sacred to the spirits of the royal women. She tells us that in certain rites performed at these capitals the chief himself salutes to the ground in front of this

house and prays to 'our mothers who bore us and suckled us
and carried us on skins on their backs'. Behaviourally, the
persisting strength of the bond is clearly revealed in the way in
which adults who are seriously ill or in great pain, that is to say
who feel themselves to be in extremis, will moan continuously,
calling on the mother: *'nafwa mayo ee'*, 'I am dying, mother.'
Nevertheless, the essential point remains, as Ritchie emphasises,
that the hatred is not completely abrogated. Aroused in early
infancy and then repressed, it lives on in the unconscious, and
in later life it comes to colour attitudes to a whole range of
matters as well as to influencing the response to a variety of
situations.

Conclusion

It is time now to try and draw together the manifold strands
that have gone into this chapter. The starting point for the
whole analysis, as indicated earlier, was the hint I detected in
the Dublin interviews that I was concerned with people who
had difficulty in coming to terms with their aggressive impulses
of which they were in some obscure way deeply afraid.
Exploring, with the aid of psychoanalytic theory, the experience
of childhood in these African societies helps, I believe, to remove
some of this obscurity. There are, of course, great gaps in my
information on many vital points, but the evidence presently
available seems sufficiently strong to warrant the hypothesis
that the particular experience of child-rearing I have described
tends to produce a fixation at the oral sadistic phase of libidinal
development. The implications of this situation ramify widely
and enable us to understand more clearly some aspects of the
indigenous culture as well as forms of behaviour in a wide
variety of contexts.

I have argued, following Ritchie, that the Oedipus complex is
a fact of life among the groups being considered here, but I
have also suggested that its distinctive cast is shaped
particularly by the earlier relations of the child with its mother.
That relationship is marked by strong ambivalence, a compound
of love and hate difficult to disentangle. With regard to the
latter I have already referred to Ritchie's (1943: 32) observation
how in early infancy hatred and a lust to destroy were aroused
when her breast became 'bad' (absent) and how the infant
imagined that his own hostile impulses were responsible for
sending her away. 'As long as he retains them he cannot bring

her back, even physically, so he must get rid of the burden.' The operation of a number of psychic mechanisms, of which more in a moment, together with the support provided by the constant presence of surrounding kin and friends do help to mitigate what otherwise prove an intolerable strain. Indeed, it is important to stress that most Africans manage to cope fairly adequately with the problems of living under ordinary circumstances, particularly in their own cultural milieu, so much so indeed that, for much of the time, far from appearing to be weighed down by a burden of anxiety and guilt, they convey to the outside observer an impression of cheerful extraversion, summed up in the stereotype of 'happy, happy Africa'.[10] At the same time, it is plain that to repress a hostile impulse is not the same as to eliminate it; it remains in the unconscious, finding its expression in varying contexts through displacement or being activated under conditions of emotional stress. In the latter event, when one's defences are down, so to speak, and the ego is not in full control of the situation, there is likely to be a 'return of the repressed' which manifests itself in forms of oral aggression or other regressive behaviour displaying oral characteristics.

I have referred to the intra-psychic mechanisms by which the African handles the problems posed by his unconscious hostile impulses. The first of these takes the form of a reaction-formation. Because the consequences of giving rein to the aggressive impulses associated with the oral sadistic stage are too awful to contemplate – the dismemberment of the beloved mother – the presence of the impulse itself has to be denied. Repression here is achieved by means of an excessive reinforcement of the thought contrary to the one which is to be repressed. We have, that is to say, a pairing off of two ideas in such a way that the one is exaggeratedly conscious while its counterpart is repressed and unconscious. Such a reaction-formation, I suggest, serves to explain the emphasis on the integrity of the person which, I have argued, is an important feature of the local ethos and underlies the concept of liability for injury in customary law.

But what of the other side of the coin, reflected in the practice of various forms of bodily mutilation? From one point of view, these must be seen in their political context as an instrument of policy: the resort to physical violence in many of these instances is deliberate and rational. But the matter also has a psychological dimension, particularly when regarded from the subject's point of view. Here we have to take account of a second mechanism, that of projection. Ritchie speaks of the African projecting his own intolerably evil emotions and impulses onto his father and thus persuading himself that he is good again. This relationship with the father is again one of ambivalence, and lays the foundation for the dominant attitude that develops towards all figures of authority. I would myself argue that, where a group like the Bemba is concerned, the position is more complex than Ritchie allows. Here, I suggest, a 'splitting' mechanism operates whereby all hostility towards the father can be denied and readily displaced onto the mother's brother. However, in the case of more 'remote' authority, such as the chief, the ambivalence that is so much a part of the child's relations with both parents emerges in its full intensity. The chief combines the attributes of both mother and father in regard to the aspects of nurturance and generosity, but he is also essentially a threatening and punitive figure. In terms of my whole argument, it seems no accident that Richards's informants should have found it wholly appropriate that Chitimukulu and the other senior chiefs should belong to the *Bena Ng'andu*, the Crocodile clan, because, they said, the crocodile is a creature that tears the common people to pieces with its teeth – an especially vivid image of oral aggression. It is, I submit, their own oral sadism that is projected onto the chief, while his own acts of cruelty represent the merited punishment for their unconscious hostility. A chief is thus required and expected to be both loving and punitive, and it is this fact which accounts for the complex blend of awe, admiration, and fear towards their traditional rulers that Richards has described so well, but which she also found so puzzling.

In his own discussion Ritchie has suggested a number of behavioural implications that stem from the psychic conflicts generated by the African's infantile experiences. He was particularly concerned with the African response to education, but he also argues, for example, that early disappointment with the mother comes in adult life to colour the whole attitude towards women and underlies many features of the approach to marriage and divorce. As we have seen earlier, marriage in this part of Africa tends to be extremely unstable. This implies not merely a high frequency of divorce, but also a weakness in the psychical bonds between husband and wife. Factors of social structure clearly contribute to this situation, but account also needs to be taken of the way these interact with psychological variables. The nursing mother sets up a standard of women, and in so far as the individual remains psychically bound to her throughout life, he unconsciously demands the same standard of perfection in all women - which few can achieve. But disappointment goes further than this; for however perfect the mother was in the first years, there came the inevitable moment of 'betrayal'. Thus, the wife, an unconscious surrogate of the mother, becomes the object of the same ambivalence. From this point of view, frequency of divorce and remarriage expresses the unending quest for the faithful mother and underlies perhaps the practice of what Bemba call *ukubwekeshanya*. This refers to the fact that a couple, long divorced, who have then gone through a series of other marital partners, sometimes in the end return to one another. In remarriages of this kind, or in unions which have achieved stability, the parties may perform the act known as *chipingo*. *Chipingo*, a term which, incidentally, is also used in speaking of the Testaments of the Bible, creates such a strong bond between them that thereafter divorce is said to be impossible. In this rite the husbar.d eats a piece of *bwali* ('porridge') which he has previously dipped in his wife's vagina. The symbolism of the act appears to fuse sexual and nurturant roles: the faithful, loving mother has been rediscovered. But such rediscovery apparently is rare, and more usually it is the element of conflict that is most evident to the observer. As previously mentioned, mutual suspicion, constant bickering, and, particularly where one or other of the parties is drunk, fighting are recurring features of relations between spouses. It is no part of my argument that all cases of fighting between husband and wife will involve oral aggression, as in the case cited earlier in the chapter, merely that its incidence is likely to be greater in societies and cultures of the kind with which we have been concerned here than in certain others. The case cited[11] was far from unique in my experience of hearings in urban and rural courts, but its chief importance here is in pointing to a hypothesis which could be tested by further comparative research.

I now turn finally to the African response to Federation. From the very outset Africans had made it clear beyond doubt that they were utterly opposed to the proposed development,

and much of the campaign they waged against Federation can
be handled adequately employing the conventional categories
of political science or political sociology. There were, however,
other aspects of African behaviour to be witnessed in that
context that require one to go further than this if one is to
explain satisfactorily the emotional factors that were also
present in the situation. I have suggested that, given in
particular the ineffectiveness of African opposition at that time,
and their powerlessness to influence the outcome, the whole
issue represented a crisis of attachment and dependence,
reviving unconscious memories of infantile experiences that
were charged with psychic conflict. The administration, 'their
father and mother', to whom they were accustomed to look for
protection, was now on the point of abandoning them to
European 'ogres'. The anxiety that these circumstances
provoked are, I think, clearly expressed in the outbreak of the
poison scares. Regrettably, when in the field I forsook the
opportunity to explore the symbolic significance that attached
to sugar and meat, though I believe that the context itself
makes plain, at least in the case of sugar, the fusing of genital
and oral images and anxieties.[12] The fear that they were being
poisoned, that is to say, has to be understood in the context of
the child's early relations with the mother. For if, as Ritchie
(1943: 23) puts it: 'The mother, the breast and her milk -
together with the self-preservative and the erotic joy associated
with them - are for ever the pattern of "goodness", what is it
that represents ultimate "badness"?' The answer would appear
to be the mother who destroys, whose milk, instead of giving
sustenance, yields only poison. Here, again, the mechanism of
projection is at work. The aggressive impulses towards the
mother being repressed, the situation is unconsciously interpreted
as though it were the mother who was seeking to destroy her
children and whose gifts of food had, therefore, to be rejected.
In the resurgence of the *munyama* cult we appear to find a
similar fusion of phallic and oral elements: the inoculation with
a hypodermic needle, and the sucking of blood, leading to loss
of will and possibly disappearance or death. Some remarks of
Ernest Jones (1949: 120) are of interest in this connection. He
writes:

> When the more normal aspects of sexuality are in a state of
> repression there is always a tendency to regress towards
> less developed forms. Sadism is one of these, and it is the

earliest form of this - known as oral sadism - that plays such an important part in the Vampire belief. The still earlier stage, the simple sucking that precedes biting, is more connected with the love side, the sadism with the element of hate.

The African belief in *munyama* and the notion of the vampire familiar in Western folklore differ in certain important respects, and it would, therefore, be a mistake to treat them as a product of identical unconscious mental processes. Unfortunately, when I was in the field I was not fully alive to the significance of these problems and my failure at the time to inquire into the matter more systematically prevents me from exploring the question further here. Nevertheless, it would seem to be a point of considerable interest that the resurgence of the *munyama* cult should have occurred at a time of widespread emotional upheaval. As I have argued, the Federation issue was widely perceived by Africans, at an unconscious level, as reviving memories of threats to their sexuality. In this situation, *munyama* reflected the breakdown of trust on which all viable systems of social relationships must rest, and the predominant mood of fear and hostility; that the central activity of *munyama* is believed to be the sucking of the blood of its victim exhibits in yet another guise the theme of oral aggression.

Earlier in this chapter I referred briefly to a number of methodological issues raised by Gluckman in the symposium *Closed Systems and Open Minds*. Since the position he adopted there remains pertinent and continues to command respect (see, for example, Fortes 1980), it may be of interest to offer some comments on it in the light of the present analysis. In their conclusion to the volume, as part of the task of 'clarifying the relations between disciplines', Devons and Gluckman define a number of procedures by which, say, a social anthropologist demarcates his field of study. Integral to this whole approach is the 'duty of abstention' which, they point out (Gluckman 1964: 168), involves a rule of disciplined refusal to trespass on the fields of others. This theme is well illustrated in the discussion of the relations of social anthropology and psychoanalysis, where they cite with approval Turner's argument in the same volume that the *precise sources* of unconscious feeling and wishes may be irrelevant to the social anthropologist. The latter is 'interested in the fact that emotion is evoked and not in the specific quality of its constituents. He may indeed find it

situationally relevant for his analysis to distinguish whether
the emotion evoked by a specific symbol possesses the gross
character, say, of aggression, fear, friendliness, anxiety or sexual
pleasure. But he need go no further than this' (1964: 239). These
remarks, of course, have to be read in their proper context; they
are not intended to lay down, prescriptively, a general rule. As
Devons and Gluckman make clear on more than one occasion,
whether one needs to go further depends on the nature of the
problem set. In so far as this chapter makes use of certain
psychoanalytic ideas, it offers ample illustration of some of the
procedures that Devons and Gluckman identify and define -
incorporation and abridgement, both postulated and in some
instances at least, I believe, validated. But in so far as I have
been concerned with aggression, the particular forms it takes
under certain conditions, and the unconscious mental factors
underlying them, I have plainly gone much further than Turner
found necessary for his purposes. In the restricted sense in
which they employ the term, I think it is plain that Devons and
Gluckman would regard much of my analysis as having
overstepped the limits of naivety.

That serious pitfalls and snares await those who do not
recognise the 'limits of naivety' Devons and Gluckman's
discussion brings out very clearly, and in straying into other
fields, I do not myself claim, nor can indeed hope, to have
avoided all of them. But even if these difficulties are overcome,
the major objection to 'trespass' appears to be that it is likely to
be an impediment to 'an understanding of those aspects of
reality which are properly the concern of one's own discipline'
(1964: 167). There are two assumptions here, both closely
related: one concerns the definition and fixity of disciplinary
boundaries; the other the question of agreement on the basic
paradigm in terms of which we select our problems and present
our analyses. I discuss the latter point first.

For Gluckman, clearly, the subject of social anthropology
was, in broad terms, fairly well settled; its special concern was
with the significance of custom in the relations between persons
and, beyond this, with the systematic interdependence that
exists within the body of custom itself (1966: 256; compare
Gluckman 1965a: 300). Whether such a view would be
universally, or even generally, accepted within the profession I
do not need to consider. I need simply note that, since in their
introduction Devons and Gluckman define social anthropology

operationally in terms of what its practitioners have been doing during the past fifty years, the emphasis on custom or institution hardly seems to do justice to the range of matters with which contemporary social anthropologists concern themselves. But the more important consideration is that a consistent stress on custom would appear to exclude areas of inquiry in a way that is difficult to justify on grounds of logic. Consider some of the issues touched on in the present chapter. In discussing the concept of liability in customary law, and the implicit assumptions which underlie the decisions of African judges in such cases, we are in the realm of ideas. Such assumptions go to make up the structure of what I call here the ethos of a society; its exploration is usually seen as part of the task of those anthropologists whose work is integrated around the concept of culture.[13] Again, in dealing with courts we are at the same time dealing with people in a number of social roles, including their role as subjects in relation to the political authorities; such roles go to make up a structure of social relationships, the study of which is also a proper concern of the social anthropologist. Social relationships are often described in terms of mutual expectations defined by the appropriate norms of behaviour, but if we examine more closely the aspects of behaviour that enter into any social relationship we are likely to find that together they form a continuum, imperceptibly shading into one another. Thus, for example, entering into a subject's relations with his chief there will be elements of regular and obligatory behaviour on both sides, that is custom in the strict sense. However, we may also observe modes of behaviour that are regular or recurring, and even expected, but which are not mandatory. The ferocity and cruelty of Bemba chiefs in the past offer examples of this. Yet further along the continuum we may find behaviour that is both regular and expected (in a statistical sense), but which, in fact, flouts the accepted norms appropriate to the relationship in question. Instances of this kind are found in my chapter in the discussion of the relationships of the parties to a marriage, where brawling and fighting will commonly be observed or recorded between spouses, but can hardly be regarded as customary, that is institutionalised behaviour. Finally, at the other end of the continuum, there is behaviour which can best be described perhaps as 'spontaneous' in the sense that, within the framework of some set of social relationships, it represents a response or reaction to a particular situation. Such behaviour may not be regular in the sense that it can be recorded on separate occasions throughout the period of observation but it is not, therefore, necessarily to be regarded as random. Its regularity depends on other criteria and relates rather to the way in which certain types of situation tend to be perceived. Much in the African response to Federation exhibited behaviour of this kind.

Given, then, that we have to deal with this kind of 'gradient' in behaviour, by what logical criteria do we decide to include certain modes as legitimate concerns of our discipline, and to exclude others? The drawing in this way of sharp lines of demarcation not only turns out, on closer inspection, to be arbitrary but it also precludes us from going on to ask a number of interesting questions. For example, how far and in what ways ideas and various modes of behaviour that appear on the surface to belong to quite different domains of social life, or to be otherwise quite unrelated, may, in fact, be interconnected. I believe that I have shown that such a thread of connection runs through those aspects of ethos and behaviour that I have discussed in this chapter, but this emerges only because I was prepared to give full weight to the emotional component in behaviour, exploring it rather than simply taking it as given.

There is today an increasing recognition that no academic discipline is wholly self-sufficient; that meaningful problems arise which require us from time to time to cross conventional disciplinary boundaries. *Closed Systems and Open Minds* was an attempt to state the theoretical issues that this situation creates. The approach enunciated by Devons and Gluckman predicates a view of scientific activity in which each discipline is discrete, defining itself, so to speak, by its focus on some particular set of systematic connections and interdependencies. On this view, for example, psychoanalysis is concerned with processes going on within the individual human psyche, and therefore can have no part in explaining events in the socio-cultural domain, which is subject to its own regularities the investigation of which is the task of the sociologist or social anthropologist. It is true, of course, that psychoanalysts are concerned with the structure of the human personality and with intra-psychic processes, but what Devons and Gluckman leave out of account is that where individuals, brought up within the same culture and physical environment, display similar behaviour responses and emotional reactions in certain situations, then the rigid distinction between what are the concerns of the psychologist and what are those of the sociologist become less easy to maintain. Judged in terms of its impressive record of achievement in the field of social anthropology, there is no question but that powerful arguments can be mustered in favour of the 'closed systems' approach. But this approach, with its emphasis on discreteness, implies a view of the relations between disciplines akin to the way in which sovereign nation-states conduct their foreign relations with one another. This is hardly likely to be very helpful when so many of the interesting questions thrown up by the anthropologist's own field data are seen to arise in the interstices between disciplines, and involve the interaction of sociological as well as other kinds of variables. Nor is it an answer in such circumstances to hand the problem over to some specialist in another discipline, since its practitioners, too, are bound by the same interdiction on 'trespass'. As Barnes (1971: 268) has remarked, the position adopted by Devons and Gluckman appears 'to be aimed more at delimiting an intellectual niche for social anthropology rather than at finding the most satisfactory solutions to problems presented by data from the real world'. To this one needs to add a point of a rather different kind. For what is at issue is not a technical question about boundaries; it is rather, as I think Spiro's (1979) paper 'Whatever Happened to the Id?' brings out clearly, the way our conceptions of anthropology tend to be tied to, or to project, a particular image of man (compare Geertz 1973; Spiro 1978). From this point of view, as it now seems to me, an anthropology that is unprepared to explore affect ties itself to a model of man that simply leaves too much out of account. No one, of course, will seriously question the claim that every scientist has to work within circumscribed limits; but it is no less plain that advancing our understanding in any field of intellectual endeavour also requires from time to time the redefinition, and thus the transcending, of those limits.

Notes

Introduction

1. This is not a purely personal observation. Kees van Donge, a Dutch anthropologist who spent some time at the University of Zambia, has remarked (1985: 73) that the pre-independence literature was seldom recommended reading there in the 1970s. 'The end of colonization seems almost to have been a point of discontinuity in the study of Zambian societies.' I may add that when I published my study *Urbanization and Kinship* (1981) I sought, with the aid of my publishers, an arrangement with the University of Zambia that would have made the book available to readers in Zambia at a much reduced price. After lengthy correspondence, we were finally advised that no courses were being offered at the University for which the book was suitable.
2. The volume, edited by Meyer Fortes and Evans-Pritchard, was first published in 1940; a fifth impression appeared in 1955.
3. My copy of this is a cyclostyled abridged translation. The author's name was not given.
4. Gluckman was fond of remarking that he could not read Marx, but could and did read Engels.
5. Also worth mentioning here is that while the index to his textbook *Politics, Law and Ritual in Tribal Society* (1963a) carries many references to Durkheim, to Marx there is none at all.

Chapter 1

1. How I came to embark on this study may itself be of some interest. Briefly, I had been awarded a scholarship by the Colonial Social Science Research Council, enabling me to spend a year as a postgraduate student in the Department of Anthropology at the London School of Economics to prepare myself for a field study of customary law in Africa. Initially the idea was that I would carry out the study among the Embu Meru of Kenya, working under the local supervision of Dr Gunther Wagner. Wagner was a German anthropologist who had done distinguished work in East Africa in the 1930s but, during the Second World War, so I came to understand, he had served as a high-ranking German officer there. Very late in the day it occurred to someone at the Colonial Office that to have a young Jewish researcher working under Wagner's supervision was not an appropriate arrangement, and another project had to be found for me. I suspect that what happened then was that Sir Gilbert Rennie, then Governor of Northern Rhodesia, and on a short visit to London, was button-

holed by someone at the Colonial Office and persuaded that a study of the African Urban courts there could be of considerable interest.

2. In his own brief account of the affair, Mitchell (1977: 313) speaks of having been visited one evening in London by the Secretary of the Chamber of Mines, who asked for my withdrawal from the Copperbelt. The apparent discrepancy between our two accounts is readily explained. At the time I was not aware that Mitchell had first been approached about the matter while he was on a visit to England. He returned from this trip in good time for our Conference at the Institute.

3. The story has an ironic aftermath. Some years later, when I held an appointment at the Australian National University (ANU), Canberra, and had been conducting research in Papua New Guinea, I received an invitation to lunch at Parliament House with a prominent Australian public figure and a senior official of Con Zinc Rio Tinto. Con Zinc Rio Tinto at that point were engaged in opening up a new copper mine on Bougainville, Papua New Guinea. The Con Zinc man had recently returned from a tour of the copper mines in other parts of the world to confer with colleagues there and discover what could be learnt from their experience. He visited, of course, the Zambian Copperbelt, where he discussed a variety of problems relating to the employment of local labour. He was advised that he should seek the services of an anthropologist! Learning somehow that I was at the ANU, he had sought me out to see if I would be prepared to go to Bougainville.

4. Before this happened, we did succeed in staging a single performance of a version of Dickens's *A Christmas Carol*. The performance itself went off quite well, but from my own point of view it was the process of getting the production off the ground that proved to be most instructive. We needed, of course, someone to play the part of Mrs Cratchit, Tiny Tim's mother. It proved to be very difficult to find an African woman who was prepared to appear on stage. Eventually we were able to persuade the wife of one of the members, who was a schoolteacher, to play the part. Rehearsals went off quite well, but for the actual performance Mrs Cratchit came on stage wearing a full-length evening dress and long white gloves. Very simply, for a member of Ndola's African elite at that time to have appeared in public attired in clothes that were more fitting to the role of a poor housewife would have been quite unthinkable.

5. A rather different aspect of this ambiguity in the relations of government and anthropologist emerged in regard to the report on the Urban courts I was required to submit at the conclusion of the study. This report, which included at the request of the Colonial Social Science Research Council my recommendations concerning all the various aspects of the Urban courts system, was submitted to the Colonial Office, who in turn passed it on to the Northern Rhodesia Government, seeking the latter's approval for the publication of the report. The Northern Rhodesia Government did agree to publication – but on condition that the recommendations were not included in the published version. In this way presumably it avoided commitment to taking any action in the matter. The other point that emerges from this episode – fairly obvious, but also readily overlooked – is that within a power structure different interests are apt to be involved at different levels of the hierarchy.

6. Mitchell (1977: 316) reproduces the original editorial, but also includes a reply by Vic Turner and Merran McCulloch (then Administrative Secretary of the Institute) as well as the editor's response to it.

7. Anthropologists who were on the staff of the Rhodes-Livingstone Institute at this time would return to the University of Manchester in order to write up their research in the Department of Anthropology, whose head was then Professor Max Gluckman, a former Director of the Institute. Back in England a number of them, with Gluckman himself, did publicly engage in the campaign against Federation. Within Northern Rhodesia itself, however, so far as my knowledge goes, none was a member of Congress, took part in Congress rallies, or otherwise actively participated in the campaign against Federation. To criticisms of his political involvement made by colleagues Gluckman replied in his paper 'Anthropology and Apartheid: the Work of South African Anthropologists' (1975).

Chapter 2

1. The Copperbelt comprises a narrow strip which extends from the railway at Ndola westward some 200 miles along the border of the Belgian Congo (now Zaire). I employ the term here to cover the urban districts of Chingola, Kitwe, Luanshya, Mufulira, and Ndola. Ndola itself is not a mine township, and does not fall within the 'Copperbelt proper', but it forms the administrative and commercial centre for the area.

2. 'Already in 1931, and still more so in 1932, emigration [of Europeans] considerably exceeded immigration, owing in part to the completion of construction in the mines, but mainly to the fall in the price of copper.' (Kuczynski 1949: 2, 419)

3. I speak here of 'conflict of interest' rather than simply of conflict since the latter term refers more properly to the lines of cleavage operating within the structure as a whole. Of course, 'conflicts of interest' may be an index or reflection of such conflict in this wider sense.

4. This is an informal court composed of Tribal Elders or Tribal Representatives handling minor disputes arising within the Municipal location or the mine compound. Those cases which could not be settled here went on to the Urban court.

5. I omitted to find out if Cewe was a pagan, though this was unlikely. Mwamba was a staunch Roman Catholic.

6. The implication was that the woman had a lover. See also below p. 187.

7. The marriage arrangements were conducted in Bembaland by the girl's matrilineal kin.

8. This, and other passages, come from the manuscript of Gluckman's book *The Judicial Process Among the Barotse of Northern Rhodesia*, which he kindly allowed me to read. He had already formulated the concept of the 'reasonable man' in Barotse jurisprudence, observing how Lozi judges assessed the behaviour of litigants against standards of 'the reasonable and customary behaviour of specific social positions'. Independently, I had arrived at a very similar view of procedure in the Urban courts, which I have summed up here in the expression 'normative man' (compare Epstein 1954).

9. Cases in the 'conflict of law' are those in which the parties base their claims on opposed tribal customs. Thus, a Bemba might claim damages against a Lenje whose child had accidentally damaged his property. Such a claim might be good in Bemba law, but under Lenje law the rule might be that no liability attaches to the parents for the acts of their children if committed accidentally. The laws here are opposed, and the court must decide what law governs the case.

10. In Bemba custom the process whereby a 'young man wins economic independence from his father-in-law and gains paternal authority in his own right' is often protracted, and may take a varying number of years (Richards 1940a: 51 *et passim*).

Chapter 4

1. These hotels, of course, were intended to cater for a European clientele. It is worth mentioning, therefore, that it was in Ndola that the first African hotel in the country was officially opened, towards the end of 1955.

2. Among the Lamba of the Ndola District the onset of the slump in the closing of the open-cast mine at Bwana Mkubwa still marks an important point in dating events (Dr V. W. Turner, personal communication).

3. Under the terms of the African Housing Ordinance the Location Superintendent has a discretion to allow an unemployed man to remain in possession of the house for a further month provided he can pay the rent himself. In my experience, few Africans are aware of this provision and my impression is that so great is the demand for housing that in any case the discretion is rarely exercised.

4. See Mitchell (1951), whose evidence suggests that newcomers move about during the first five years of their residence on the Copperbelt and then settle down in one town. This is also reflected to some extent in African trade unions, where the greater the stability of labour the stronger the tendency to join a union (compare Mwewa 1958).

5. During 1955 there were widespread reports of stoning incidents in which cars were attacked by riotous mobs after accidents involving Africans, frequently irrespective of the race of the driver and whether in fact the particular car had been involved in the accident or was merely stopping to offer assistance. In a similar sort of incident at Chingola some 2,000 Africans rioted after an African worker was accidentally killed by a moving crane. Different interpretations will no doubt be placed upon these events, but it is at least clear that they cannot be satisfactorily explained by an easy reference to the presence of loafers alone. While it is true that many of those arrested for their part in the riot at Chingola were 'unauthorised persons' living on the mine compound without permission, they were not 'loafers' for they were, in fact, in employment elsewhere in the town. Parasites and rogues who live on their wits there may be - as there are in every town - but my own view is that the dimensions of the 'loafer' problem as commonly conceived are grossly exaggerated. What emerged plainly from the Chingola incident were the dimensions of the housing problem.

6. After the meeting the District Commissioner commented to me that

the Advisory Council had his full sympathy. On the other hand, he
explained, one could not let the police down too badly. The whole
business had put him in a very difficult position!

7. In this generally unsettled atmosphere it is hardly surprising that
   Africans should sometimes have appeared unduly credulous and ready
   to believe the worst, and that the wildest rumours should receive
   widespread and ready acceptance. At the time of the arrests the
   rumour soon got around that the government was rounding up the
   tax defaulters and dispatching them to work on the great dam being
   built at the Kariba Gorge. Among Africans the area was commonly
   regarded as a 'death-trap' and for a week or more the clerks were
   scarcely able to cope with the long queues of Africans coming hastily
   to pay their overdue taxes.

8. In the meantime a residence permit, renewable weekly at a cost of
   three pence, entitles one to reside legally in the location with friends or
   relatives. The whole situation lends itself readily to graft and all
   manner of intrigue.

9. The relationship involved here has to be understood in the light of the
   principle of positional succession, and the identification of alternate
   generations (see Cunnison 1956).

10. Most of the major denominations of organised Christendom are
    represented in the town. Roman Catholics constitute the largest
    single group, while in recent years the Watchtower sect (Jehovah's
    Witnesses) has emerged as an influential and highly organised body
    (see Chapter 7). There has been little of an African separatist movement
    in the country.

11. The word adultery is commonly used to translate a vernacular term –
    bucende in Bemba – which covers heterosexual relations of any kind
    which take place outside marriage.

Chapter 6

1. The following incident, typical of its kind, was related to me by an
   African Education Officer who had studied in England. He was
   walking along the street of a Copperbelt town when it started to rain.
   He took shelter in a nearby building. Noting his smart dress and
   appearance a European accosted him and said in Fanagolo: 'So you've
   left off wearing skins.' The African replied in English that he did not
   understand Kitchen Kaffir but the European at once got angry and
   told him to clear off.

2. Charlie, of course, was just a name with which he greeted nearly
   everybody.

3. Bemba is the language of the Bemba 'proper', the largest and formerly
   one of the most powerful tribes in the country, but it is also the
   mother tongue, with certain minor dialectal variations, of a number
   of other groups, for example, Aushi, Chishinga, Lunda, Tabwa, etc.

4. In one instance this led a group of Nyasaland Africans to break away
   and found an independent church, using another vernacular.

5. I use the word 'almost' advisedly. White (1951) reports, for example,
   that despite the large number of migrant labourers to the Copperbelt
   from the Balovale District very few from that area acquired any
   proficiency in speaking Bemba.

6. These examples show how two separate but coincident processes enter into the adoption of English words. In the first place the English word is assimilated to the phonemic structure of the Bantu language. Simultaneously, the initial sound (or sounds) of the English word is assimilated to the class morpheme prefix most similar to it. In this way the loan word becomes a member of the class of nouns marked in Bemba by that particular prefix. Thus, the nearest a Bemba speaker can get to say 'glass' is *kalashi*, which becomes a noun of the class taking the prefix *ka-*.

7. The Bemba terms for money are *ndalama* and *lupya* (pl. *mpya*), both of which are loan words of an earlier vintage. *Ndalama* is the same word as the Nyanja *ndarama*, for which Nyanja dictionaries give the derivation *ndala* ('whiteness', i.e. silver). But the correct etymology is probably the Arabic *dirhema*, a small coin, from the Greek *drachma* (see Curator's Note in Quiggin 1949). *Ulupya* is the Indian rupee and presumably harks back to the days when Indian troops were used by Johnston in pacifying the Lake Nyasa region.

8. *Pace* Gower, the only other current expression deriving from army experience that I came across was *ukuya ku cuti* (to go on leave), or, in its Copperbelt denotation, to go on a short visit to the rural areas. Picked up by African troops serving in the Far East, the expression appears to derive from the Hindi word *chut*, female genitalia.

9. This is the meaning given in the White Fathers' *Bemba–English Dictionary*, but I have not been able to discover the derivation of the term.

10. The *kanyangu*, or mine compound policeman introduces yet another urban social personality. They are the 'cow peas' boys. The expression originated on the mines, where a food rationing system used to operate. The compound police who controlled the queues at the Feeding Store were held to be in a position to get extra rations, of which cow peas, *nyangu*, were a prominent item.

11. A girl who is offered a mere pint may even feel herself slighted. The following incident was reported by one of my assistants. A girl had seated herself beside a man at the Bottle Store, and he offered her a pint of bottled beer. She asked for a quart, remarking that pints were given only to skinny, unattractive women. The man went off and fetched two quarts, for which she rewarded him with 'lelo ndedupela *wonder tango, my dear*' [today I will show you a really wonderful 'dance'].

12. *Ukupanga four*, that is to make four (legs), is also sometimes used for the act of sexual intercourse.

13. References to current events are also sometimes found where we might least expect them. Thus, at football matches a popular player setting off on a solo run would be cheered on with the cry *Mau Mau*. Again at the time of the Suez Crisis, and the blocking of the canal, one young woman who had won herself a reputation because of her many lovers was promptly nicknamed Miss Suez Canal.

14. In this context the prefix *Ci-* is an index of language as, for example, Ci-Bemba, the Bemba language or language of the Ba-Bemba, the Bemba people.

Chapter 7

1. According to figures kindly made available to me by Mr H. Arnott, the missionary in charge of the Society's office in Luanshya, the average number of persons taking part actively in their teaching work throughout the country in 1950 was 13,560. By 1955 these figures had risen to 24,370. These figures, it should be stressed, do not include all those who might describe themselves as Watchtower members but who were only active from time to time. Recent indications are that a high rate of growth has been maintained; Hodges (1976) gives the average number of those who were fully active in the previous year as 54,289.

2. A considerable literature has by now grown up around the early Watchtower. The most comprehensive treatment of its vicissitudes up to the period of the Second World War is to be found in Dr Sholto Cross's unpublished D.Phil. thesis (1973). Various aspects have also been discussed in other publications by Cross and other writers cited elsewhere in the text.

3. Falling between these two periods is another covering the late 1930s and 1940s – which includes, of course, the war years – for which unfortunately I have little or no information. Plugging the gap might prove to be a rewarding task for a Central African historian.

4. According to Witnesses, Gondwe was expelled from their community in 1945 for 'wife-changing' (Cross 1970: 181).

5. de Jager was an important witness before the Commission of Inquiry into the Disturbances on the Copperbelt in 1935. His testimony sheds interesting light on the teachings and work of Jehovah's Witnesses in Northern Rhodesia, but mostly his concern was to dissociate the Witnesses from the Watchtower, which he insisted were two distinct bodies.

6. As one man expressed it: 'It's like water. Look how many things are made from water: tea, beer, *bwali* [porridge]. All these are different, but they're all made of water.'

7. For the annual Memorial, when Witnesses celebrated Christ's death, an attendance record was kept. This showed that in 1955 74,720 were present.

8. Perhaps I should emphasise here that I am reporting how our respondents perceived – or had been schooled to perceive – the situation. I am not offering my own understanding of that situation. From the point of view of an external observer, the freedom to ask questions and the exercise of independent judgement are not necessarily the same thing (compare Beckford 1975: 120).

9. CCAR stands here for the Church of Central Africa in Rhodesia, a grouping of Protestant denominations, of which for present purposes the main ones are Free Church, London Missionary Society and the Church of Scotland.

10. Lehmann's figures were drawn from an investigation undertaken by the Christians' Council in Luanshya and Mufulira in 1953. How the data were assembled is not indicated. Mitchell's figures derive from a more intensive study: a random 10 per cent survey of all dwellings occupied by Africans in a local authority, industrial, domestic, and African township areas throughout the Copperbelt.

11. 'Skilled' here, and in the table, refers to jobs carried out by men who had received proper training: bricklayers, carpenters, plumbers, and the like. But it should be noted here that no provision as yet existed in law for apprenticeship for Africans. Increasing numbers were applying to be trade-tested under a scheme organised by the Labour Department, but in the circumstances 'skill' was likely to be a fairly elastic term.

12. I have omitted from the table the small category of police included in Mitchell's original data as well as the unemployed and those for whom the relevant information was not available. This explains why the percentage columns do not add up to 100. IA is the index of association: this provides a measure of the observed frequency of some particular occurrence as against what could be expected if purely random processes were at work. The value of 1:0 in this context means that the observed frequency coincides exactly with the expected; the further above or below 1, the more one is entitled to speak of the actual number in the category as representing a higher or lower proportion of the universe in question than could be anticipated on grounds of pure chance.

13. A photograph of the substantial Kingdom Hall at Twapiya, the African Township just outside Ndola, is given in Cole (1955). The opposite page, incidentally, carries a photograph of an assembly at Kitwe in 1952, when 18,000 attended.

14. With over 100 ethnic groups represented in the African population of the Copperbelt, I have not felt it necessary to include all of them in the table. Those that are, however, do give a fair coverage of all parts of the country except the south, the numbers from there on the Copperbelt being relatively small. For the sake of convenience I speak of northern (Aushi, Ng'umbo, Chishinga, Lunda of Kazembe, Bemba, Mambwe, and Inamwanga), central (Lala, Lamba, Lenje, and Kaonde), and western (Lozi, Lovale, Ndembu) groups; while there is substantial overlap, there is no precise coincidence with the similarly named Provinces.

15. It must not be assumed, of course, that the statements of one's informants or respondents necessarily reflect accurately official doctrine. What was said here about hell, for example, appears to express a personal syncretism: traditional Christian teachings on hell were among a number of orthodox doctrines which Pastor Russell had early found difficulty in accepting (see Beckford 1975: 2, 12).

16. This position was by now, in general terms, so well understood by others that Congress leaders themselves felt compelled on occasion to seek biblical arguments to counter those of the Witnesses. So, for example, when a meeting to discuss the forthcoming boycott was called at Twapiya, the Congress spokesman had evidently expected a large turnout of Witnesses, many of whom lived in the African Township, and prepared himself accordingly. Thus, part of his speech was built around a passage from Lamentations, which he cited to show that the Bible did not oppose involvement in politics, but in fact encouraged people to become politically engaged. Few Witnesses, however, had attended the meeting, and there was none to argue with him.

17. It is interesting to note in this regard Dr Lehmann's (Taylor and Lehmann 1961: 112) comment that the most progressive in developing

a relationship between the sexes in a way that showed Christian freedom were probably the Watchtower members. It should also be noted here, moreover, that the Witnesses were now beginning to seek a more accommodating approach to various customary arrangements and to rethink their position on such matters as bride-wealth and polygyny (see, for example, *The Watchtower*, 1956).

18. For a more detailed discussion of this and other issues related to gender identity on the Copperbelt, see Epstein (1981).

19. Intriguing questions are raised here about the differential appeal of the Society to African men and women. Tables 7.3 and 7.4 present some data on the point: it is apparent that in a number of ethnic groups in which the Witnesses are strongly represented female members outnumber males, but there are also striking exceptions, and the picture is far from clear-cut. Clearly, this is an aspect of the broader problem that cries out for more systematic research in which survey methods would be supplemented by more intensive modes of inquiry that would include detailed case-histories and interviews to probe women's perceptions of the situation.

20. It is sometimes said that Witnesses show a lack of sociability and warmth in social relations (for example, Beckford 1975: 86). This did not strike me as being the case on the Copperbelt. One point worth mentioning in this connection is the heightened sense of meaning the expression 'brothers and sisters' was likely to have for a people accustomed to a classificatory system of kinship terminology (compare Epstein 1981: 247).

21. It may be worth mentioning in this connection that Jehovah's Witnesses was still a proscribed organisation in the neighbouring Belgian Congo (Zaire), presumably because of the historical association with Watchtower, which had also flourished there in an earlier day.

22. In one case, for example, the preacher was said to have referred to *mupula mpako*. This is a shrub that grows in the hollow of a tree, sometimes eventually killing the tree itself. This was interpreted as a clear reference to the position of the African *vis-à-vis* the European.

23. I say perhaps here because Mitchell's survey data reveal relatively few Nsenga and Kunda as Jehovah's Witnesses. A much higher proportion (23 per cent) was found among Nsenga and Kunda interviewed in my own study in Ndola. In the latter case, however, the number of respondents was small (twenty-six); nor did the households we called at constitute a true random sample of the population at large.

24. The map presented by Martin (1977: 100) is interesting in this regard. This shows the areas of most intense Watchtower activity in the northern parts of the country: Watchtower influence extended in an arc from Mansa (Fort Rosebery) to the west of the Bemba right round to Isoka to the east, but the great heartland of Bemba country itself had not been penetrated. In another account of Watchtower in the Northern Province, Meebelo (1971: 137) wonders why the Bemba seem not to have been as ready converts as were the Mambwe or Namwanga, and suggests that because leaders of Watchtower were all members of tribes they had previously subjugated the Bemba responded to their doctrine as another attempt at political assertion by their erstwhile subjects. While there may be an element of truth in this, it seems likely that chiefs and missionaries alike were more concerned with Watchtower preaching against authority. Martin's

account (1977: 163, 165) is again interesting here, for he points out that in the 1930s Chitimukulu, the Bemba Paramount Chief, had forbidden Watchtower preachers to enter his territory, and that the White Fathers had taken steps 'to combat the forces of paganism' through the development of a number of Catholic organisations such as the Legion of Mary. With regard to the position of Watchtower in the far north-west of the country, I do not know enough of the local situation to speak with any confidence, and would merely suggest that examining the role of the Lozi might repay attention. Right from the beginning the Barotse had sought to control missionaries and to prevent them spreading their influence to those parts of the country, such as Balovale, over which for many years the Lozi continued to claim hegemony.

25. Interesting comment on this accommodationist stance is to be found in some remarks (cited in Assimeng 1970: 110) of the Resident Minister for the Central Province in post-independence Zambia: 'There were no Watchtower troubles during the colonial days. They all saluted the Union Jack and sang the British National Anthem. Now that Zambia is an independent state, they have resorted to a campaign of insults.'

Chapter 8

1. The metaphor, while technologically apt, would also convey to an African audience overtones not immediately apparent to someone unfamiliar with African religious thought. The verb *ukubumba* (to mould a pot) also expresses the wider sense of to create, and the term *Kabumba* (the Potter) is frequently used when referring to Lesa, the Supreme Being.

2. While I gratefully acknowledge the stimulus I have received from Mannoni's (1956) discussion of the dependence complex, I find it difficult to go along with his argument all the way. The complex, as he acknowledges, is not peculiar to the Malagasy; it is shared by children whatever their environment. But Mannoni argues for the persistence of dependence among the Malagasy 'as an essential part of their personality, which is constructed along very different lines from our own'. The whole of this argument is built on the opposition of dependence and inferiority. Apart from the objections that have been raised by Fanon (1970: 76), it seems to me that dependency needs to be counterposed not to inferiority but to autonomy, which is no less a need of the developing personality. For a discussion along these lines, see Epstein (1971). It is also important to note here that the fear of abandonment is not tied solely to the complex of dependence. Thus, a major theme of the second volume of Bowlby's study *Attachment and Loss* is the fear that can be aroused at the possibility that an attachment figure will be inaccessible or unresponsive. For further comment on the concepts of dependence and attachment, see note 9 below.

3. Stated quantitatively, the position was that in Southern Rhodesia, with a population in 1950 of around 2 million Africans and 130,000 Europeans, 33 per cent of the land available had been set aside for the *exclusive* use of the African people, and 50 per cent for the *exclusive* use of Europeans. By contrast, in Northern Rhodesia, which then had a population of 1.8 million Africans and 36,000 Europeans, 6 per cent

had been set aside as Crown Land, 34 per cent was accounted for by Native Reserves and Barotseland, and the remaining 60 per cent was Native Trust Land (Cmd. 8235, 1951).

4. Ritchie explains that he had no African women among his analysands. The perspective adopted here therefore is, unfortunately, that of the male only.

5. Little Hans did have relations with other children in Vienna, but their character serves only to underline the point being made here. Thus, on one occasion his father took him to the skating rink and *introduced* (my italics) him to the young daughters of a friend. There is also reference to a visit to the house made by a five-year-old cousin. The rarity of these contacts is suggested by the fact that Hans embraced his cousin tenderly, saying 'I *am* so fond of you' (Freud 1909: 15).

6. I am referring here, of course, to the situation in the rural areas. In towns the position is somewhat different, though even here the proximity of houses to one another, and the fact that much domestic activity is carried on out-of-doors rather than within the four walls of the house, means that there is less radical discontinuity than one might otherwise be disposed to assume. Quite apart from this, the vast majority of urban-dwellers in the 1950s had, in fact, been born in villages.

7. Malinowski's views on these and related matters drew him into heated controversy with the psychoanalyst Ernest Jones. For more recent discussion of some of the issues raised there, see Gluckman (1964: 236–9), Parsons (1969), and Spiro (1982). Since the pattern of familial relations among Bemba and related peoples parallel so closely that of the Trobrianders, it may be worth mentioning one important point of ethnographic difference. Unlike the Trobrianders, the Bemba do acknowledge physiological paternity; but, interestingly, Bemba dogma attributes the more important role in procreation to the woman. The child is held to be made from the blood of a woman, which she is able to transmit to her male and female children. A man can possess this blood in his veins, but he cannot pass it on to his children; his semen is said merely to activate the foetus in the womb (Richards 1934: 276; 1950: 222).

8. In recent years there has been a considerable build-up in research by physiologists and paediatricians on different aspects of lactation and its varying implications for later development. I am grateful to Dr Mavis Gunther, herself a leading worker in this field, for drawing my attention to a study on the factors influencing lactation performance in rural Gambia (Whitehead *et al.* 1978). This showed, among other things, that during the rains breast-milk output was adversely affected. The fall-out was not due to a reduced frequency of feeding but to a reduction in the average amount of milk consumed at each feed. The report adds that the adequacy of the maternal diet was almost certainly a causal factor in these seasonal variations.

With regard to the second issue – the effects on the child – of considerable interest are some observations of Ainsworth (1967: 26) in the course of her study of Ganda infancy. She reports that five Muslim mothers attributed a dwindling milk supply to the month-long Ramadan fast, during which they could not eat between sunrise and sunset. Ainsworth comments: 'Perhaps regular meals are required to maintain lactation – or, more likely – regular intake of fluids.

Perhaps the tension and irritation induced by fasting had an adverse effect on lactation or made the mother believe that lactation was affected. In any event some effect communicated itself to the babies because they were fussy and irritable during visits made in the Ramadan period. . . . It was easy to interpret their fussy crying as an indication of hunger.' Ainsworth also observes (p. 105) that among the most commonly reported reasons for crying on the part of the babies was hunger. I have already noted earlier Freeman's description of a Samoan baby who when hungry responded to the mother in irate fashion.

9. It should be noted here that Ritchie's view of the mother–child bond is tied very closely to the concept of dependence or dependency. The assumptions underlying much of the earlier psychoanalytic use of these terms were that a child became linked to its mother because he was dependent on her as the source of physiological gratification, and that all later social-dependency relations with others were considered to come about through generalisation from the initial dependency relationship with the mother. The work of Bowlby and his colleagues has raised serious questions about the tenability of these views and Bowlby himself (1969: 279) has pointed to the confusion that is likely to result when the term dependence is also used to cover the distinctive form of behaviour he has come to call attachment. In a more recent discussion of the two concepts, a close collaborator of Bowlby, Ainsworth (1972: 97), has suggested the need to see them as supplementary rather than competing ones: 'although the connotations of attachment and dependency are by no means identical, there is substantial overlap between them'. This overlap occurs because they are rooted at the point of origin of social relations, though in different ways. The view I have followed here is that dependence derives from the initial powerlessness of the child; in speaking of its later manifestations in adult life, I have sought to confine use of the term to situations involving dominance and subordination, recalling the infantile situation and the mutual adjustments that this implies.

10. Of interest here are the perceptive observations of two early officials in Bemba country: 'It has become traditional to invest the native of Africa with the attributes of a good-natured, happy child. Smiles, laughter, neglectfulness, carelessness of what the morrow may bring – these are, it would seem, the signs by which we know him. But is it really so? Watch the face of the adult native in repose. Surely in the dark eyes there is a kind of unconscious sadness? Are there not lines upon the forehead and about the mouth that seem to argue an incessant anxiety, unrecognized, perhaps unfelt, yet nonetheless existent?' (Gouldsbury and Sheane 1911: 8)

11. Running through some of my field-note files after preparing a draft of this essay, I came across a number of other cases involving biting, but in no other did my records show a reference to the swallowing of the part bitten. I should also note that the case I have cited was not selected for discussion because it involved an act of biting. At the time I presented my first analysis of it, I did not attach any significance whatsoever to this fact.

12. Some comments of Audrey Richards are relevant here. She records (1940b: 93) that in the symbolism of the *cisungu* ceremonies – the puberty rites for Bemba girls which traditionally were linked to the

ceremonies of marriage – the husband is represented as the roaring lion or the destroying flame of fire. He himself appears on the concluding night of the ceremonies as a hunter with a bow and arrow. He sings a song beginning 'I have tracked my game through the forest and now I am killing the meat', and fires his arrow at a spot on the wall under which the bride sits submissively. The subsequent act of intercourse is referred to as 'eating the *cisungu*' (*kulye cisungu*).

As for sugar, as such this was not part of the traditional indigenous diet, but already in the 1930s Richards (1939: 55) noted that among the Bemba it had become almost a necessity and that children returning to the village who had spent time in the towns found it difficult to take *bwali* – the standard dish of 'porridge' – without it. Adults, however, take it chiefly with tea, which has also become a regular part of the diet; African taste demands that it be saturated with sugar. In this form, I conjecture, it 'recalls' the sweetness of the mother's milk. At the same time, it seems to me, the other properties of sugar – its whiteness and granularity – make it an apt symbol for semen and the capacity of women to bear children. That this would be consistent with African thought is suggested by some comments of Turner, who has discussed on a number of occasions the various meanings that Ndembu attach to whiteness, among them the begetting or bringing forth of young. The Ndembu hold that semen is quite white and remains in the woman as 'a seed of life' (Turner 1968: 75). Elsewhere (1967: 61) he mentions that in certain ritual contexts powdered white clay is explicitly likened to semen. He also describes (1967: 135) how, in the context of the girl's puberty ritual, the whiteness of the *mudyi* tree (which exudes a milky latex) is related to the white beads that are draped on a miniature bow and placed in the apex of the novice's seclusion hut. His informant, Muchona, explained: 'These beads stand for her capacity to reproduce, her *lusemu* – from *kusema*, "to bear children or beget".'

13. It may be of interest to recall here that when Gluckman once gave a seminar in his Department introducing some of the key themes he was to develop in his book *The Ideas in Barotse Jurisprudence* (1965b), he was deeply hurt when some of his junior colleagues complained that its subject-matter was not social anthropology.

References

Abraham, K. 1968 (or. 1924). 'A Short Study of the Development of the Libido'. In *Selected Papers on Psychoanalysis*. London: Hogarth Press.

African Representative Council Proceedings (ARCP). 1948. Lusaka: Government Printer.

Ainsworth, M. 1967. *Infancy in Uganda: Infant Care and the Growth of Attachment*. Baltimore: Johns Hopkins Press.

Ainsworth, M. 1972. 'Attachment and Dependency: a Comparison'. In Gewirtz, J. (ed.), *Attachment and Dependence*. Washington, D.C.: Winston.

Assimeng, J. M. 1970. 'Sectarian Allegiance and Political Authority: the Watch Tower Society in Zambia, 1907-35'. *Journal of Modern African Studies* 8: 97-112.

Banton, M. 1959. 'Review of *Politics in an Urban African Community*'. *Man (OS)* 59: 34.

Barnes, J. A. 1951. *Marriage in a Changing Society*. Manchester University Press: Rhodes-Livingstone Paper No. 20.

Barnes, J. A. 1954. 'Class and Committees in a Norwegian Island Parish'. *Human Relations* 7: 39-58.

Barnes, J. A. 1955. 'Race Relations in the Development of Southern Africa'. In Lind, A. W. (ed.), *Race Relations in World Perspective*. Honolulu: University of Hawaii Press.

Barnes, J. A. 1971. *Three Styles in the Study of Kinship*. London: Tavistock Publications.

Beckford, J. A. 1975. *The Trumpet of Prophecy: a Sociological Study of Jehovah's Witnesses*. Oxford: Blackwell.

Bledisloe, Lord. 1939. *Rhodesia-Nyasaland Royal Commission Report*. London: Her Majesty's Stationery Office.

Bott, E. 1957. *Family and Social Network*. London: Tavistock.

Bowlby, J. 1952. *Maternal Care and Mental Health*. Geneva: World Health Organisation.

Bowlby, J. 1969. *Attachment and Loss*. I, *Attachment*. London: Hogarth Press.

Bowlby, J. 1973. *Attachment and Loss*. II, *Separation*. London: Hogarth Press.

Brown, R. 1973. 'Anthropology and Colonial Rule: the Case of Godfrey Wilson and the Rhodes-Livingstone Institute, Northern

Rhodesia'. In Talal Asad (ed.), *Anthropology and the Colonial Encounter*. London: Ithaca Press.

Brown, R. 1979. 'Passages in the Life of a White Anthropologist: Max Gluckman in Northern Rhodesia'. *Journal of African History* 20: 525-41.

Cesara, M. 1982. *No Hiding Place: Reflections of a Woman Anthropologist*. London: Academic Press.

Chagnon, N. A. 1968. *Yanomamo: the Fierce People*. New York: Holt, Rinehart and Winston.

Cmd. 8233. 1951. *Report of the Conference on Closer Association of the Central African Territories*. London: Her Majesty's Stationery Office.

Cole, D. T. 1953. 'Fanagolo and the Bantu Languages in South Africa'. *African Studies* 12: 1-9.

Cole, M. 1955. *Jehovah's Witnesses: the New World Society*. New York: Vantage Press.

Colson, E. 1953. *The Makah Indians*. Manchester: Manchester University Press.

Colson, E. and Gluckman, M. (eds). 1951. *Seven Tribes of British Central Africa*. London: Oxford University Press for the Rhodes-Livingstone Institute.

Comhaire-Sylvain, S. 1949. 'Le Lingala des Enfants Noirs de Léopoldville'. *Kongo-Overzee* 15: 239-50.

Cross, Sholto 1970. 'A Prophet not without Honour'. In C. Allen and R. W. Johnson (eds), *African Perspectives: Papers Presented to Thomas Hodgkin*. Cambridge: Cambridge University Press.

Cross, Sholto 1973. 'The Watch Tower Movement in South Central Africa 1908-1945'. Unpublished D.Phil. thesis, Oxford University.

Cross, Sholto 1977. 'Social History and Millennial Movements: the Watch Tower in South Central Africa'. *Social Compass* 24: 83-95.

Cunnison, I. G. 1951. 'A Watch Tower Assembly in Central Africa'. *International Review of Missions* 40: 456-69.

Cunnison, I. G. 1956. 'Perpetual Kinship: a Political Institution of the Luapula Peoples'. *Rhodes-Livingstone Journal* 20: 28-48.

Dennis, N., Henriques, F. and Slaughter, C. 1956. *Coal is Our Life*. London: Eyre & Spottiswoode.

Devereux, G. 1969. *Reality and Dream: the Psychotherapy of a Plains Indian*. New York: New York University Press.

Dotson, F. 1951. 'Voluntary Associations among Urban Working-class Families'. *American Sociological Review* 16: 687-93.

Douglas, M. 1959. 'Review of Tribal Cohesion in a Money Economy'. *Man (O.S.)* 59: 168.

Epstein, A. L. 1953. *The Administration of Justice and the Urban African*. Colonial Research Series No. 7. London: Her Majesty's Stationery Office.

Epstein, A. L. 1954. *Juridical Techniques and the Judicial Process*. Manchester: Manchester University Press: Rhodes-Livingstone Institute Paper No. 23.

Epstein, A. L. 1958. *Politics in an Urban African Community*. Manchester: Manchester University Press.

Epstein, A. L. 1964. 'Urban Communities in Africa'. In M. Gluckman (ed.), *Closed Systems and Open Minds*. Edinburgh: Oliver & Boyd.

Epstein, A. L. 1969. 'Injury and Liability in African Customary Law in Zambia'. In M. Gluckman (ed.), *Ideas and Procedures in African Customary Law*. London: Oxford University Press.

Epstein, A. L. 1971. 'Autonomy and Identity: Aspects of Political Development on the Gazelle Peninsula'. *Anthropological Forum* 2: 427-43.

Epstein, A. L. 1978. *Ethos and Identity: Three Essays in Ethnicity*. London: Tavistock Publications.

Epstein, A. L. 1979. 'Unconscious Factors in the Response to Social Crisis: a Case Study from Zambia'. *The Psychoanalytic Study of Society* 8: 3-39.

Epstein, A. L. 1981. *Urbanization and Kinship: the Domestic Domain on the Copperbelt of Zambia 1950-56*. London: Academic Press.

Epstein, A. L. 1992. *In the Midst of Life: Affect and Ideation in the World of the Tolai*. Berkeley: University of California Press.

Erikson, E. H. 1968. *Identity: Youth and Crisis*. New York: Norton.

Erikson, E. H. 1969. *Gandhi's Truth*. New York: Norton.

Evans-Pritchard, E. E. 1940. *The Nuer*. Oxford: Clarendon Press.

Fanon, F. 1970. *Black Skin, White Masks*. London: Paladin Books.

Fenichel, O. 1946. *The Psychoanalytic Theory of Neurosis*. London: Routledge.

Firth, R. W. 1936. *We, the Tikopia*. London: Allen and Unwin.

Firth, R. W. 1951. *Elements of Social Organization*. London: Watts.

Firth, R. W. 1975. 'Max Gluckman'. *Proceedings of the British Academy* 61: 479-96.

Fishman, J. (ed.), 1968. *Reader in the Sociology of Language*. The Hague: Mouton.

Fortes, M. 1980. 'Anthropology and the Psychological Disciplines'. In E. Gellner (ed.), *Soviet and Western Anthropology*. London: Duckworth.

Fortes, M. and Evans-Pritchard, E. E. (eds), 1940. *African Political Systems*. London: Oxford University Press.

Fraenkel, P. J. 1959. *Wayaleshi*. London: Weidenfeld & Nicolson.

Frankenberg, R. 1967. 'Economic Anthropology: One Anthropologist's View'. In R. W. Firth (ed.), *Themes in Economic Anthropology*. London: Tavistock Publications.

Frankenberg, R. 1978. 'Economic Anthropology or Political Economy?: the Barotse Social Formation - a Case Study'. In J. Clammer (ed.), *The New Economic Anthropology*. London: Macmillan.

Freeman, J. D. 1974. 'Kinship, Attachment Behaviour and the Primary Bond'. In J. Goody (ed.), *The Character of Kinship*.

Cambridge: Cambridge University Press.

Freud, A. 1949. *The Ego and the Mechanisms of Defence*. London: Hogarth Press.

Freud, S. 1909. *Analysis of a Phobia in a Five-Year-Old-Boy*. S.E. 10. London: Hogarth Press.

Gann, L. H. 1964. *A History of Northern Rhodesia*. London: Chatto & Windus.

Garbett, K. 1970. 'The Analysis of Social Situations'. *Man* 5: 214-27.

Geertz, C. 1973. 'The Cerebral Savage: on the Work of Claude Levi-Strauss'. In *The Interpretation of Cultures*. New York: Basic Books.

Gluckman, H. M. 1943a. *Essays on Lozi Land and Royal Property*. Rhodes-Livingstone Paper No. 10.

Gluckman, H. M. 1943b. *Administrative Organization of the Barotse Native Authority*. Rhodes-Livingstone Communication No. 10.

Gluckman, H. M. 1945. 'The Seven Year Research Plan of the Rhodes-Livingstone Institute'. *Rhodes–Livingstone Journal* 4: 1-32.

Gluckman, H. M. 1949. *An Analysis of the Sociological Theories of Bronislaw Malinowski*. Rhodes-Livingstone Paper No. 16.

Gluckman, H. M. 1950. 'Kinship and Marriage among the Lozi of N. Rhodesia and the Zulu of Natal'. In A. R. Radcliffe-Brown and C. D. Forde (eds), *African Systems of Kinship and Marriage*. London: Oxford University Press.

Gluckman, H. M. 1955. *The Judicial Process Among the Barotse of Northern Rhodesia*. Manchester: Manchester University Press.

Gluckman, H. M. 1958 (orig. 1940, 1942). *Analysis of a Social Situation in Modern Zululand*. Rhodes-Livingstone Paper No. 28. Manchester: Manchester University Press.

Gluckman, H. M. 1963. 'Gossip and Scandal'. *Current Anthropology* 4: 307-16.

Gluckman, H. M. 1965a. *Politics, Law and Ritual in Tribal Society*. Oxford: Blackwell.

Gluckman, H. M. 1965b. *The Ideas in Barotse Jurisprudence*. New Haven: Yale University Press.

Gluckman, H. M. 1975. 'Anthropology and Apartheid: the Work of South African Anthropologists'. In M. Fortes and S. Patterson (eds), *Studies in African Social Anthropology*. London: Academic Press.

Gluckman, H. M. (ed.). 1964. *Closed Systems and Open Minds*. Edinburgh: Oliver & Boyd.

Gouldsbury, C. and Sheane, J. 1911. *The Great Plateau of Northern Rhodesia*. London: Edward Arnold.

Gower, R. H. 1952. 'Swahili Borrowings from English'. *Africa* 22: 154-6.

Grillo, R. 1989. 'Anthropology, Language, Politics'. In R. Grillo (ed.), *Social Anthropology and the Politics of Language*. Sociological Review Monograph. London: Routledge.

Hall, R. A. 1955. *Hands Off Pidgin English*. Sydney: Pacific Publications.

Harré, R. and Secord, P. F. 1972. *The Explanation of Social Behaviour*. Oxford: Blackwell.

Hellmann, E. 1949. 'Urban Areas'. *Handbook of Race Relations in South Africa*. London: Oxford University Press.

Hodges, T. 1976. *Jehovah's Witnesses in Central Africa*. London: Minority Rights Group.

Hoebel, E. A. 1942. 'Fundamental Legal Conceptions in Primitive Law'. *Yale Law Journal* 51: 951-66.

Hooker, J. R. 1965. 'Witnesses and Watchtower in the Rhodesias and Nyasaland', *Journal of African History* 6: 91-106.

Jones, E. 1949. *On the Nightmare*. London: Hogarth Press.

Krystal, H. 1971. 'Trauma: Considerations of its Intensity and its Chronicity'. In H. Krystal and W. G. Niederland (eds), *Psychic Traumatization: After effects in Individuals and Communities*. Boston: Little, Brown.

Kuczynski, J. 1949. *Demographic Survey of the British Colonial Empire*. London: Oxford University Press.

Lanternari, V. 1963. *The Religions of the Oppressed*. London: McGibbon & Kee.

LaPiere, R. T. 1954. *A Theory of Social Control*. New York: McGraw Hill.

Leach, E. R. 1963. 'Review of *Order and Rebellion in Tribal Africa*'. *New Statesman* 65: 156.

Leach, E. R. 1973. 'Ourselves and the Others'. *Times Literary Supplement* pp. 771-2.

Lehmann, D. See Taylor, J. V. and Lehmann, D. A.

Llewellyn, K. N. and Hoebel, E. A. 1941. *The Cheyenne Way*. Norman: University of Oklahoma Press.

Long, N. 1968. *Social Change and the Individual*. Manchester: Manchester University Press.

Magubane, B. 1971. 'A Critical Look at Indices used in the Study of Social Change'. *Current Anthropology* 12: 419-45.

Mannoni, O. 1956. *Prospero and Caliban: the Psychology of Colonization*. London: Methuen.

Martin, C. J. 1977. 'Social Movements in Northern Rhodesia, 1907-35'. Unpublished M.Phil. thesis, University of London.

Marwick, M. 1965. *Sorcery in its Social Setting*. Manchester: Manchester University Press.

Mayer, A. 1962. 'System and Network: an Approach to the Study of Political Process in Dewas'. In T. N. Madan and G. Sarana (eds), *Indian Anthropology Essays in Memory of D. N. Majumdar*. Bombay: Asian Publishing House.

Mayer, A. 1966. 'The Significance of Quasi-Groups in the Study of Complex Societies'. In M. Banton (ed.), *The Social Anthropology of Complex Societies*. London: Tavistock Publications.

Meebelo, H. S. 1971. *Reaction to Colonialism: a Prelude to the*

Politics of Independence in Northern Zambia, 1893-1939.
Manchester: Manchester University Press.

Mitchell, J. C. 1951. 'A Note on the Urbanization of Africans on the Copperbelt'. *Rhodes-Livingstone Journal* 12: 20-7.

Mitchell, J. C. 1956a. *The Yao Village.* Manchester: Manchester University Press.

Mitchell, J. C. 1956b. *The Kalela Dance.* Rhodes-Livingstone Paper No. 27. Manchester: Manchester University Press.

Mitchell, J. C. 1956c. 'The African Middle Classes in British Central Africa'. In *Development of a Middle Class in Tropical and Subtropical Countries.* Brussels: Incidi pp. 222-33.

Mitchell, J. C. 1957. 'Aspects of African Marriage on the Copperbelt of Northern Rhodesia'. *Rhodes-Livingstone Journal* 22: 1-30.

Mitchell, J. C. 1974. 'Social Networks'. *Annual Review of Anthropology* 3: 279-99.

Mitchell, J. C. 1977. 'The Shadow of Federation, 1952-55'. *African Social Research* 24: 309-18.

Mitchell, J. C. 1983. 'Case and Situation Analysis'. *Sociological Review* 31: 187-211.

Mitchell, J. C. (ed.). 1969. *Social Networks in Urban Situations.* Manchester: Manchester University Press.

Mitchell, J. C. and Epstein, A. L. 1959. 'Occupational Prestige and Social Status among Urban Africans in Northern Rhodesia'. *Africa* 29: 22-39.

Moore, R. J. B. 1942. 'Native Wages and Standards of Living in Northern Rhodesia'. *African Studies* 1: 142-8.

Muensterberger, W. 1976. 'Psyche and Environment: Sociocultural Variations in Separation and Individuation'. *Psychoanalytic Quarterly* 38: 191-216.

Mwewa, P. B. 1958. *The African Railway Workers Union, Ndola.* Rhodes-Livingstone Communication No. 10.

NRG (Northern Rhodesia Government Publications). 1931. *Annual Report, Native Affairs.* Lusaka: Government Printer.

NRG. 1950. *Annual Report, African Affairs (Western Province).* Lusaka: Government Printer.

NRG. n.d. *Evidence . . . into the Disturbances on the Copperbelt* (1935). Lusaka: Government Printer.

Parsons, A. 1969. 'Is the Oedipus Complex Universal? The Jones-Malinowski Debate Revisited and a South Italian "Nuclear Complex"'. In W. Muensterberger (ed.), *Man and His Culture: Psychoanalytic Anthropology after Freud.* London: Raap & Whiting.

Peel, J. D. Y. 1968. *Aladura: a Religious Movement among the Yoruba.* London: Oxford University Press for International African Institute.

Pickford, R. W. 1954. *The Analysis of an Obsessional.* New York: Norton.

Pike, R. 1954. *Jehovah's Witnesses.* London: Watts.

Powdermaker, H. 1962. *Copper Town: Changing Africa*. New York: Harper & Row.

Powdermaker, H. 1967. *Stranger and Friend: the Way of an Anthropologist*. London: Secker & Warburg.

Quick, G. 1940. 'Some Aspects of the African Watch Tower Movement in Northern Rhodesia'. *International Review of Missions* 24: 216-26.

Quiggin, A. H. 1949. *Trade Routes, Trade and Currency in East Africa*. Occasional Papers of the Rhodes-Livingstone Museum No. 5. Livingstone.

Ranger, T. O. 1975. 'The Mwana Lesa Movement of 1925'. In T. O. Ranger and J. Weller (eds), *Themes in the Christian History of Central Africa*. London: Heinemann.

Richards, A. I. 1932. *Hunger and Work in a Savage Tribe*. London: Routledge & Kegan Paul.

Richards, A. I. 1934. 'Mother-right among the Central Bantu'. In E. E. Evans-Pritchard *et al.* (eds), *Essays Presented to C. G. Seligman*. London: Kegan Paul.

Richards, A. I. 1939. *Land, Labour, and Diet in Northern Rhodesia*. London: Oxford University Press.

Richards, A. I. 1940a. *Bemba Marriage and Modern Economic Conditions*. Rhodes-Livingstone Paper No. 4. Manchester: Manchester University Press.

Richards, A. I. 1940b. 'The Political System of the Bemba Tribe - North-eastern Rhodesia'. In M. Fortes and E. E. Evans-Pritchard (eds), *African Political Systems*. London: Oxford University Press.

Richards, A. I. 1950. 'Variations in Family Structure among the Central Bantu'. In A. R. Radcliffe-Brown and C. D. Forde (eds), *African Systems of Kinship and Marriage*. London: Oxford University Press.

Richards, A. I. 1963. 'The Life of Bwembya'. In M. Perham (ed.), *Ten Africans*. London: Faber.

Richards, A. I. 1968. 'Keeping the King Divine'. *Proceedings of the Royal Anthropological Institute* pp. 23-35.

Richmond, A. H. 1961. revised edn. *The Colour Problem*. Harmondsworth: Penguin Books.

Ritchie, J. F. 1943. *The African as Suckling and Adult*. Rhodes-Livingstone Paper No. 9. Manchester: Manchester University Press.

Roberts, A. 1976. *A History of Zambia*. London: Heinemann.

Rossetti, C. 1985. 'B. Malinowski, the Sociology of "Modern Problems" in Africa and the "Colonial Situation".' *Cahiers d'Etudes africaines* 100: 477-503.

Rotberg, R. 1965. *Christian Missionaries and the Creation of Northern Rhodesia*. Cambridge, Mass.: Harvard University Press.

Rotberg, R. 1966. *The Rise of African Nationalism: the Making of Malawi and Zambia, 1873-1964*. London: Oxford University Press.

Sampson, A. 1958. *The Treason Cage*. London: Heinemann.

Scholem, G. 1973. *Sabbatai Sevi: the Mystical Messiah*. Princeton: Princeton University Press.

Shepperson, G. 1953. 'Ethiopianism and Nationalism'. *Phylon* 14: 9-18.

Shepperson, G. 1963. 'Church and Sect in Central Africa'. *Rhodes-Livingstone Journal* 33: 82-94.

Shepperson, G. and Price, T. 1958. *Independent African: John Chilembwe and the Nyasaland Rising of 1915*. Edinburgh: Edinburgh University Press.

Siegel, B. 1989. 'The "Wild" and "Lazy" Lamba: Stereotypes on the Central African Copperbelt'. In L. Vail (ed.), *The Creation of Tribalism in Southern Africa*. London: James Currey.

Sovietskaia Etnografia. Vol. 3. 1948. 'The Functional School of Ethnography in the Service of British Imperialism'.

Stevenson, W. C. 1967. *Year of Doom, 1975: the Inside Story of Jehovah's Witnesses*. London: Hutchinson.

Spiro, M. E. 1978. 'Culture and Human Nature'. In G. D. Spindler (ed.), *The Making of Psychological Anthropology*. Berkeley: University of California Press.

Spiro, M. E. 1979. 'Whatever Happened to the Id?' *American Anthropologist* 81: 5-13.

Spiro, M. E. 1982. *Oedipus in the Trobriands*. Chicago: Chicago University Press.

Taylor, J. V. and Lehmann, D. A. 1961. *Christians of the Copperbelt: the Growth of the Church in Northern Rhodesia*. London: SCM Press.

Tempels, P. 1959. *Bantu Philosophy*. Paris: Plon.

Turner, V. W. 1957. *Schism and Continuity in an African Society*. Manchester: Manchester University Press.

Turner, V. W. 1964. 'Symbols in Ndembu Ritual'. In M. Gluckman (ed.), *Closed Systems and Open Minds*. Edinburgh: Oliver & Boyd.

Turner, V. W. 1967. *The Forest of Symbols*. Ithaca: Cornell University Press.

Turner, V. W. 1968. *The Drums of Affliction*. Oxford: Clarendon Press.

van Donge, J. K. 1985. 'Understanding Rural Zambia Today: the Relevance of the Rhodes-Livingstone Institute'. *Africa* 55: 60-76.

van Velsen, J. 1967. 'The Extended-case Method and Situational Analysis'. In A. L. Epstein (ed.), *The Craft of Social Anthropology*. London: Tavistock Publications.

The Watchtower. 1956. New York: Watch Tower Bible and Tract Society. September.

Watson, W. 1958. *Tribal Cohesion in a Money Economy*. Manchester: Manchester University Press.

Welensky, R. 1964. *4000 Days*. London: Collins.

Werbner, R. 1984. 'The Manchester School in South-Central Africa'. *Annual Review of Anthropology* 13: 157-85.

Western Province Provincial Council Proceedings (WPPCP). 1950.
Lusaka: Government Printer.

Whalen, W. J. 1962. *Armageddon Around the Corner: a Report on Jehovah's Witnesses*. New York: John Day Co.

White, C. M. N. 1951. 'Modern Influences upon an African Language'. *Rhodes-Livingstone Journal* 11: 66-71.

White Fathers 1947. *Bemba-English Dictionary*. Chilubula.

Whitehead, R. G. *et al.* 1978. 'Factors Influencing Lactation Performance in Rural Gambian Mothers'. *Lancet* 2: 178-81.

Wilson, B. R. 1973. *Magic and the Millennium*. London: Paladin.

Wilson, G. 1941. *The Economics of Detribalization*. Rhodes-Livingstone Papers Nos 5-6. Manchester: Manchester University Press.

Wirth, L. 1956. 'Urbanism as a Way of Life'. Reprinted in *Community Life and Social Policy*. Chicago: University of Chicago Press.

Worsley, P. 1957. *The Trumpet Shall Sound: a Study of Cargo Cults in Melanesia*. London: McGibbon & Kee.

Young, J. Z. 1971. *An Introduction to the Study of Man*. Oxford: Clarendon Press.

Index

Abraham, K., 187
affect, study of, in anthropology, xxvi
African Mine Workers Trade Union (AMWTU), xii, xiii, 10, 11
    and the ANC, 179
    leadership in, 47
African National Congress (ANC), xiii, xvii, 47, 78
    in aftermath of Federation, 14
    boycott organised by, 140-1
    and the campaign against Federation, 178-80
    formation of, 178
African Representative Council, 178
African Salaried Staff Association, emergence of, 15
Ainsworth, M., 218, 219
anthropology
    and colonial rule, 16
    and settler opinion, 19
Anti-Federation Action Committee, 3
Arnott, H., 129, 141, 142, 145, 150, 214
Assimeng, J., 157, 217
associations, 77-9
attachment, 192, 194, 217, 219
Attlee, C., 172, 173
authority, as maternal, perception of, 185

Banton, M., xviii
banyama see vampires
Barnes, J. A., xiv, 52, 80, 82, 88, 93, 182, 186, 207
Beckford, J., 127, 129, 130, 139, 148, 214, 215, 216
Beer Hall, 111-13

bodily mutilation, among Bemba, 167-9, 199, 200
Booth, Joseph, 122
Bott, E., 52, 81, 82-3, 88
Bowlby, J., 189, 192, 193-4, 217, 219
Broken Hill (now Kabwe), x, 4, 17, 182
Brown, R., xix, xx, 16-17
Bwana M'Kubwa, 22, 55, 64, 211

case-method, use of, xi-xii, xxiii, 25
castration
    fears, 185, 197
    threat of, 192
Cesara, M., 126
Chagnon, N., 1
Chamber of Mines, and anthropological research, 9, 11, 17
Chambeshi, A., 6
Chapoloko, J., 9
Chilembwe Rising, 122, 123, 125
CiBemba, dominance of, 105
CiCopperbelti, xv, xvi, 115
Codrington, R. E., 167, 168
Comhaire-Sylvain, S., 105
Cole, D. T., 100
Cole, M., 215
Colson, E., 83
    and Gluckman, M., 40
Comrie, W., 119
conflict
    and change, 22
    interest in, xii
Cross, S., 122, 123, 151, 214
Cunnison, I., 127, 128, 212

dependence
    Federation as crisis of, 202

230